Travel and Tourism

for BTEC National Award, Certificate & Diploma

Book One

Ray Youell

Published by Travel and Tourism Publishing Limited.

www.tandtpublishing.co.uk
info@tandtpublishing.co.uk

First published 2005

British Library Cataloguing in Publication Data is available from the British Library on request.
ISBN 0 9550190 0 1

Designed and typeset by Jenks at Cambrian Printers
Cover design image courtesy of Airtours plc
Printed in the UK by Cambrian Printers, Aberystwyth

Table of Contents

Note: Unit numbers exactly follow the Edexcel specifications

I am grateful for the help and support of many individuals and organisations in completing this book. Arabella Stewart did an excellent job on researching photos, while Jenks and the team at Cambrian Printers handled the typescript very professionally. But, as ever, the biggest thanks go to Sue, Megan and Owen.

The publishers extend thanks to the following for granting permission to reproduce images and logos throughout the book:

Airbus
Association of British Travel Agents (ABTA)
Association of Independent Tour Operators (AITO)
Bicester Village Tourist Information Centre
bmi
Borough of Telford & Wrekin
British Airways
Brittany Ferries
Canvas Holidays
Center Parcs
Columbus Travel Guides, Swanley, Kent (Tel: 01322 616344 Fax: 01322 616323)
Cunard
Dartmoor Tourist Association
easyJet
Eurostar
Federation of Tour Operators
First Choice
Holiday Inn
InterContinental Hotels and Resorts
Keycamp Holidays
Manchester United
Marriott Hotels and Resorts
National Express

New Orleans Visitor and Convention Bureau (Romney Caruso)
Passenger Shipping Association
Photo of Grand Canyon courtesy of Scottsdale Convention & Visitors Bureau
Czech Tourism
Saga Holidays
Shearings
South West Tourism (www.visitsouthwest.co.uk)
Superbreak
The Eden Project
Thomas Cook
Thomsonfly
Travel Weekly
Travelcare
Travelodge
TTG (Travel Trade Gazette)
TUI UK
Virgin Atlantic Airways
VisitBritain
Welcome to Excellence
Wotton Travel Limited
www.info-costablanca.com
YHA

Introduction

Travel and Tourism for BTEC National Award, Certificate and Diploma Book 1 is written specifically for BTEC National travel and tourism courses. Exactly matched to the specifications, the book covers all the core units for the Award, Certificate and Diploma, plus specialist units for the Certificate and Diploma, as follows:

BTEC National Award (Core Units)

- Unit 2 The Business of Travel and Tourism
- Unit 3 Marketing Travel and Tourism Products and Services
- Unit 4 Tourist Destinations
- Unit 5 Customer Service in Travel and Tourism

BTEC National Award (Specialist Units)

- Unit 1 The Travel and Tourism Industry
- Unit 7 Retail Travel Operations
- Unit 11 Tour Operations

BTEC National Certificate and Diploma (Core Units)

- Unit 1 The Travel and Tourism Industry
- Unit 2 The Business of Travel and Tourism
- Unit 3 Marketing Travel and Tourism Products and Services
- Unit 4 Tourist Destinations
- Unit 5 Customer Service in Travel and Tourism
- Unit 6 Working in the Travel and Tourism Industry

BTEC National Certificate and Diploma (Specialist Units)

- Unit 7 Retail Travel Operations
- Unit 11 Tour Operations
- Unit 21 Work-based Experience within the Travel and Tourism Industry
- Unit 22 Travel and Tourism Residential Study Visit

The companion book *Travel and Tourism for BTEC National Award, Certificate and Diploma Book 2* (ISBN 0 9550190 1 X) includes a further 8 specialist units that contribute towards the Certificate and Diploma.

How to use this book

Each unit includes:

1. An introductory page – giving details of the content and assessment for the unit;
2. Clearly-labelled sections – exactly covering the specification content for the unit;
3. Activities – based on the assessment criteria to help you learn more;
4. Focus on industry – short practical statements of how the travel and tourism industry implement key topics in the unit;
5. Weblinks – Internet links to organisations and topics in the unit;
6. Case studies – longer examples of organisations and topics included in the unit, with questions to expand your knowledge;
7. Unit summary – concise overview of key topics covered in the unit;
8. Test questions at the end – to build your knowledge of what's been covered in the unit;
9. A sample assignment – covering all the grading criteria for the unit.

About tandtONLine

Everybody who buys this book can register for free access to tandtONLine, a brand new web resource for travel and tourism students and staff. It gives you a host of extra features that are regularly updated by academic staff and industry experts, including:

- Latest news from the travel and tourism industry;
- Key statistics on UK, European and global tourism;
- Glossary of common terms and key definitions;
- Links to useful websites;
- Top tips for students on completing assignments;
- Extra staff teaching resources linked to textbooks (PowerPoint slides, worksheets, links to websites featured in the book, suggestions for extra reading, etc.).

Register by going to www.tandtonline.co.uk and completing the online registration form using the unique book code found on the inside back cover.

I hope you find this book a useful companion for your BTEC course and wish you well in your studies.

Ray Youell
Aberystwyth
March 2005

INTRODUCTION TO THE UNIT

Travel and tourism is often referred to as 'the world's biggest industry', providing income and jobs for millions of people across the globe. It is a very dynamic and high profile industry, which attracts young and old alike to develop careers in one of the most vibrant industries in the world.

This unit gives you the opportunity to learn more about travel and tourism, its development and the many organisations that are involved in the industry. You will also explore the structure of the industry and the many factors that affect travel and tourism, today and into the future. It will provide you with a sound base from which to develop a detailed understanding of the industry through the other units you will study on your course.

WHAT YOU WILL STUDY

During the course of this unit you will:

1. Investigate the **development** of the travel and tourism industry;
2. Examine the **structure** of the travel and tourism industry;
3. Explore the **roles and responsibilities of organisations** that provide travel and tourism products and services;
4. Explore **factors** that affect the travel and tourism industry.

You will be guided through the main topics in this unit with the help of the latest statistics, examples and industry case studies. You should also check out the weblinks throughout the unit for extra information on particular organisations or topic areas and use the activities to help you learn more.

ASSESSMENT FOR THIS UNIT

This unit is internally assessed, meaning that you will be given an assignment (or series of assignments) to complete by your tutor(s) to show that you have fully understood the content of the unit. A grading scale of pass, merit or distinction is used for all internally assessed units, with higher grades awarded to students who show greater depth in analysis and evaluation in their assignments. An assignment for this unit, which covers all the grading criteria, can be found on page 59. Don't forget to visit www.tandtONLine.co.uk for all the latest industry news, developments, statistics and tips to help you with your assignments.

Unit 1

SECTION 1: THE DEVELOPMENT OF THE TRAVEL AND TOURISM INDUSTRY

Travel and tourism has developed into one of the world's most important industries, with more than 760 million international tourist trips globally in 2004. It is also one of the fastest-growing sectors of the UK economy, worth £74 billion to the economy in 2003 and employing 2.2 million people. To understand fully the present position and future growth of travel and tourism, it is useful to delve back into history to explore some important milestones and trends. However, first we must spend a little time investigating just what we mean by 'travel and tourism'.

What is travel and tourism?

It's not easy to find a single definition of travel and tourism that everybody can agree with! Some people make a distinction between 'travel' and 'tourism' in the definition, with 'travel' being the movement of people from one place to another using different types of transport, while 'tourism' covers the whole phenomenon of people visiting destinations for a variety of reasons, plus the industry that supports this. However, one thing everybody can agree with is that travel and tourism is big business! The industry generates billions of pounds internationally and supports more than 120 million jobs across the world. Travel and tourism is also a part of 'leisure', since we go on holidays and day visits during our leisure time (log on to the 'key terms and definitions' section of www.tandtONLine.co.uk for more on definitions in travel, tourism and leisure).

The World Tourism Organisation (WTO), a specialist agency of the United Nations and recognised as the leading international body in international tourism, states that tourism comprises:

'...the activities of persons travelling to and staying in places outside their usual environment for not more than one consecutive year for leisure, business and other purposes'.

Probably the most widely-accepted definition of tourism in use in the UK today is:

'Tourism is the temporary, short-term movement of people to destinations outside the places where they normally live and work, and activities during their stay at these destinations; it includes movement for all purposes, as well as day visits or excursions' (Tourism Society 1976).

Both definitions clearly show that people we think of as tourists are:

- Away from their normal place of residence (although they will be returning home);
- On a visit that is temporary and short-term;
- Engaged in activities which would normally be associated with travel and tourism;
- Not necessarily staying away from home overnight: they may be on a day-trip or excursion;
- Not always away from home for holiday purposes: they could be on business or visiting friends and relatives (VFR), but would still qualify as tourists.

WEBLINK

www.world-tourism.org and www.tourismsociety.org

Check out these websites for information on the work of the World Tourism Organisation and the Tourism Society.

Unit 1

Different types of tourism

It's very important to remember that tourism isn't just about going abroad! There is a common misconception in Britain that travel and tourism is only concerned with taking overseas holidays; this couldn't be further from the truth. Research shows that British people take nearly three times as many tourist trips in the UK compared with visits abroad, but the majority do prefer overseas destinations for their main holidays. Tourism in the UK employs more than 2.2 million people and is a major industry in places as far afield as Cornwall, the Scottish Borders, the Lake District, York and Snowdonia.

There are three main types of tourism:

Domestic tourism: when people take holidays, short breaks and day trips in their own country, e.g. a family from Manchester enjoying a two-week holiday in a caravan in Scarborough.

Incoming/inbound tourism: this is when people enter a country from their own country of origin or another country which is not their home, e.g. Monsieur and Madame du Pont from Dijon sampling the delights of Edinburgh as part of a driving tour of Scotland.

Outbound tourism: this is when people travel away from the country where they normally live, e.g. the family from Manchester deciding to give Scarborough a miss this year and taking a week's holiday at Disneyland Paris instead.

ACTIVITY

Carry out a survey of the rest of your group to find out how many people took their last holiday abroad and what proportion stayed in the UK. Draw a bar chart showing the results you collected. Ask the members of your group to tell you the main reasons for taking holidays abroad and draw a pie chart showing their answers.

Why do people travel?

Contrary to popular belief, travel and tourism isn't just about taking holidays! People travel for all sorts of reasons and the industry is usually divided into leisure tourism, business tourism and visiting friends and relatives (known as VFR). Figure 1.1 shows the main travel purposes under each of these categories.

Unit 1

TOURISM

LEISURE TOURISM

- Holidays
- Short breaks
- Day visits
- Sport
- Education
- Culture and religion
- Social and spiritual

VISITING FRIENDS AND RELATIVES (VFR)

- Long holidays
- Short breaks
- Day visits

BUSINESS TOURISM

- Business meetings
- Conferences and conventions
- Exhibitions and trade fairs
- Incentive travel

Fig. 1.1 Why people travel

WEBLINK

www.bacd.org.uk

Check out this website for more information on the importance of business and conference tourism.

As you can see from Figure 1.1, leisure tourism includes many of the activities that most people think of as 'tourism', such as taking holidays and short breaks. Business tourism, including conferences, business meetings and trade fairs, is an increasingly important sector since it is often of high value and earns hoteliers, caterers and transport operators significant income. Indeed, many city-based travel agents operate a separate department geared exclusively to the needs of business clients.

Visiting friends and relatives (VFR) is also an important contributor to tourism revenue. You may be wondering how it is that somebody who stays for free with a friend or relative in their home is helping tourism in an area. The answer is that the visitor, although enjoying free accommodation, is likely to spend money on other goods and services in the locality, such as food, entertainment and transport, so contributing to the local economy. Indeed, the very fact that he or she is not paying for accommodation may well be an incentive to spend more on such things as eating out and entertainment.

Figures from the United Kingdom Passenger Survey (UKPS) show that British people made a total of 151 million overnight trips within the UK for all purposes in 2003, of which:

- 70.5 million (47 per cent) were holidays;
- 22.3 million (15 per cent) were on business;
- 54.8 million (36 per cent) were visits to friends and relatives;
- 3.4 million (2 per cent) were for other miscellaneous reasons.

Unit 1

HOLIDAYS	• A short break in Milan • A two-week family holiday to the Costa del Sol • A trip to a theme park in Orlando
HEALTH AND FITNESS	• A walking tour of the Andes • A cycling holiday in Spain • A tennis holiday in the Algarve
SPORT	• A weekend break to the Belgian Grand Prix in Spa • Visiting Barcelona to watch Newcastle play a match • A short break to the UK swimming championships in Sheffield
EDUCATION	• A French student taking an English language course in London • A weekend canoeing course in Wales • A week at an Open University summer school in Reading
CULTURE AND RELIGION	• A pilgrimage to Lourdes in the Pyrenees • A visit to Scotland to study Celtic music • A weekend exploring churches in Cornwall
SOCIAL AND SPIRITUAL	• A weekend reflexology course • A group of friends visiting Spain for the first time • A week-long meditation course in the Lake District

Fig. 1.2 Examples of leisure tourism

Fig. 1.3 Examples of business tourism

BUSINESS MEETINGS	• A salesman attending a meeting in Brighton • Two Manchester-based company directors going to their annual general meeting in Belfast • A Member of the European Parliament travelling to Brussels for meetings with EU officials
EXHIBITIONS AND TRADE FAIRS	• Travel agents visiting the World Travel Market in London • A tourist board officer attending the British Travel Trade Fair in Birmingham • A plastics buyer travelling to a trade fair in Copenhagen
CONFERENCES AND CONVENTIONS	• Delegates attending a political party conference in Brighton • Double-glazing sales people travelling to their annual sales convention in Bristol • A group of lawyers attending a conference on EU law
INCENTIVE TRAVEL	• A weekend golfing break at the Belfry for an employee who achieves top yearly sales for a company • A free holiday to Paris for a designer completing an important project on time for a client • Two weeks in the Caribbean for an employee who clinches a multi-million pound contract for a company

Some examples from each of the categories shown in Figure 1.1 will help to give a clearer understanding of the meaning of travel and tourism. Leisure tourism examples are shown in Figure 1.2 and different examples of business tourism are given in Figure 1.3.

Unit 1

ACTIVITY

Business tourism is often considered to be 'high value' tourism. Why do you think this is? Can you think of ways that travelling for business reasons has changed in recent years and what factors are likely to affect business travel in the future?

WEBLINK

www.staruk.org.uk

Check out this website for the latest data on business tourism in the UK.

FOCUS ON INDUSTRY – Business tourism

According to figures on StarUK, business tourism in the UK was worth more than £9 billion to the economy in 2002. UK residents made 23.3 million business trips, while trips by overseas visitors coming to Britain on business amounted to 7.2 million. Non-residential conferences had an estimated value to the economy of £2.9 billion and residential conferences £4.4 billion. These are the estimated direct income to venues and take no account of delegate or organiser expenditure outside the venue on, for example, entertaining, eating out, transport, shopping, etc.

1945	World War Two finished
1949	First overseas package holiday by air offered by Vladimir Raitz of Horizon Holidays
1950	Worldwide international tourist arrivals totalled 25 million
1950	Car ownership in the UK reached 2.3 million
1958	More than 1 million passengers crossed the Atlantic by ship
1958	Boeing 707 aircraft launched
1965	Lord Thomson took the first steps towards creating Thomson Holidays
1968	First cross-Channel hovercraft service introduced
1969	The Development of Tourism Act established the English, Wales and Scottish Tourist Boards, plus the BTA (British Tourist Authority) – now VisitBritain
1970	Introduction of the Boeing 747 'jumbo jet'
1970	Car ownership in the UK reached 11 million
1974	The then number one UK tour operator Clarkson went into liquidation
1976	Concorde came into service
1982	UK people made 20 million visits of all kinds abroad
1986	The number of UK package holidaymakers topped 10 million for the first time
1989	Worldwide international tourist arrivals topped 400 million
1989	Tim Berners-Lee invented the Internet
1991	The Intasun holiday company ceased trading
1994	Channel Tunnel opened
1994	easyJet launched
1994	National Lottery launched in the UK
1998	25.7 million overseas came to Britain, spending more than £12 billion
1999	UK government's tourism strategy Tomorrow's Tourism launched
2002	UK people made more than 59 million visits abroad, including 40 million holidays
2002	Car ownership in the UK reached 22 million
2003	Concorde taken out of service
2003	50 per cent of UK households had access to the Internet
2003	Value of UK tourism reached £74 billion, employing 2.1 million people
2003	24.7 million overseas visitors came to Britain
2004	Worldwide international tourist arrivals reached a record 760 million
2004	A record 27.5 million overseas tourists visited Britain
2005	Airbus A380 'super jumbo' aircraft unveiled

Historical development of travel and tourism

Travel for purposes of trade, religion, leisure, education and to fight in battles goes far back in history, but for the purposes of this unit we are only concerned with developments in travel and tourism since the end of World War Two in 1945.

Key events and milestones post-1945 to the present day

Mass tourism, i.e. the movement of large numbers of people across the globe for tourism, has grown dramatically since the end of the

Fig. 1.4 Milestones in the development of travel and tourism since 1945

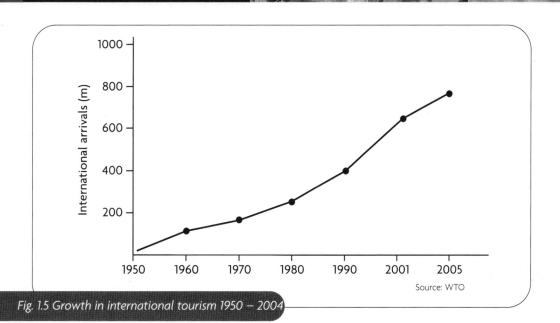

Fig. 1.5 Growth in international tourism 1950 – 2004

Second World War (1939 – 1945). Figure 1.4 lists the key milestones in the development of travel and tourism since 1945.

Figure 1.4 shows us that tourism has grown into a major economic activity, both in the UK and worldwide. If we concentrate on the figures for international arrivals, i.e. the number of people travelling around the world for leisure, business and VFR purposes, this has grown from just 25 million in 1950 to more than 760 million in 2004. Figure 1.5 charts this growth in international tourism more fully and shows just how dramatic the growth has been since the 1950s.

ACTIVITY

Using Figures 1.4 and 1.5 for reference, write a newspaper article that describes the development of the travel and tourism industry. Your headline is 'Fifty Years of Tourism Growth'. You should expand on the points listed in the Figures and carry out some research of your own to add to these facts. Your article should be no more than 750 words long.

This activity is designed to provide evidence for P1.

Three particular factors mentioned in Figure 1.4 – increasing car ownership, the development of jet aircraft and the growth of the package tour – have had far-reaching impacts on the development of travel and tourism since 1945.

Increasing car ownership

The increase in car ownership after the Second World War provided individuals with greater freedom and flexibility in the use of their leisure time. People travelled further afield, exploring new areas of the British coast and countryside. The number of private cars on the roads of Britain rose steeply from 2.3 million in 1950 to 11 million in 1970. In 2002 the figure exceeded 22 million vehicles.

Although this rise in car ownership has brought increased freedom and flexibility, it has highlighted a number of issues of concern. Firstly, the upward trend in the ownership of cars has resulted in a drop in demand for traditional types of public transport. The use of trains for holiday travel has fallen dramatically since 1945 and statistics for coach travel show a similar downward trend. This fall in demand for public transport has led to cuts in services and, in the case of the railways, the closure of unprofitable lines. Those living in the remoter rural areas of Britain have been particularly affected by these service reductions and the loss of choice in their travel arrangements.

A second consequence of the growth in car ownership in the UK has been the rise in associated environmental problems, including pollution, congestion and the loss of land to further road building. These problems are particularly acute in many of Britain's historic cities and scenic countryside areas. In many National Parks, for example, the volume of cars is having a damaging effect on the landscapes and wildlife habitats, often spoiling what the visitors have come to see and enjoy. These problems have led to calls for cars to be banned from some areas or their use strictly controlled. The Congestion Charge is now firmly established in London, while popular tourist cities, including Canterbury, Cambridge and York, have introduced measures such as 'park and ride' schemes, cycle hire and parking restrictions to help alleviate their traffic problems. Managers in the Peak District National Park encourage the use of public transport by working in partnership with local bus and train operators.

Cycle hire schemes can help ease congestion

The development of jet aircraft

One positive outcome of the Second World War was the rapid advance in aircraft technology, which led to the growth of a viable commercial aviation industry in Britain and the USA. The surplus of aircraft from 1945 onwards, coupled with the

Unit 1

business flair of entrepreneurs such as Harold Bamberg of Eagle Airways and Freddie Laker, encouraged the development of holiday travel by air. Comet aircraft were used in the 1950s, but it was not until the introduction of the faster and more reliable Boeing 707 jets in 1958 that we began to see the possibility of air travel becoming a reality for the masses of the population. The 1960s saw a surge in demand for scheduled and charter flights, the latter being combined with accommodation, transfers and courier services to form the overseas 'package tour' that is so familiar today.

A Virgin Atlantic Boeing 747

The growth of package tours

Vladimir Raitz of Horizon Holidays is credited with having organised the first modern package tour by air (also called an 'inclusive tour') when he carried a party of holidaymakers to Corsica in 1949. The holiday consisted of travel in a 32-seater DC3 aircraft and full-board accommodation in tents! From a modest start with just 300 passengers carried in its first year of operation, Horizon repeated the formula in subsequent years with increasing success. The 1960s saw the beginning of the rapid increase in the number of package holidays sold. Destinations such as the coastal areas of Southern Spain, the Balearic Islands and Greece became favourite locations for British and other European travellers. The convenience of an all-inclusive arrangement, coupled with the increased speed which the new aircraft brought, caught the imagination of the British travelling public. Today, package holidays are under threat from the growth of low-cost airlines and the Internet, which allow people to make up their own holidays and bypass travel agents and tour operators. Mintel's Travel Trends report showed, for the first time, that package holidays made up less than half of all overseas holidays sold to British people in 2003.

Unit 1

Recent developments in the travel and tourism industry

The pace of development in travel and tourism has increased in recent years, due mainly to new developments in technology, not least the growth of the Internet. Recent developments can be grouped under three headings – transport, changes in distribution systems and industry restructuring.

Transport developments

Transport for tourism is constantly changing to meet customer demands for safer, faster, more comfortable and more affordable travel. Transport operators also have to adapt to society's growing concern for the environment by developing new types of environmentally-friendly travel.

One of the most important developments in the transport sector in recent years has been the introduction of low-cost airlines, helped by the growth in Internet use. The low-cost carriers, including easyJet, Ryanair and bmibaby, offer a cheap, 'no frills' service to people looking to travel on a budget. They are able to offer cheap fares by keeping support services to a minimum and selling direct to travellers via the Internet and telephone, thereby saving travel agents' commission charges. They also use smaller regional, airports that charge lower landing fees and the airlines sell ranges of add-on products, such as travel insurance, 'phone cards, car hire, rail tickets and accommodation on a commission basis. The low-cost carriers are a serious threat to the longer-established 'full service' airlines, which are having to cut their prices and alter their services to compete.

WEBLINK	FOCUS ON INDUSTRY – bmibaby low-cost airline
www.bmibaby.com *Check out this website for more information on bmibaby.*	bmibaby, a subsidiary company of British Midland Airways (bmi), was set up in January 2002 and carried over 7.6 million passengers in its first three years of operation. The airline has expanded very rapidly, establishing bases at 5 UK airports – Nottingham East Midlands, Birmingham, Manchester, Cardiff and Durham Tees Valley. The company flies to 20 destinations in 7 different countries, operating 340 flights per week during the summer 2004 season.

Other recent developments in transport for tourism include the introduction of 'super ships' by cruise lines and the development of high-speed train services, both of which are covered in detail later in this unit.

Unit 1

Changes in distribution systems

The last few years have seen a revolution in the way we book holidays, flights and other travel products and services. Developments in technology have opened up completely new methods for companies to distribute their travel and tourism products and new ways for customers to buy. No longer is it necessary to visit a travel agency for information or to make a booking, although many people still prefer the more personal service that agents offer. Some of the most notable recent changes in distribution include:

- The Internet – this has revolutionised the way many people now buy their travel and tourism products and services. Travellers can make their own bookings for flights, car hire, accommodation, travel insurance, etc. on their computer at a time that is convenient for them. These 'unpackaged holidays' do away with the need for a tour operator or travel agent. The Internet has also led to the growth of so called 'e-retailers', for example ebookers, lastminute.com and Expedia;
- Call centres – many of the larger holiday companies, e.g. Thomas Cook and Thomson, operate call centres (sometimes called contact centres) where large numbers of trained staff provide details of holidays and take telephone bookings from customers;
- Digital and cable TV – companies such as Sky Travel and Thomas Cook TV offer programmes and features selling holidays to all parts of the world. Viewers are directed to the company's website or call centre to make a booking.

ACTIVITY

Log on to the websites of ebookers, lastminute.com and Expedia, and compare the three sites in terms of – products on offer, site design, ease of use, general travel information and other features.

The Internet has changed the way we book holidays

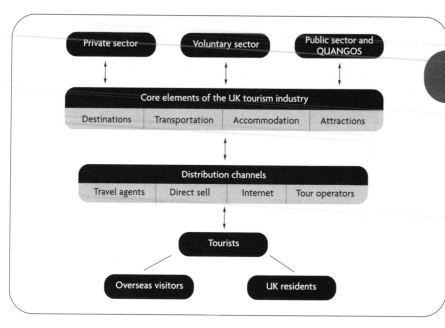

Fig. 1.6 Structure of the UK travel and tourism industry

As you can see from Figure 1.6 travel and tourism is a complicated business! The focus of all activity in travel and tourism is satisfying the needs of tourists, whether they are on a day visit, short break, annual holiday or an extended stay. The core elements of the industry — destinations, transportation, accommodation and attractions — are supplied by a mixture of private, voluntary and public sector providers, ranging from multi-million pound companies such as Virgin Holidays and British Airways, to small businesses and local councils which provide tourist facilities and tourist information for visitors. QUANGOS (quasi-autonomous, non-governmental organisations), such as VisitBritain and the Wales Tourist Board, are funded from public money to help develop and promote tourism. Tour operators put together holidays and short breaks, which are sold through travel agents, direct to the public or via the Internet.

ACTIVITY

Working in a small team, carry out some research into which sectors of the travel and tourism industry are found in your local area. Use the diagram in Figure 1.6 as your starting point. Make a note of the names of the companies or organisations represented, their purpose and whether they are in the private, public or voluntary sector.

The following sections of this unit look in detail at the main sectors of the travel and tourism industry, starting with transport.

Transport

Having good transport networks is essential for a successful travel and tourism industry, whether people are on business, travelling for leisure or visiting friends and relatives. Transportation for tourism can be divided into air, road, rail and sea. The most common types of transport in each of these categories are:

Unit 1

- Air – scheduled services, charter flights, 'low-cost' carriers, air taxis;
- Road – private car, coach, taxi, bus, bicycle;
- Rail – regional services, inter-city routes, high-speed services, steam trains;
- Sea – ferries, cruise ships, yachts.

Travel by private car is the most popular mode of transport used for tourist trips in the UK, as Figure 1.7 demonstrates.

Type of transport	% of trips
Car	73
Train	12
Bus/Coach	4
Organised coach	2
Motor caravan	1
Plane	5
Other	3

Fig. 1.7 Types of transport used by UK people for tourist trips in 2003

Figure 1.7 shows that nearly three-quarters of all tourist trips are made by car, with just 12 per cent by train and 6 per cent by coach travel of various types. Although travel by plane in the UK accounts for just 5 per cent, this is the fastest-growing transport sector, with low-cost airlines in particular offering new routes to more regional airports.

The following sections of this unit look in detail at each of the four main types of transport, starting with air travel.

Air travel

The rapid growth in international tourism in the last 50 years has been closely linked to the growth in air travel. Advances in aircraft technology have led to increases in aircraft capacity and the development of planes with far greater flying ranges. Deregulation of air travel has increased competition between airlines and helped to keep fares low on an expanding network of routes. Aviation is a major UK industry, carrying 200 million passengers per year. The government expects this number to double by 2020 and has outlined plans for airport expansion to deal with this growth. The *Future of Air Transport White Paper* published in November 2004 gives details of these plans, which include growth at a number of airports, including Stansted, Birmingham and Newcastle.

The growth in air travel has led to a rapid expansion of the associated infrastructure needed to cope with business and leisure tourists, such as airport terminals, runways, access roads and parking facilities. This often leads to opposition by local people who are most affected by increased noise and other environmental impacts.

- The Strategic Rail Authority (SRA) – deals with all train-related matters, such as planning and co-ordinating the rail networks;
- The Health and Safety Executive (HSE) – looks after health and safety on the railways;
- The Office of Rail Regulation – is independent of the government and regulates the national rail network.

Network Rail is responsible for revitalising Britain's railways, after its predecessor Railtrack went into administration in 2001. Network Rail is a non-profit engineering company, which aims to maintain, improve and upgrade every aspect of the railway infrastructure, including track, signalling systems, bridges and viaducts, tunnels, level crossings and stations. Including Eurostar and the new Trans Pennine Express, there are 26 train operating companies in the UK, which together make up the Association of Train Operating Companies (ATOC). They have the responsibility for running the trains, through-ticketing, railcards and the National Rail Enquiries telephone and Internet service.

Rail travel is an altogether more environmentally friendly mode of transport, but one that has lost popularity with UK tourists in recent years. Tourist trips by train are now at only 15 per cent of their 1951 level. There are, however, one or two growth areas in tourist travel by rail, notably short breaks in cities and the popularity of narrow-gauge scenic railways, particularly in Wales. Some operators have successfully exploited the market for 'nostalgia' travel by introducing rail holidays, e.g. the Venice-Simplon Orient Express, which is sometimes chartered for special excursions in the UK, and the Great Little Trains in Wales steam-powered services. Eurostar services from London to Paris, Lille and other European destinations have fuelled the growth in short breaks to cities on the continent.

ACTIVITY

Carry out some research into companies that offer specialist holidays by train in the UK and overseas. Present your findings as a series of factsheets.

Travel by sea

Sea travel in UK tourism is dominated by the ferry companies which operate services between the UK and Ireland, Scandinavia and the near continent, principally France, Belgium and the Netherlands. There is fierce competition on the cross-Channel routes and the number of ferry services has fallen dramatically since the opening of the Channel Tunnel in 1994. Faster, more frequent and more comfortable cross-Channel services, using new generation 'super ferries' and hydrofoils, have given ferry passengers faster and more comfortable services. Companies have introduced new products, such as short Channel cruises and day trips to buy food and drink ('booze cruises'), in order to increase their income.

Unit 1

Cruising

Cruising is an area of travel and tourism that is growing steadily and expanding its customer base. Whereas in the past cruising was seen as the preserve of the elderly, rich and famous, today it appeals to a far wider cross-section of customers, including families, young people and groups. Prices for some cruise products have fallen as the major tour operators have entered the market. For the first time in 2003, one million British people took a cruise of one sort or another. Major cruise lines include Royal Caribbean International, Princess Cruises, Cunard and P&O.

Cruising in the Antarctic

WEBLINK

www.oceanvillageholidays.co.uk

Check out this website for more information on Ocean Village cruises.

FOCUS ON INDUSTRY – Ocean Village

Launched in 2003, Ocean Village is a new cruise ship from P&O that is attracting a younger type of cruise passenger and contributing significantly to the rise in popularity of cruising generally in the UK. Catering for singles, couples and families, Ocean Village offers informal cruising in the Mediterranean and Caribbean. The cruises also offer passengers a range of activities away from the ship, such as cycling, diving and windsurfing.

Travel agents

Travel agents are in business to sell holidays and other travel products to a wide range of customers. They are the retail arm of the travel and tourism industry, i.e. in the same way that a clothes shop sells products to shoppers, travel agencies retail their 'products' to the general public. Indeed, the term 'travel shop' is commonly used to refer to travel agency premises. The one major difference between these two types of retail outlets, however, is that, unlike the clothes retailer, travel agencies do not buy in 'stock' in advance, but rather react to the wishes of their customers before contacting the holiday companies.

There are around 6300 travel agency outlets in the UK that are members of the Association of British Travel Agents (ABTA) – see case study in unit 7 on page 310 . Most are leisure travel agents, catering for the needs of people going on holidays and short breaks. Business travel agents specialise in travel arrangements for business people, including designing itineraries, booking flights and accommodation.

Thomas Cook agency in Birmingham

Travel agencies in the UK are either independently-owned or part of a chain of agencies owned by a single company (often referred to as the 'multiples'). In recent years, the numbers of multiple agencies have grown at the expense of the independent agents. At the time of writing, the 'big four' multiple agencies (with number of branches in brackets) are:

1. Thomson (860)
2. Going Places (670)
3. Thomas Cook (616)
4. First Choice (202)

Each of these multiples is owned by a major tour operator, a process known as 'vertical integration'. For example, Going Places is part of the MyTravel Group, while Thomson Travel Shops are owned by Thomson, the UK's number one tour operator, which is itself part of the German-controlled TUI Group. You can learn more about vertical integration in unit 11 on page 333.

Travel agencies are going through a period of significant change at present. Developments in new technology, particularly the Internet and digital TV, are giving customers a host of new ways to buy their holidays and travel products direct, rather than using an agent. Travel agencies are responding by reducing the number of high street premises, developing their own Internet operations, opening holiday hypermarkets and setting up call centres to answer queries and take bookings from customers.

WEBLINK

www.thomascook.com

Check out this website for more information on Thomas Cook.

FOCUS ON INDUSTRY – Thomas Cook call centres

Thomas Cook runs one of the UK's leading travel telephone sales operations, employing 700 people in call centres in Peterborough, Birmingham and Falkirk. The centres operate 7 days a week and are equipped with the latest communications technology, accepting calls generated through Thomas Cook TV, the company's Internet site and advertising.

Unit 1

Travel agents act on behalf of two parties when they carry out their work, the customer, referred to as the client, on whose behalf they are making the travel arrangements and the company that is supplying the travel product. This company is sometimes referred to as the 'principal', and may include:

- Tour operators;
- Airlines;
- Coach companies;
- Hotels;
- Car hire firms;
- Ferry companies;
- Train operators;
- Cruise lines;
- Theatres.

Travel agents earn their income through commission from the principals whose products they sell. The commission payment is usually expressed as a percentage and varies according to the product being sold and the commission policy of the principal.

You will learn more about travel agents in unit 7 (see page 287).

ACTIVITY

Make a list of the travel agencies in your area and find out whether they are independents or part of a 'chain'.

Tour operators

Tour operators are the holiday companies that many of us use when booking a UK or overseas trip. In the UK at present there are 1052 tour operator office members of ABTA. Unlike travel agents, who sell holidays and a range of other travel products, tour operators actually assemble the different parts of a holiday, by dealing with airlines, accommodation providers, coach companies and other service providers. If we consider that travel agents are the retail arm of the travel business, then tour operators can be likened to wholesalers, since they buy in 'bulk' from these suppliers of travel services, break the bulk into manageable packages and offer the finished product for sale via a travel agent or direct to the customer. The package is sold for an all-inclusive price, which is generally lower than if the component parts of the holiday had been booked individually by the holidaymaker. Figure 1.8 shows the role of tour operators and their position as intermediaries between the suppliers of travel products and travel agents.

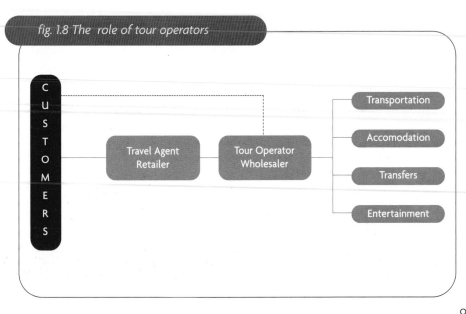

fig. 1.8 The role of tour operators

Figure 1.8 also shows that some tour operators deal direct with their customers rather than selling through travel agents. In the case of foreign package holidays booked by British people, the majority of customers use the services of a travel agent rather than booking direct with the operator. Developments in technology, however, have meant that growing numbers of people are using the Internet, digital TV, Teletext or 'direct sell' operators like Portland Holidays Direct to book their holidays. Companies that sell direct stress that, since they don't have to pay a commission to a travel agent, they are able to pass this saving on to the client who should benefit with a cheaper holiday. Also, many specialist tour operators prefer to deal directly with their clients and provide a more personal service. The more specialist the holiday product on offer, the more likely it is that the customer will deal direct with the operator, for example skiing holidays from companies such as Inghams and mountain exploration tours offered by operators such as Himalayan Kingdoms.

WEBLINK

www.portland-direct.co.uk and www.teletext.co.uk

Check out these websites for more information on the holiday products offered by these 'direct sell' companies.

Types of tour operators

There are approximately 600 UK-based tour operators, most of which are small companies specialising in a particular destination of type of product. Tour operators can be grouped into one of the following four categories:

- Mass-market operators;
- Specialist operators;
- Domestic operators;
- Incoming tour operators.

Unit 1

Mass-market operators

These operators sell high volumes of holidays and include some of the best-known names in the industry, such as Thomson (TUI), MyTravel, Thomas Cook and First Choice Holidays. According to data from the CAA (Civil Aviation Authority), these 'big four' companies organised package holidays and flights for around 12.6 million UK travellers in 2004, accounting for 45 per cent of all such products sold. As well as offering popular Mediterranean holiday destinations, tour operators are selling more packages to long-haul destinations, such as Florida, the Caribbean, Australia, New Zealand and the Far East, as travellers seek out new destinations and experiences.

ACTIVITY

Choose one of the 'big four' tour operators (Thomson, MyTravel, Thomas Cook or First Choice Holidays) and, working in a small group, find out about the history of the company, the 'products' that it sells, the destinations it flies to and the names of some of the other travel companies that are part of the same group. Researching on the Internet and in brochures should give you all the information you need.

How do you think that the 'products' offered by mass-market tour operators might change in the next 10 years? What about the role of the travel agent? How might that change in the future?

This activity is designed to provide evidence for P2 and P4.

WEBLINK

www.thomascook.com

Check out this website for more information on Thomas Cook tour operations.

FOCUS ON INDUSTRY – Thomas Cook tour operations

Thomas Cook UK is owned by Thomas Cook AG, a German company formerly known as C & N Touristic. It is currently the second largest travel group in Europe (after TUI) and the third largest in the world. Thomas Cook UK is a vertically-integrated travel group, since it owns its own sales outlets (travel agencies, call centres, Internet sites, TV channel), airline and tour operating business. Leading brands in its tour operating business include Thomas Cook, JMC and Sunset. It also boasts a number of specialist products serving 'niche' markets, e.g. Thomas Cook Signature, Latitude, Club 18-30, Flexiletrips, Neilson, Style Holidays and Sunworld Ireland.

Specialist operators

Although less well known than the mass-market operators, there are literally hundreds of specialist tour operators in the UK travel and tourism industry providing holidays and short breaks. They range from companies selling short breaks to Rome and adventure tours in the Amazon to sporting holidays in Brazil and wine tours in Italy – the variety is breathtaking! In general, specialist operators are becoming more popular as customers look for a more individual type of experience than package holidays offer. Many specialist operators are members of AITO, which we investigate in the following case study.

WEBLINK

www.aito.co.uk

Check out this website to help answer the questions in this case study and for more information on AITO and its member companies.

THE ASSOCIATION OF INDEPENDENT TOUR OPERATORS

CASE STUDY – AITO (the Association of Independent Tour Operators)

Introduction

AITO is a trade organisation representing around 160 of Britain's specialist tour operators. Its members are independent companies, most of them owner-managed, specialising in particular destinations or types of holiday. AITO was established in 1976, mainly in response to the problems posed for smaller travel companies by a sudden, sharp increase in financial bonding requirements following the collapse of a number of major tour operators. Today, AITO is increasingly recognised as the official voice of the smaller, specialist tour operator.

AITO's aims

The common aim of all AITO members is to provide the highest level of customer satisfaction by concentrating on three main pillars – choice, quality and service. It is a source of pride to the Association that AITO companies dominate the consumer-voted travel awards every year in various categories.

The AITO Quality Charter

All members of AITO adhere to its Quality Charter, covering the following elements:

- Exclusive membership – AITO sets criteria regarding ownership, finance and quality which must be satisfied before new companies are admitted to membership. All members are required to adhere to a Code of Business Practice, which encourages high operational standards and conduct.

- Financial security – AITO members are required to protect money paid by customers to the member for any holiday sold under the AITO logo and to comply with UK government regulations in this respect. Members submit details of their bonding and guarantee arrangements to the Association on a regular basis.

- Accurate brochures and websites – all members do their utmost to ensure that all their brochures and other publications, print or electronic, clearly and accurately describe the holidays and services offered.

- Professional service and continual improvements – all members are committed to high standards of service and believe in regular and thorough training of employees. Members continually seek to review and improve their holidays. They listen to their customers and always welcome suggestions for improving standards.

- Monitoring standards – AITO endeavours to monitor quality standards regularly. All customers should receive a post-holiday questionnaire, the results of which are scrutinised by the Association.

- Responsible tourism – all members acknowledge the importance of AITO's responsible tourism guidelines, which recognise the social, economic and environmental responsibilities of tour operating. Those demonstrating their achievements beyond the pure acceptance of this principle are recognised by the award of 2 or 3-star status.

- Customer relations – all members endeavour to deal swiftly and fairly with any issues their customers may raise. In the unlikely event that a dispute between an AITO member and a customer cannot be settled amicably, AITO's low-cost Independent Dispute Settlement Service may be called upon by either side to bring the matter to a speedy and acceptable conclusion.

CASE STUDY QUESTIONS

1. In what ways is AITO different to ABTA?
2. What methods does AITO use to help promote its members?
3. Name three AITO member companies that specialise in holidays to France and three that feature city breaks.
4. How does AITO help to develop more environmentally sustainable tourism?

Unit 1

Domestic operators

WEBLINK

www.wallacearnold.com
and
www.shearingsholidays.com

Check out these websites for details of the products on offer and to get the latest news on the possible merger.

Although British holidays have not been 'packaged' to the same extent as trips abroad, there are a number of UK operators that put together tours for the home market. Probably the best-known are coach operators, such as Shearings and Wallace Arnold, which are currently in talks on a possible merger. Both offer value-for-money products geared mainly to older age groups, the so called 'grey market'.

The packaging of UK short breaks has been something of a success story in recent years. Companies such as Superbreak have led the development of city and country breaks offered for sale through travel agencies. Some local authorities, keen to boost their visitor numbers, have worked with tour operators to feature their particular destinations in brochures and tour programmes.

WEBLINK

www.superbreak.com

Check out this website for details of Superbreak products.

Special interest groups are well catered for by domestic operators. Activity holidays are growing in popularity and operators, large and small, are emerging to cater for the demand, for example YHA Holidays, PGL, HF Holidays and Cycleactive. Companies offering specialist services and facilities, ranging from sketching holidays to ballooning breaks, are being increasingly sought by people looking for something unusual to do in their leisure time.

Hotel groups and marketing consortia, for example Best Western Hotels, have created and marketed domestic tours for some time, often in conjunction with coach companies. The competitive situation that has arisen in the hotels sector in recent years has forced some hotel groups to widen their customer base, by developing themed breaks, activity breaks, special interest tours and hosting weddings.

Incoming tour operators

WEBLINK

www.bitoa.co.uk

Check out this website for the latest news on incoming tourism from UKinbound.

Incoming, or inbound, tour operators supply holidays and travel products for overseas visitors to Britain. Some are based in the countries where the visitors originate, while others operate from the UK. Some are little more than handling agents offering a transfer or 'meet and greet' service on behalf of an agent or tour operator. Others, such as Gullivers Sports Travel, Pathfinders and Evan Evans Tours, offer complete package tours of the UK, which are sold through overseas agents. The packages are often themed, including tours based on British heritage, gardens or castles. Approximately 270 incoming tour operators in the UK are members of UKinbound (formerly BITOA – the British Incoming Tour Operators' Association).

You will learn more about tour operators in unit 11 (see page 331).

Unit 1

Trade associations and regulatory bodies

Trade associations are found in all areas of the economy, from the motor industry to the brewing sector. They are set up to represent the interests of companies operating in particular industry sectors and to make sure that the voice of their sector is heard. Many trade associations draw up codes of conduct which lay down the minimum standards under which member companies are expected to conduct their everyday business with customers and suppliers. Key trade associations in travel and tourism are ABTA (see case study in on page 310), AITO (see case study on page 28), UKInbound, the British Hospitality Association, the Confederation of Passenger Transport UK and the Federation of Tour Operators (FTO) — see case study on page 337 They provide advice and support for their members, and lobby central and local government to get a better deal for their member companies on issues such as taxation, regulations and funding.

All travel and tourism operators have a duty to serve the travelling public safely, fairly and efficiently. It is the job of regulatory bodies of all kinds to make sure this happens and to provide redress to the travelling public if things go wrong. Regulatory bodies exist at different levels in travel and tourism:

- Global — bodies such as ICAO (International Civil Aviation Organisation) regulate international air transport services;
- European — the European Commission introduces consumer protection measures for travellers, such as the Package Travel Regulations and Distance Selling Regulations;
- National — the UK government is responsible for legislation concerning, for example, health and safety at tourist attractions and airport security;
- Local — local authorities carry out a great deal of work on matters such as trading standards and inspections of hotels, restaurants and other food premises.

WEBLINK

www.caa.co.uk

Check out this website for more information on the work of the CAA.

FOCUS ON INDUSTRY – The Civil Aviation Authority (CAA)

The CAA is the UK's independent aviation regulator and controller of air traffic services. Its main areas of work are economic regulation, airspace policy, safety regulation and consumer protection. It manages the UK's largest system of consumer protection for travellers, the Air Travel Organisers' Licence or 'ATOL'.

ACTIVITY

Log on to the CAA's website and make notes on how the ATOL system works. Pay particular attention to whether travellers are covered by an ATOL if they buy their air ticket and accommodation separately. Present the information you find as a factsheet.

Unit 1

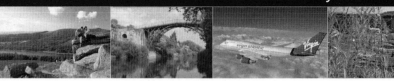

Accommodation and catering

The accommodation and catering sector, often simply called 'hospitality', is an important revenue earner in UK travel and tourism. It includes all types of accommodation that people use for leisure/business tourism and visiting friends and relatives, plus the full range of catering establishments available to visitors, from restaurants and fast-food outlets to pubs and bars. Figures from the United Kingdom Tourism Survey (UKTS) and International Passenger Survey (IPS) show that spending on accommodation by domestic and overseas visitors to Britain in 2002 was more than £11.8 billion, representing 31 per cent of total visitor spending. This made accommodation the single largest sector of tourist spending in 2002, ahead of eating out (21 per cent), shopping (19 per cent) and travel within the UK (16 per cent).

The hospitality sector is also a significant employer in the UK, as the following June 2003 figures from the DCMS website indicate:

- Hotels and other tourist accommodation   392,700 employees
- Restaurants, cafés, etc.   590,400 employees
- Bars, pubs and nightclubs   568,200 employees

Taken together, employment in the hospitality sector totals more than 1.5 million, representing over 70 per cent of all UK travel and tourism jobs. Figure 1.9 gives some examples of the importance of employment in this sector for individual companies.

Hotel	Number of Employees
Jarvis Hotels	6000
Centre Parcs	5000
Travelodge	4000
Shearings Holiday Hotels	2000
Celtic Manor Resort	650
Gleneagles Hotel	600

Fig. 1.9 Examples of employment in the accommodation sector

Unit 1

The accommodation sector in the UK is dominated by commercial enterprises, providing a wide range of hotels, guesthouses and self-catering accommodation. The main non-commercial suppliers of accommodation are the Youth Hostels Association (YHA), universities and colleges, and premises operated by religious groups.

Llangollen YHA

Popularity of accommodation

Data from the UKTS indicates that staying with friends and relatives was the most popular type of accommodation used by British people on tourist trips in 2003, accounting for 42 per cent of all accommodation used. This aside, staying in a hotel, motel, guesthouse or B&B were the most popular paid accommodation choices, with 29 per cent of all accommodation.

Types of accommodation

Visitors to Britain and UK residents can choose to stay in a wide range of establishments, all of which can be classified as 'accommodation'. For example, there are city-centre hotels, motels, farm guesthouses, country house hotels and self-catering cottages. For those looking for something a little different, the Landmark Trust specialises in self-catering accommodation in unusual settings, including a lighthouse and a former railway station!

WEBLINK

www.landmarktrust.org.uk

Check out this website for details of Landmark Trust properties.

UK accommodation can be classified in a number of ways, for example independent or part of a chain (e.g. Holiday Inn, Jarvis Hotels), commercial or non-commercial, static or mobile, urban or rural. However, it is most commonly classified as either serviced or self-catering, depending on the level of service offered.

Serviced accommodation

As its name implies, the term 'serviced accommodation' is used when a service is provided along with an overnight stay, for example meals and housekeeping. Hotels are the most common type of serviced accommodation, but the category also includes motels, guesthouses, bed and breakfast (B&B) establishments, inns, youth hostels and farm guesthouses. The British Hospitality Association estimates that there are approximately 22,000 hotels and guesthouses registered with the UK tourist boards with an additional

accommodation at timeshare properties elsewhere in the world. Although most commonly associated with overseas resorts, there are many timeshare properties in the UK. One of the first was developed on the banks of Loch Rannoch in Scotland in 1974. Most UK timeshare developments are found in the rural areas of Britain, including the Lake District, North Yorkshire, Scottish Highlands and Cornwall. As well as self-catering villas, cottages and log cabins, apartments in seaside resorts and city centres are also available on a timeshare basis.

Camping and caravanning are excellent choices for those looking for good value self-catering accommodation. The owners of many camping and caravanning sites have invested heavily in recent years, to provide their customers with an enhanced range of facilities, including swimming pools, fitness suites, entertainment and restaurant facilities, aimed principally at the family and youth market. Touring caravans are particularly popular with older age groups, many of whom are members of the Caravan Club or the Caravan and Camping Club of Great Britain.

WEBLINK

www.hoseasons.co.uk

Check out this website for more information on Hoseasons.

FOCUS ON INDUSTRY – Hoseasons Holidays

Hoseasons Holidays is a long established self-catering company, specialising in holiday parks, lodges, country cottages and boating in Britain, plus holiday parks and apartments in Europe. The company also offers boating holidays in France and Belgium. It is the leading independent holiday booking service in the UK, arranging holidays for more than 1 million customers every year. Over one-third of the company's business comes from people who have been with Hoseasons before and a further one-third comes from friends and relatives of those who have booked previously. Hoseasons employs more than 200 staff to handle its reservations, systems and marketing, dealing with 2 million telephone calls and website hits each year. It has recently invested heavily in its online booking facility.

Accommodation grading standards

Accommodation grading schemes are a way that tourist boards can classify accommodation according to the quality of facilities and standards of service on offer in a particular establishment. Customers use these schemes when selecting where to stay, with the expectation that their accommodation will be a fair reflection of the grade that it has been given. In the UK, the national tourist boards have used different schemes in the past based on crowns, stars, keys and a variety of other symbols. There are also schemes on offer from the motoring organisations. This has caused confusion amongst visitors, but from 2005-2006 VisitBritain, VisitScotland, the Wales Tourist Board, AA and RAC have designed common standards across all the British accommodation grading systems currently in place. Tour operators sometimes use their own grading schemes to classify accommodation, e.g. Thomson has its 'T' system, with the greater number of Ts indicating higher quality accommodation.

Unit 1

Public sector organisations

The 'public sector' consists of all government departments, public bodies and local authorities that provide services to the public. Public sector involvement in UK travel and tourism can be traced back to before Victorian Times when many 'resorts', both inland and on the coast, benefited from investment in tourist facilities by their local councils. However, central government recognition of the economic importance of tourism did not come until as late as 1969, with the passing of the Development of Tourism Act. This first piece of tourism legislation, now more than 30 years old, still applies today, although the nature and scale of the industry has changed dramatically. The Act established the British Tourist Authority (now VisitBritain), English Tourist Board (now part of VisitBritain), Wales Tourist Board and Scottish Tourist Board (now VisitScotland). The Northern Ireland Tourist Board was not included in the Act since it had already been established in 1948.

Public sector bodies play a major role in travel and tourism in the UK, as you can see from Figure 1.10, which shows the relationships between the various organisations with an interest in UK tourism.

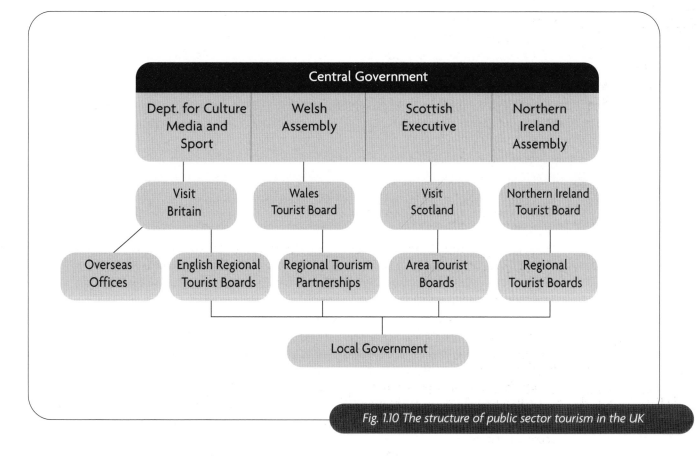

Fig. 1.10 The structure of public sector tourism in the UK

Unit 1

Figure 1.10 shows us that public sector involvement in UK travel and tourism occurs at three levels:

1. National – through the work of government departments, national tourist boards and government agencies;
2. Regional – activities undertaken by Regional Development Agencies (RDAs) and Regional Tourist Boards (RTBs);
3. Local – through local authorities.

Tourism at national level

WEBLINK

www.culture.gov.uk

Check out this website for more information on the work of DCMS in UK tourism.

The Department for Culture, Media and Sport (DCMS) is responsible for UK tourism policy. It sets the agenda for tourism, supports the industry to improve what it has to offer, provides funding and helps to promote a positive image of Britain abroad. In 1999, it published the national tourism strategy *Tomorrow's Tourism*, which was concerned with the framework for UK tourism, achieving quality, developing sustainable tourism and monitoring progress. This was updated in July 2004 when DCMS launched *Tomorrow's Tourism Today*, an action plan setting out the responsibilities of public and private sector organisations in the key areas of marketing, quality, skills and data collection.

Other government departments have an indirect involvement with aspects of tourism, e.g. the Department for Transport (DfT), Department for Environment, Food and Rural Affairs (defra), Department for Education and Skills (DfES), and Foreign and Commonwealth Office (FCO).

WEBLINK

www.fco.gov.uk

Check out this website for more information on the Foreign and Commonwealth Office and its travel and tourism support activities.

FOCUS ON INDUSTRY – The Foreign and Commonwealth Office (FCO)

The purpose of the FCO is to work for UK interests in a safe, just and prosperous world. It does this with some 16,000 staff based in the UK and in its overseas network of more than 200 diplomatic offices. As part of its service to UK citizens, the FCO offers advice to travellers. This can be before they start their journey, while in a destination or on their return home. The FCO's website has very detailed, up-to-date information on known risks to visitors in countries around the world. It offers advice on such matters as terrorist threats, travel health, child sex tourism and sustainable tourism.

Unit 1

National Tourist Boards

The UK has four National Tourist Boards:

- VisitBritain – responsible for promoting the whole of Britain abroad and England to the British;
- Wales Tourist Board – concerned with improving the economic and social prosperity of Wales through effective marketing and development of tourism;
- VisitScotland – exists to support the development of the tourism industry in Scotland and to market Scotland as a quality destination;
- Northern Ireland Tourist Board – responsible for the development, promotion and marketing of Northern Ireland as a tourist destination.

The National Tourist Boards are funded mainly from central government sources, channelled through the DCMS, Welsh Assembly Government, Scottish Executive and Northern Ireland Office/Assembly.

ACTIVITY

Choose one of the four National Tourist Boards and carry out some research to find out its aims and objectives, structure, funding sources and the range of products and services it offers.

This activity is designed to provide evidence for P3 and P4.

Tourism at regional level

The launch of Regional Development Agencies (RDAs) in England in 1999 marked a change in government support for regional tourism. Up to that time, Regional Tourist Boards (RTBs) took the lead in all tourism-related matters. Now, the RDAs are funded from central government to promote economic development, including tourism, in their areas. In most regions, the RDAs work with the RTBs to develop future plans for tourism development and marketing. There are currently 9 Regional Tourist Boards in England and 4 Regional Tourism Partnerships (RTPs) in Wales, as shown in Figure 1.11.

Unit 1

Fig. 1.11 Regional tourism structure in England and Wales

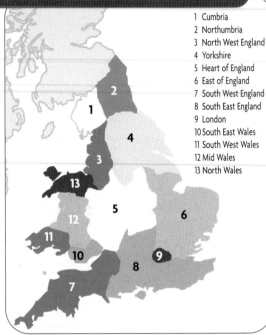

1 Cumbria
2 Northumbria
3 North West England
4 Yorkshire
5 Heart of England
6 East of England
7 South West England
8 South East England
9 London
10 South East Wales
11 South West Wales
12 Mid Wales
13 North Wales

The Welsh Regional Tourism Partnerships (RTPs) were set up in 2002 to cover North, Mid, South West and South East Wales. Their principal role is to lead the implementation of four regional tourism strategies which seek to improve the competitive performance of tourism so that it makes a better contribution to the economic and social prosperity of Wales. The RTPs work in partnership with the Wales Tourist Board, local authorities, tourism businesses and other organisations to undertake a range of marketing, product investment and business support activities on behalf of the tourism industry.

Local authorities and tourism

District, city and county councils in the UK are keen to develop tourism in their areas as a way of injecting income into the local economy and creating much needed employment. Many support the establishment of local tourism groups and associations that bring together the private and public sector. The Local Government Act of 1948 gave local authorities the powers to set up information and publicity services for tourists. This was reinforced by the Local Government Act 1972 which empowered them to publicise their areas for tourism and provide facilities for visitors.

Today, there are few local authorities in the UK that are not actively involved in some way with promoting their areas to tourists; places as diverse as Brighton and Berwick, Newcastle and Nottingham, Scarborough and Shrewsbury, are all competing for a slice of the 'tourism pound'. The scale of involvement is very variable, ranging from authorities with a single person given the responsibility for tourism development and promotion, to councils with separate tourism departments under a Director of Tourism. Some local authorities see tourism as a natural extension of their planning function and house their tourism officer and staff in this department. Other local councils consider that tourism is an integral part of economic development, while some view tourism, and particularly the marketing and promotion of tourism, as a PR activity which lends itself very well to their press and PR department.

Local authorities use their resources to provide as wide a range of tourism facilities and services that finances will allow. In a typical area, this might include:

- Promotional leaflets, brochures and websites;
- Parks and gardens;
- Theatres;

WEBLINK

www.wtbonline.gov.uk

Check out this website for more information on the work of the Regional Tourism Partnerships in Wales.

Unit 1

- Museums;
- Tourist information centres (TICs);
- Accommodation booking services;
- Sports and leisure centres;
- Outdoor activity centres;
- Art and craft galleries.

Regardless of how tourism development is organised within a particular local council, it is clear that it will remain a vital and increasing part of the work of local authorities in the future.

ACTIVITY

Do some research to find out how your local authority is involved in tourism, i.e. what is the structure, what marketing does it carry out, what are the aims and objectives for tourism, etc. Make a presentation to the rest of your group on your findings.

This activity is designed to provide evidence for P2 and P3.

Salisbury TIC

Tourist attractions

The tourist boards estimate that there are approximately 6,400 tourist attractions in the UK. Attractions are a vital part of the UK and international travel and tourism industry, since they are often the single most important reason why tourists visit an area. People have different ideas about exactly what we mean by an 'attraction'; a person living in the West Midlands may think of Drayton Manor Park or Warwick Castle as tourist attractions. People from the south of England might mention Thorpe Park, The London Eye or the Eden Project. Those living in Wales may include St Fagans, Snowdonia or Powys Castle on their list of attractions, while residents of Scotland might well mention Aviemore, Edinburgh Castle or the Burrell Collection in Glasgow. The people of Northern Ireland would surely put the Giant's Causeway or Waterfront Hall in Belfast towards the top of their list of tourist attractions.

ACTIVITY

Carry out your own survey of staff and students to find out which 'dream destination' they would choose and why.

Customers

Customers come in all shapes and sizes! Travel and tourism companies have to cater for people from a wide variety of cultural backgrounds, of different ages, travelling to different types of destinations, in groups or individually, on a package or independent tour, on business, visiting friends and relatives, etc. This complexity, together with the way that customers' needs are constantly changing, is a real challenge to the travel and tourism industry. The general ageing of the population (the so-called 'grey market') is giving travel and tourism organisations the opportunity to develop products and services for a section of the population that is living a longer, active life with a reasonable level of disposable income.

The 'grey market' offers opportunities for travel and tourism companies

Time

There is a gradual change in the pattern of taking holidays, as holiday entitlement grows, flexitime becomes more common and people choose to work more part-time and home-based. Many people talk of the decline of the traditional two-week holiday, but the reality in many parts of the UK and abroad is that it is just as important as it has ever been. What's happening is the growth of short breaks, but these are tending to be in addition to the long holiday, not replacing it. Short breaks in the UK, Europe and even further afield have been a major growth area in travel and tourism in recent years.

Activities

WEBLINK

www.aito.co.uk

Check out this website for more information on activity holidays with AITO members.

Activity tourism is a boom area of the travel and tourism industry at the moment. More people are choosing to do something more active than just sitting on the beach for their main holiday or short break. Activities such as cycling, skiing, walking and water sports of all kinds are growing in popularity, with a wide range of different customers. Many companies that offer activity holidays are members of the Association of Independent Tour Operators (AITO).

Unit 1

Technology

The travel and tourism industry has always been quick to use new technology to exploit new business opportunities. We have seen earlier in this unit that the growth in use of the Internet is revolutionising how travel and tourism products are sold to customers. Many new transport developments, such as the introduction of the Airbus A380 'super jumbo' aircraft and improvements in rail services, are driven by technology.

In hotels, high-speed Internet connections are becoming more popular in rooms and wireless connectivity is available in the public areas of a growing number of establishments. Perhaps not surprisingly, new hotels in Asia are at the forefront of developments in technology, e.g. Hong Kong's Langham Place Hotel has state-of-the-art telephony and TV systems for guests.

WEBLINK

www.aviemorehighlandresort.com

Check out this website for more information on the Aviemore Highland Resort.

FOCUS ON INDUSTRY – Aviemore Highland Resort

The new Aviemore Highland Resort, managed by MacDonalds Hotels and Resorts, is one of the first hotels to offer an interactive e-TV system in every room. Guests can access recently-released movies and more than 10,000 songs. It also offers links to radio stations from around the world, Internet access through the TV and online computer games.

Politics

Political acts such as war and terrorism can have devastating impacts on a destination and its travel and tourism industry. This is particularly true when the destination is heavily reliant on tourism and has few other economic activities. The effects of the 9/11 disaster on world travel still persist today, while recent bombings in Bali, Nairobi, Madrid and Cairo, have immediate impacts on tourism, although most destinations eventually recover lost trade.

Health and safety

In the same way that political acts can have serious consequences on an area's travel and tourism industry, natural disasters can do the same. For example, erupting volcanoes, flash floods, earthquakes and avalanches can wipe out tourist areas. The tsunami of 26 December 2004 was one of the world's most devastating natural disasters of recent times, killing nearly 300,000 people across a range of countries, including Indonesia, the Maldives and Sri Lanka. Reports from the World Tourism Organisation (WTO) suggest a drop in tourism of as much as 70 per cent in the Maldives, when January 2003 figures are compared with those of the same month in 2004. Health scares, such as SARS and Asian bird flu, can also affect tourism.

Closer to home, the outbreak of foot and mouth disease (FMD) in 2001 had a devastating impact on tourism in many rural parts of Britain. Research carried out for the Countryside Agency estimated a loss of £2-3 billion in tourism revenue in 2001.

UNIT SUMMARY

This introductory unit has considered one of the most vibrant industries in the world, offering a wide range of career opportunities to people of all ages. You have studied the main developments in travel and tourism over the past 50 years, examined some recent changes, such as the growth in use of the Internet, and considered some future trends. The unit has looked in detail at the complex structure of the travel and tourism industry, with its many industry sectors, regulatory bodies and public sector organisations. You have considered the many interrelated factors that affect the travel and tourism industry today, including technological developments, security concerns and changes in society. Throughout the unit you have been shown examples from many sectors of the travel and tourism industry. The case studies on AITO and English Heritage investigated how two organisations met their aims and objectives.

If you have worked methodically, by the end of this unit you should have:

- Investigated the development of the travel and tourism industry;
- Examined the structure of the travel and tourism industry;
- Explored the roles and responsibilities of organisations that provide travel and tourism products and services;
- Explored factors that affect the travel and tourism industry.

You are now in a position to complete the assignment for the unit, under the direction of your tutor. Before you tackle the assignment you may like to have a go at the following questions to help build your knowledge on the travel and tourism industry.

Test your knowledge

1. How has the growth in the use of the Internet affected the travel and tourism industry?
2. What is the Federation of Tour Operators (FTO)?
3. What is the role of the public sector in travel and tourism?
4. Explain the term 'quango' and give an example in travel and tourism.
5. How are call centres changing the way that holidays and other travel products are sold?
6. What is 'vertical integration'?
7. Name 3 members of AITO.
8. What is an ATOL?
9. What is the role of the CAA?
10. What is the 'grey market' and why are travel and tourism organisations so interested in it?

Unit 1

11. What is the difference between a charter and scheduled air service?

12. Why are accommodation grading schemes important?

13. What is the main role of VisitBritain?

14. How do the Regional Development Agencies influence tourism developments in England?

15. What role do local authorities play in tourism development and marketing?

UNIT 1 ASSIGNMENT: The travel and tourism industry

Introduction

This assignment is made up of a number of tasks which, when successfully completed, are designed to give you sufficient evidence to meet the Pass (P), Merit (M) and Distinction (D) grading criteria for the unit. If you have carried out the activities and read the case studies throughout this unit, you will already have done a lot of work towards completing the tasks for this assignment.

Scenario

You have always liked the idea of a career as a travel writer and have been lucky enough to secure a holiday job with Max Landers, a freelance travel writer who regularly writes for the national daily and Sunday newspapers. Max has been asked to write a series of 3 articles for the travel section of the Sunday Times, focusing on:

1. The development and structure of the travel and tourism industry;
2. The products and services provided by travel and tourism organisations;
3. Factors affecting the travel and tourism industry.

Max has asked you to help research the factual side of these articles for him and wants you to present the information as a series of Word documents so that he can incorporate them easily into his articles. He has asked you to carry out the following tasks.

Task 1

Your first document should include descriptions of the following:

(a) The development of the travel and tourism industry;

(b) The structure of the travel and tourism industry;

(c) The roles and responsibilities of different types of organisations in the travel and tourism industry (to include responsibilities to the customer, other organisations and the industry).

These tasks are designed to provide evidence for P1, P2 and P3.

The document should also:

(d) Explain how key developments have shaped the structure of the travel and tourism industry;

(e) Evaluate the effectiveness of the current structure of the travel and tourism industry to respond to customer needs and external factors.

These tasks are designed to provide evidence for M1 and D1.

Task 2

Your second document should:

(a) Describe the products and services provided by organisations in the travel and tourism industry;

(b) Analyse the range of products and services provided by different organisations in the travel and tourism industry.

These tasks are designed to provide evidence for P4 and M2.

Task 3

Your third and final document should:

(a) Describe current factors affecting the travel and tourism industry today;

(b) Analyse two factors that are having a significant effect on the travel and tourism industry today;

(c) Evaluate the effect of two factors that are having a significant effect on the travel and tourism industry today and recommend how the industry should respond, justifying your recommendations.

These tasks are designed to provide evidence for P5, M3 and D2.

The Business of Travel and Tourism

INTRODUCTION TO THE UNIT

We saw in the last unit that travel and tourism is made up of a many interrelated business sectors, such as travel agents, airlines, accommodation, tour operators and attractions. They vary from very large, global enterprises to very small, local businesses all working together to supply travel products and services as efficiently as possible to a wide variety of customers.

This unit gives you the opportunity to learn more about the different types of organisations found in the travel and tourism industry, including those that provide support of one kind or another. You will also examine a range of financial and administrative systems used in the industry, relating to banking, payments and sales. Finally, you will explore management and communication systems in travel and tourism, considering different types of ownership, staffing, technology and staff responsibilities.

WHAT YOU WILL STUDY

During the course of this unit you will:

1. Investigate different types of travel and tourism organisations, their **ownership** and the organisations that provide **support;**
2. Examine **financial and administrative systems** within the travel and tourism industry;
3. Explore **management structures and communication** systems in the travel and tourism industry.

You will be guided through the main topics in this unit with the help of the latest statistics, examples and industry case studies. You should also check out the weblinks throughout the unit for extra information on particular organisations or topic areas and use the activities to help you learn more.

ASSESSMENT FOR THIS UNIT

This unit is externally assessed, meaning that you will need to complete an Integrated Vocational Assignment (IVA) covering units 2 and 3. This is set by Edexcel and marked by your tutor(s), who will tell you how long you have to complete the assignment and what access you will have to support and resources. A grading scale of pass, merit or distinction is used for the IVA, with higher grades awarded to students who show greater depth in analysis and evaluation. A practice IVA assignment, which covers the grading criteria for this unit, can be found on page 95. Don't forget to visit www.tandtONLine.co.uk for all the latest industry news, developments, statistics and tips to help you with your IVA.

Unit 2

Unit 1 demonstrated that travel and tourism is a very wide-ranging industry, made up of many different sectors. In the following section of this unit we investigate the types of organisations found in travel and tourism, including those that provide support to new and established businesses.

Understanding the private, public and voluntary sectors

Organisations in travel and tourism are often put into one of three categories:

1. Private sector;
2. Public sector;
3. Voluntary sector.

Private sector travel and tourism

The great majority of travel and tourism organisations operate in the private sector. This means they are commercial businesses whose primary aim is to make a profit. The majority of airlines, accommodation providers, travel agencies, tour operators, attractions and support organisations are private sector enterprises. Some are very big companies, but most are small and medium-sized enterprises (SMEs), employing up to 250 people, or micro-businesses with fewer than 10 employees. Private sector businesses are financed from a variety of sources, such as bank loans, the owners' private funds, money from friends and relatives, investments by shareholders and business grants. You will learn more about the different types of private sector businesses later in this unit.

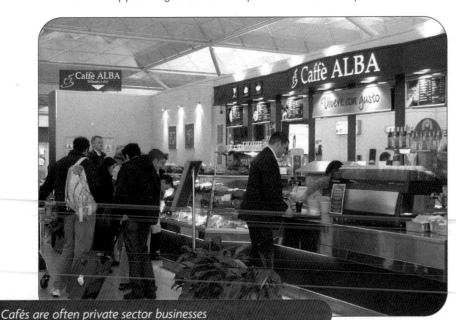

Cafés are often private sector businesses

Unit 2

Public sector organisations

Public sector travel and tourism organisations play an important role in helping to market destinations and provide a range of services to encourage tourism development. Unlike the private sector, public sector bodies are not primarily concerned with making a profit, but have wider social and economic objectives, e.g. creating jobs through tourism and improving tourist facilities for visitors and local people. As we saw in unit 1, public sector travel and tourism organisations in the UK exist at different levels:

1. National – through the work of government departments, National Tourist Boards and government agencies;
2. Regional – activities undertaken by Regional Development Agencies (RDAs) and Regional Tourist Boards (RTBs);
3. Local – through local authorities.

The government sets the policy for tourism development and looks to the National and Regional Tourist Boards to help deliver high quality products, services and destinations for visitors. They do this by working in partnership with local authorities, Regional Development Agencies (RDAs) and private sector businesses. Public sector organisations are funded from the central government, local authorities and the European Union (EU).

ACTIVITY

Carry out some research into the different public sector organisations that are involved with travel and tourism in your own area. Include national organisations (e.g. VisitBritain, Wales Tourist Board, etc.), regional bodies (e.g. Regional Development Agencies, Regional Tourist Boards, etc.) and local authorities (e.g. your local council). Don't forget to include any government agencies that provide support services to travel and tourism businesses, for example training and business advisory services.

This activity is designed to provide evidence for P1.

Voluntary sector travel and tourism

Not all travel and tourism facilities and services in Britain are provided solely by private and public sector organisations. A third important source of provision, the voluntary sector, also plays an important part in the travel and tourism industry. The voluntary sector includes charities, trusts and non-governmental organisations (NGOs) involved in:

Unit 2

- Conservation/environment;
- Community activities;
- Sustainable tourism;
- Heritage;
- Minority groups;
- Youth organisations;
- Cultural/entertainment organisations.

Voluntary organisations vary enormously in their size and aims. At one end of the scale, a small group of like-minded people may decide to set up a tourism association in a town or form a group to clear rubbish from local beaches. At the other there are large, voluntary sector organisations such as the National Trust and the Youth Hostels Association (YHA). Pressure groups play an important part in highlighting issues and campaigning for change in travel and tourism, for example Tourism Concern and the Travel Foundation. Voluntary organisations at local, national and international level often receive advice and financial help from both the public and private sector, sometimes in the form of grants or sponsorship.

YHA York

WEBLINK

www.yha.org.uk

Check out this website for more information on the YHA.

FOCUS ON INDUSTRY – YHA

The Youth Hostels Association (YHA) was founded in 1930 with the aim of promoting love, care and understanding of the countryside in principle and in practice. It currently has 226 Youth Hostels in England and Wales that welcome more than 2 million overnight stays every year. The YHA makes a major contribution to the UK travel and tourism industry by generating revenue and providing jobs. It employs up to 1350 staff in total, including approximately 600 who are seasonally employed, 500 employed all year round in Youth Hostels and 150 in the national headquarters at Matlock in Derbyshire.

Types of organisations

Travel and tourism organisations come in all shapes and sizes! Most are small and medium-sized companies employing quite small numbers of staff and specialising in a particular travel product or service. The following sections of this unit examine the different types of organisations found in the travel and tourism industry, starting with independents.

Independent organisations

These tend to be businesses that are either too small to be part of a bigger group or whose owners choose to trade independently. Many travel agents and tour operators in the UK are independents, as are the majority of hoteliers and other accommodation providers. Independents are also well represented in the tourist attractions sector and amongst the businesses that provide support services to the travel and tourism industry, such as taxi drivers, chauffeurs, coach companies, tour guides and marketing professionals. Independent organisations can often provide a more personalised service than is on offer from companies that are part of a larger group or chain. Owners of independent organisations like the freedom and flexibility that comes with this type of organisation. Many independents in travel and tourism become members of trade associations, such as the Association of British Travel Agents (ABTA), Associations of Independent Tour Operators (AITO) or the British Hospitality Association (BHA). You can learn more about ABTA and AITO in the case studies on pages 310 and 28 respectively.

Miniples/multiples

Unlike independents, which tend to be small and specialist, some travel and tourism businesses are part of much larger company groups. We saw in unit 7 that travel agencies are sometimes part of 'miniple' or 'multiple' branch structures. Miniples are companies with small numbers of branches, often in a particular geographical area. They pride themselves on being able to give independent advice on holiday choices and a personal service to their clients. Having a branch network gives miniples the chance to negotiate more favourable terms with principals. Multiple agents operate 'chains' of retail outlets under a single brand name and are some of the most familiar companies in the UK travel and tourism industry, for example Thomas Cook, Thomson, Going Places and First Choice. They are part of large, vertically-integrated organisations with interests in tour operations and airlines in this country and abroad.

Hotels can also be part of bigger groups, either owned by a parent company, eg Marriott Hotels, or part of a marketing group such as Best Western. Visitor attractions can also be part of larger organisations, e.g. the Tate has four galleries – Tate Britain and Tate Modern in London, Tate Liverpool in the Albert Docks and Tate St Ives in Cornwall, while the National Museums and Galleries of Wales has seven attractions spread across the country.

Unit 2

Franchises

Buying a franchise is a way of taking advantage of the success of an established business. The 'franchisee' buys a licence to use the name, products, services and management support systems of the 'franchisor'. Payment for the franchise may be through an initial fee, ongoing management charges, a share of the franchisee's turnover, or a combination of all three. A franchise business can take different legal forms; most are sole traders, partnerships or limited companies. Whatever the ownership structure, the franchisee's freedom to manage the business is limited by the terms of the franchise agreement. Franchises have a number of advantages over other types of business start-ups, for example:

1. The product or service has already been tested by other businesses;
2. Larger, well-established franchisors have national advertising campaigns;
3. Some franchisors offer training programmes for franchisees;
4. Good franchisors can also help secure funding for new franchisees.

WEBLINK

www.british-franchise.org

Check out this website for more information on the British Franchise Association.

Disadvantages of franchising include the fact that a share of the franchisee's turnover goes to the franchisor, which reduces overall profits, the franchisee's freedom to manage the business is limited and initial fees can be high.

Franchise arrangements are fairly common in travel and tourism, particularly in the catering sector, e.g. O'Briens Irish Sandwich Bars, Domino's Pizza, McDonalds and Subway sandwich outlets. Some car rental branches are also run as franchises, for example Budget and Hertz. The Global Travel Group is a franchise operation in the travel agency sector.

ACTIVITY

Select one of the franchise operations mentioned above and carry out some more research into how the business operates and how to start a franchise with the company.

This activity is designed to provide evidence for P1.

International organisations

Many travel and tourism companies operate internationally in more than one country, including airlines, tour operators and hotel groups. Some of the biggest companies are known as multinational corporations, with their headquarters in one country and a number of 'satellite' operations in a variety of countries around the world, e.g. Marriott Hotels and Resorts, Avis, InterContinental Hotels and Holiday Inn. Working internationally opens up new markets for businesses and allows them to take advantage of cost savings on labour,

Unit 2

WEBLINK

www.world-tourism.org

Check out this website
for more information on
the World Tourism
Organisation.

materials and distribution. However, some multinationals are criticised for taking money away from destination areas, particularly in the developing world, rather than investing in them for the long-term. Many public sector organisations also operate internationally, for example the World Tourism Organisation and national tourism organisations.

Public-private partnerships

Public-private sector partnerships (PPPs) are a good way of combining the organisational benefits of the public sector with the commercial flair of private sector companies. Working in partnership is seen as essential in developing a thriving travel and tourism industry, and PPPs can allow public organisations to access private sector funding and expertise for large-scale travel and tourism projects, such as airport expansions, rail improvements and regeneration projects involving tourism.

WEBLINK

www.conferencedevon.com

Check out this website
for more information on
Conference Devon.

FOCUS ON INDUSTRY – Conference Devon

Conference Devon is a public-private partnership aimed at encouraging the growth of conference and business tourism in and to the county of Devon. The organisation provides a free venue-finding service for businesses and individuals who want to hold any type of event, from a product launch or sales conference to a wedding or corporate event. Conference Devon promotes a variety of venues, including Bovey Castle in the Dartmoor National Park, Dartington Hall and a range of hotels throughout the county. It works with local suppliers to provide a range of services for clients. The organisation markets the conference potential of the county through brochures, direct mail, personal selling and its website.

Mergers and takeovers

Mergers and takeovers are commonplace in the competitive travel and tourism industry; in fact, it is sometimes difficult to keep track of who owns what! Being a largely private sector industry means that there are always companies and entrepreneurs willing to take a risk on acquiring a new business or expanding an existing business through a merger or takeover. Mergers tend to be with the agreement of both companies, whereas takeovers can be by agreement or are sometimes 'hostile', i.e. one of the parties concerned does not want the takeover to go ahead. New acquisitions usually offer companies access to more customers, but can add significantly to company costs. This is particularly so if the company starting the merger or takeover has to borrow money to finance the deal, since it will have to make interest payments. Recent examples of acquisitions in the travel and tourism industry are the takeover of the Go low-cost airline by easyJet in 2002 for £374 million, the acquisition of Travelbag and Bridge the World by the online travel company ebookers in 2003 and the takeover in May 2005 of lastminute.com for £577 million by Sabre, owner of the Travelocity online travel business.

Unit 2

ACTIVITY

Write a 500-word news article on a takeover or merger that has occurred in the travel and tourism industry within the last three years.

This activity is designed to provide evidence for P1.

Ownership in travel and tourism

There are many ways of owning and running a company in the travel and tourism industry. Every company must have a 'legal identity' so that it is on a proper footing to deal with organisations such as HM Revenue and Customs, the new government agency responsible for all tax matters (this agency replaces the Inland Revenue, which used to deal with tax matters, and HM Customs and Excise, formerly responsible for VAT). Businesses must think carefully about the ownership structure that best suits them, since it will affect:

- Tax and National Insurance payments;
- The records and accounts that must be kept;
- Who is liable if the business runs into trouble;
- The ways the business can raise money;
- How management decisions about the business are made.

It makes good sense to get advice from an accountant, solicitor or business adviser when choosing which ownership structure to adopt.

The main types of ownership structures available to travel and tourism companies are:

1. Sole trader;
2. Partnership;
3. Private limited company;
4. Public limited company.

There are also a small number of co-operatives found in travel and tourism, the most notable being Travelcare, the UK largest retail travel agency chain, owned by the Co-operative Group.

WEBLINK

www.travelcare.co.uk

Check out this website for more information on Co-op Travelcare and its approach to business.

Sole trader

As the name suggests, a business run by a sole trader is owned and controlled by just one person. It is the simplest way to run a small business and doesn't involve paying any registration fees. Keeping records and accounts is straightforward and the owner gets to

Unit 2

keep all the profits. There are many examples of sole traders working in the travel and tourism industry, e.g. tour guides, caterers, activity instructors, business consultants, taxi drivers, etc. The main disadvantage of being a sole trader is that the owner is personally liable for any debts that the business runs up. This means that a sole trader's home and other assets may be at risk if the business runs into trouble.

Partnership

In a partnership, two or more people share the risks, costs and responsibilities of being in business. Each partner is self-employed and takes a share of the profits. Usually, each partner shares in the decision-making and is personally responsible for any debts that the business runs up. An important point about partnerships is that the decision of any one partner is binding on all the other partners; this can cause problems if one partner proves to be unreliable or untrustworthy. In travel and tourism, partnerships are common in the hospitality sector, with many pubs, cafés, restaurants, small hotels, guesthouses and inns being run as partnerships. Advantages of partnerships are that extra capital is available to invest in the business and that the responsibilities are shared by the partners.

Private limited company

Any business that has 'limited' or 'ltd.' after its name is a private limited company. 'Limited' means that the company enjoys the benefit of 'limited liability', meaning that investors in the business are liable for company debts only up to the amount that they have actually invested. This is in stark contrast to sole traders and partnerships, where individuals are personally liable for all debts. Limited companies exist in their own right, distinct from the shareholders who own them. This means that their finances are separated clearly from the personal finances of their owners. Limited companies must be registered at Companies House and must have at least one director and a company secretary. They cannot offer shares to the public, for example via the Stock Exchange. Profits are usually distributed to shareholders as dividends. Many travel and tourism companies operate as private limited companies, with examples as diverse as travel agencies, tourist attractions, country house hotels and tour operators.

Public limited company

Most small companies that want the benefit of limited liability choose to become private limited companies, but a business that sets its sights on expansion can opt to become a public limited company (plc). These are usually large organisations with hundreds or even thousands of employees. Investors in plcs have the benefit of limited liability in the same way as those investing in private limited companies. The difference lies in the word 'public',

	Advantages	Disadvantages
Sole trader	• Independence • Easy to set up • Profits retained by owner	• No limited liability • Little support • Personal responsibility for debts
Partnership	• East to set up • Skills and experience of partners • Shared responsibilities • Extra capital available from partners	• Possible disagreements between partners • No limited liability • Partners are personally liable for debts • Decisions of one partner binding on all
Private limited company	• Limited liability • Access to extra funds for expansion • Personal risk is reduced	• Must be registered with Companies House • Extra fees for registration and incorporation • Extra legal duties
Public limited company (plc)	• Limited liability • Shares can be traded on the Stock Exchange • Status as an established company • Easier to enter into mergers and acquisitions	• Sometimes slow to react to opportunities • Less confidentiality as affairs are in the public domain • Extra costs associated with large organisations • Risk of takeover by another company

Fig. 2.1 Summary of advantages and disadvantages of ownership types

meaning that the shares of a plc can be offered for sale to the public on the Stock Exchange. Plcs must have share capital of at least £50,000 before they can be set up, i.e. they must sell £50,000 worth of shares, and must have a minimum of two shareholders, two directors and a qualified company secretary. Many of the biggest names in the travel and tourism industry are plcs, for example Virgin, First Choice, easyJet, Thomas Cook, Thomson, Cosmos, Hilton Hotels and British Airways. As well as the advantage of limited liability, plcs have greater opportunities for expansion and may benefit from significant tax advantages. One disadvantage of plcs (and private limited companies too) is that there is less confidentiality since they are required to publish their accounts annually. Also, their size and structure means that they are not always able to react quickly to new market opportunities unless.the management and workforce are very flexible.

Figure 2.1 summarises the key advantages and disadvantages of the main ownership structures described above.

Support for travel and tourism organisations

Whatever type of organisation and ownership is involved, all travel and tourism organisations need support from time to time. This could be at the start of a new venture, to help an existing company expand or even to get advice on a merger or takeover.

Unit 2

The following sections of this unit look at some of the key organisations that offer help and advice to the travel and tourism industry, as shown in Figure 2.2.

Government agencies

WEBLINK

www.businesslink.gov.uk;
www.businesseye.org.uk;
www.scottish-enterprise.com;
www.bdsni.gov.uk

Check out these websites for information on Business Link, Business Eye, Scottish Enterprise and the Business Development Service in Northern Ireland.

Business Link is the brand name under which the government's Small Business Service provides services to small and medium-sized businesses in England (Business Eye does a similar job in Wales, Scottish Enterprise in Scotland and the Business Development Service in Northern Ireland). Business Link has a network of local business advisory service providers, e.g. Business Link Kent and Business Link Cumbria. All of these agencies provide general advice for new start-up and growing businesses, in areas such as finance, marketing, legal aspects, tax and business premises.

Tourist boards in the UK operate at national and regional level. The four National Tourist Boards are:

- VisitBritain – responsible for promoting the whole of Britain abroad and England to the British;
- Wales Tourist Board – concerned with improving the economic and social prosperity of Wales through effective marketing and development of tourism;
- VisitScotland – exists to support the development of the tourism industry in Scotland and to market Scotland as a quality destination;
- Northern Ireland Tourist Board – responsible for the development, promotion and marketing of Northern Ireland as a tourist destination.

At regional level, Regional Development Agencies work with Regional Tourist Boards to promote economic development through tourism. There are currently 9 Regional Tourist Boards in England and 4 Regional Tourism Partnerships (RTPs) in Wales. Support and advice for tourism businesses is available from both Regional and National Tourist Boards. The following case study shows what is available from the Wales Tourist Board.

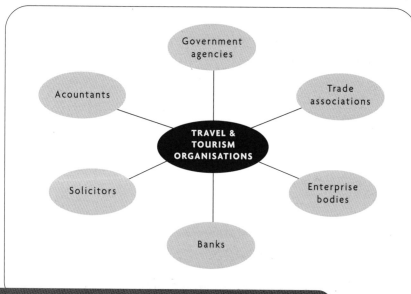

Fig. 2.2 Support organisations in travel and tourism

Unit 2

CASE STUDY – Business support from the Wales Tourist Board

Introduction

The Wales Tourist Board (WTB) was established under the 1969 Development of Tourism Act and is answerable to the Minister for Economic Development and Transport at the Welsh Assembly Government. The stated role of the Wales Tourist Board is *"to support the tourism industry and to provide the appropriate strategic framework within which private enterprise can achieve sustainable growth and success, so improving the social and economic well being of Wales".*

Business advice and support

WTB is responsible for promoting Wales as a tourism destination, carrying out research and improving the standard of visitor facilities in Wales. With funding from the European Union, WTB has developed an integrated business support package for the tourism industry. This concentrates on the need to secure competitive advantage for the industry in terms of value, quality, consistency, presentation and service. The support package is aimed at businesses that:

1. Meet the needs of key growth markets, e.g. activity tourism and short breaks;
2. Provide a competitive advantage for Welsh tourism;
3. Enhance product quality and service provision;
4. Extend the tourism season and improve profitability;
5. Provide full-time employment opportunities;
6. Demonstrate sound business planning;
7. Develop a distinctive Welsh product/experience;
8. Adopt environmentally-friendly business practices.

As part of the integrated support package, WTB provides a range of business advice and information on:

- Marketing;
- Training;
- IT and e-commerce;
- Environmental performance;
- Quality;
- Accessibility;
- 'Sense of place'.

WTB delivers these services via its website (www.wtbonline.gov.uk) and a team of specialist business advisers covering all parts of the country.

Unit 2

Developing a Successful Tourism Business Toolkit

One of WTB's most successful initiatives is its 'toolkit' aimed at developing tourism businesses. Available in paper and electronic form, the toolkit has detailed sections covering:

1. Researching your tourism business project;
2. Choosing a location and obtaining/expanding your premises;
3. Understanding legal requirements;
4. Managing your finances;
5. Designing and developing your product;
6. Providing food and drink;
7. Planning your marketing;
8. Building a winning team;
9. Delivering quality products and services;

The toolkit is primarily aimed at businesses providing serviced or self-catering accommodation, caravan and camping parks, visitor attractions, activity centres and catering establishments of all kinds, including pubs, bars, tea rooms and restaurants.

Grants for tourism businesses

WTB has a range of European-funded and other grant schemes to help raise the quality of tourism products and services in Wales, including the Event Marketing Scheme, Access Small Grant Scheme and the Visitor Amenity Scheme.

WEBLINK

www.wtbonline.gov.uk

Check out this website to help answer these questions and for more information on business advisory services provided by the Wales Tourist Board.

CASE STUDY QUESTIONS

1. Why is it in WTB's interest to offer a range of business support services to new and existing tourism businesses?
2. Log on to www.wtbonline.gov.uk and make notes on the print and electronic marketing opportunities available to businesses from the WTB;
3. What grant schemes does WTB currently have to offer tourism businesses?
4. Log on to www.tandtonline.gov.uk and make notes from the 'understanding legal requirements' section of the Developing a Successful Tourism Business Toolkit.

ACTIVITY

Carry out some research to find out what business advisory services are offered by the regional organisation with responsibility for tourism that covers your area. Use the information you find to develop a single-page information sheet that summarises the services to businesses.

This activity is designed to provide evidence for P1.

Trade associations

Trade associations exist to lobby on behalf of their members and to provide support, advice and a range of services. This often includes advice on sources of finance, business start-ups, legal matters and trade issues. Trade associations found in the travel and tourism industry include ABTA (the Association of British Travel Agents), the Association of Leading Visitor Attractions (ALVA), the Confederation of Passenger Transport UK and the British Hospitality Association (BHA). Advice from trade associations is highly valued by their members because it is very specific to their needs.

Enterprise bodies

Enterprise bodies fulfil a similar role to Business Link and Business Eye mentioned earlier in this unit. They are funded from the public purse to provide business advisory services to a wide range of industry sectors. Examples are the Welsh Development Agency, Highlands and Islands Enterprise, Scottish Enterprise and Enterprise Northern Ireland, all of which work to attract inward investment to their areas, while at the same time supporting indigenous businesses that want to start up or expand.

Banks

Banks are a popular first port of call for a business wanting to open an account or discuss financing a new venture via a business loan, commercial mortgage or overdraft facility. Many banks have small business advisers who give general business advice and can provide useful publications on business start-ups, business planning and legal aspects of running a business. Banks usually want to see a fully-costed business plan before considering an application for funding.

Unit 2

ACTIVITY

Choose one of the major banks and find out what services it provides to business start-ups, including the range of business support, types of accounts, loans, overdrafts and commercial mortgages.

This activity is designed to provide evidence for P1.

Solicitors

Solicitors can provide useful information on the many legal aspects of setting up and running a travel and tourism business, such as company incorporation procedures, contract law, employment regulations and ownership structures. They can also be called upon when disputes occur between one business and another or even between a business and one of its employees, perhaps to answer a case of unfair dismissal or breach of contract.

Accountants

Accountants handle a range of financial issues for businesses, including all tax matters, VAT, National Insurance, capital gains tax and PAYE (pay as you earn – the system for deducting income tax from employees' earnings). They can also advise on the best type of ownership structure for a travel and tourism business from a tax perspective. Accountants will use a company's trading figures to complete an annual tax return and complete a self-assessment form as appropriate.

Unit 2

SECTION 2: FINANCIAL AND ADMINISTRATIVE SYSTEMS

Sound financial and administrative systems are an essential ingredient of a successful travel and tourism organisation. Today, most systems are computer-based, but some people still prefer the reassurance of paper-based systems.

Financial systems

Accurate and easily accessible financial systems are the cornerstone of successful financial planning and control. Every travel and tourism enterprise, from the smallest bed and breakfast establishment to the largest international airline, needs to have effective financial systems in place in order to:

- Keep track of how well the organisation is performing in terms of generating revenue and controlling costs;
- Meet the legal requirements to present audited accounts at the end of each trading year;
- Make sure that its selling, purchasing and payments transactions are free from error;
- Provide continuous feedback to management to help decision-making.

In travel and tourism organisations, even employees who are not directly concerned with financial planning and control need to understand the type of information provided by accounts, such as sales volumes, pricing, cash flow and profitability. The long-term success of any organisation relies on keeping control of money and all employees contribute to this by making effective use of resources, maximising customer spending and encouraging new business.

Types of bank accounts

The most common bank account in the UK is the current account, which gives account holders a range of facilities, such as a cheque book, cheque guarantee card, credit/debit card, access to Internet banking, payment of direct debits, standing order payments and perhaps an agreed overdraft limit. Current accounts tend not to pay high rates of interest on credit balances, but some do.

Businesses nearly always open a separate business account when starting up. This ensures that all transactions associated with the business are kept completely separate from personal expenditure. It also simplifies matters when it comes to preparing accounts and completing tax returns. Banks often give new start-up businesses free banking for the first 12 or 18 months of trading, as a way of attracting new customers. It is common for a business to run a deposit account alongside its business account, with any surplus funds being transferred to the deposit account where it attracts a higher rate of interest.

Unit 2

Travel and tourism businesses that trade internationally sometimes open accounts in a foreign currency, as a way of minimising any losses associated with exchange rate fluctuations. This applies particularly to mass-market tour operators and airlines.

Receiving and making payments

Travel and tourism organisations must record all payments coming into and going out of the business. Some payments will be cash sales, when money comes immediately into the business, while others will be on credit, with payment being settled at an agreed date in the future. There are four main types of payment methods – cash, cheques, cards and electronic transfer of funds. Whichever method of payment is accepted, and depending on the policy of the individual organisation, the stages that the payment will go through are as follows:

1. Payment received by the organisation;
2. Receipt issued to customer;
3. Entry made on daily cash summary sheet;
4. Receipts and summary sheets reconciled;
5. Bank paying in slips completed;
6. Monies paid into the bank account;
7. Paying in slips stamped by bank.

Cash

Although it is becoming a little unfashionable to carry coins and notes, there are still a lot of people who wouldn't think of using anything else. Cash is the main payment method in many travel and tourism facilities, such as visitor attractions, leisure centres, museums, catering outlets and sports venues. It is usual practice to issue a receipt immediately for cash transactions, which acts as proof of purchase. Cash paid into a bank account does not need 'clearing' and is immediately credited to the organisation's account.

Cheques

Paying by cheque used to be a common payment method for customers when buying travel and tourism products and services, but cheques are gradually being replaced by card payments. They are, however, still common in business-to-business transactions. Once paid into a bank account, it will take a minimum of three working days for a cheque to be processed, during which time it remains 'uncleared'. Clearing is the process of passing the cheque to the customer's bank, debiting their account and crediting your own. Staff should always ask for a cheque guarantee card to be presented when accepting payment by cheque. Cheques for values in excess of that quoted on the card should not normally be accepted and it is safer to ask the customer to provide another form of payment. Travellers' cheques are a secure way of taking money abroad and can sometimes be used for payment in hotels and restaurants.

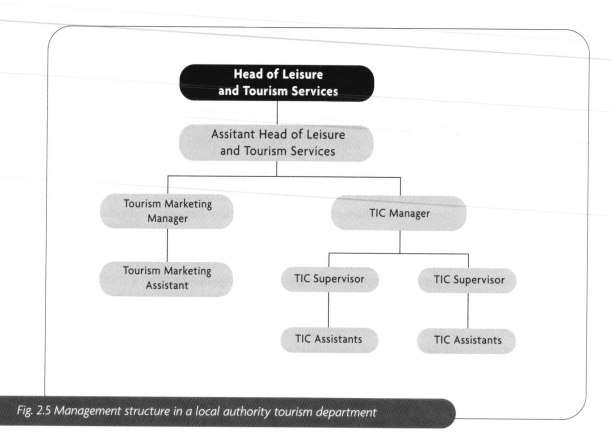

Head of Leisure and Tourism Services

Assitant Head of Leisure and Tourism Services

Tourism Marketing Manager

TIC Manager

Tourism Marketing Assistant

TIC Supervisor

TIC Supervisor

TIC Assistants

TIC Assistants

Fig. 2.5 Management structure in a local authority tourism department

Many organisations with hierarchical structures are very centralised, with power and decision making resting with a small number of powerful individuals, below which are many tiers of management. Sometimes referred to as 'steep pyramids' (see Figure 2.6), these organisations are sometimes criticised for being too bureaucratic, with decisions having to pass through a number of channels for confirmation, thus slowing up decision-making. Some public limited companies (plcs) in travel and tourism fall into this category.

Another common criticism of a centralised structure is that senior management can seem very remote from the workforce and out of touch with their everyday concerns and problems. Advocates of a centralised organisational structure would say that it has the advantage of promoting a clear corporate image for the organisation and easier implementation of common policies across very large businesses.

The shortcomings of a centralised approach have led many travel and tourism organisations to consider an alternative strategy, namely decentralisation, with less layers of bureaucracy within the organisation, resulting in faster decision-making, better communication, more senior management involvement in day-to-day activities and a positive effect on staff motivation and morale. Sometimes referred to as the 'flat pyramid', an example of this type of structure is given in Figure 2.7.

Unit 2

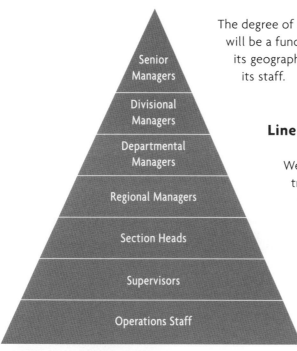

The degree of centralisation or decentralisation within an organisation will be a function of its size, the industry sector in which it operates, its geographical location, the management style and the quality of its staff.

Line and staff structures

We have seen that a typical hierarchical structure within a travel and tourism organisation consists of a number of tiers, through which responsibility, power and authority are delegated. This process is known as line management, where each employee knows to whom he or she is responsible and from whom instructions should be taken – this is their 'line manager'.

As travel and tourism organisations become more complex, the range of activities and functions carried out increases. The line management structure may then be supplemented by specialists who provide an advisory function through all departments of the organisation. These are called 'staff' structures and include:

Fig. 2.6 The steep pyramid structure

- Personnel/human resources management (HRM);
- Marketing and external communications;
- Accounting and finance;
- Research and development;
- Administration;
- Maintenance and security;
- Health and safety.

Fig. 2.7 The flat pyramid structure

Generally speaking, a 'staff' relationship describes the liaison between other employees in the organisation who are not part of the direct line of authority.

Matrix structures

Most large organisations in the travel and tourism industry operate a mixture of both 'line' and 'staff' structures, commonly referred to as a matrix structure. Figure 2.8 shows part of the matrix structure of an outbound mass-market tour operator.

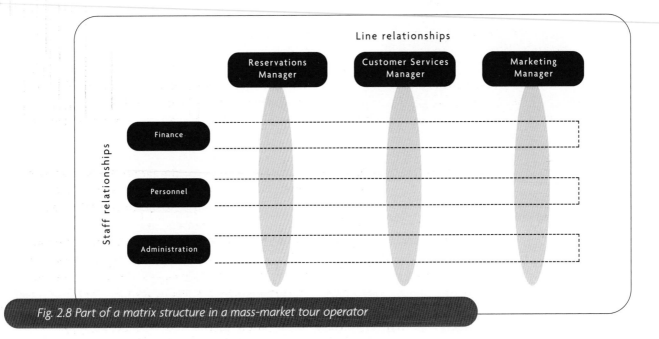

Fig. 2.8 Part of a matrix structure in a mass-market tour operator

The example in Figure 2.8 shows that 'line' relationships, where the reservations manager, for example, has responsibility for activities in his or her department, can be combined with 'staff' relationships, for example personnel, to provide an integrated and co-ordinated structure. This structure can, however, present difficulties, with friction developing between line and staff managers. Another disadvantage of the matrix structure is the blurring of lines of responsibility, lack of accountability and lengthier decision-making processes.

Functional structures

Some large travel and tourism organisations choose to develop their management structure based on the main functions carried out by the organisation. National and Regional Tourist Boards often use this structure, dividing job roles and tasks under the following functions:

1. Marketing – marketing planning, advertising, direct marketing, print, website development, travel trade activities, business and conference promotion, TIC networking;
2. Development – product development, financial help for businesses, training, business advisory services, trade relations, quality assurance, customer care;
3. Research – corporate planning, research services, policy development, planning advice;
4. Finance and administration – financial management and control, administration and personnel services, corporate press and public relations (PR), IT management.

Departmental structures

It makes sense for many travel and tourism organisations to group certain functions and activities under a particular manager and develop their organisational structure on this basis. If we take the example of a typical mass-market outbound tour operator, it will have a main UK head office, regional offices and overseas offices. The UK head office will be organised into the following departments:

- Marketing – staff employed in the marketing department are responsible for planning and developing products, which will be aimed at particular segments of the market. They focus on the selection of resorts, choice of accommodation and selection of regional UK departure airports;
- Research – a great deal of background research is undertaken to ensure that the tour operators' products have the best chance of meeting their sales potential. Research staff use a variety of sources, including internal sales data, analysis of competitors' programmes, customer comment questionnaires and financial analysis;
- Contracting – staff in the contracts department negotiate with accommodation providers over the number of beds and type of accommodation required;
- Flights – teams working on different programmes and products liaise with the flight or aviation department over how many seats they will need, which regional airports are to be used and whether day or night flights are required;
- Brochure production – teams working in the marketing department work with brochure production staff to finalise design, copy and photographs;
- Brochure distribution sales staff make decisions about how many brochures are required and to which travel agents they will be distributed;
- Promotion – marketing staff plan and co-ordinate a range of activities including advertising, direct mail, sales promotion and PR (public relations).
- Reservations – systems are developed by computer operations personnel and sales staff are fully briefed on the features of products included in the programmes;
- Agency sales support – sales representatives regularly visit travel agencies and offer product training and POS (point-of-sale) materials, such as posters and window displays;

- Administration – the administration department is responsible for producing invoices, receiving payments and issuing tickets and other documentation;
- Customer services – this department is responsible for handling complaints and queries from agents and members of the public. They try to ensure that all matters are dealt with quickly and efficiently in order to retain goodwill.

The overseas office of a major tour operator will be responsible for:

- Feeding back to head office any formal or informal research findings;
- Organising transfers to and from the accommodation and airport;
- Arranging and selling excursions and other 'extras' such as car hire;
- Finalising contracts with hoteliers and transport operators;
- The well-being, training and deployment of representatives;
- The handling of complaints and emergencies.

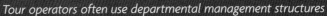

Tour operators often use departmental management structures

ACTIVITY

Working in a small team, try to find out the management structure of a local travel and tourism organisation. Present your findings as an organisation chart.

This activity is designed to provide evidence for P4.

Organisation charts

It is usual for the formal structure of a travel and tourism organisation to be shown as an organisation chart showing the levels of hierarchy. Organisation charts are very useful in giving an immediate picture of the inter-relationships between different members of staff and different departments. Organisation charts show a number of organisational features, which may include:

- Lines of communication;
- Lines of management;
- Levels of authority;
- Division of work tasks;
- Decision-making structures;
- Limits of responsibility of staff.

Unit 2

Charts vary enormously, some being very rigid while others are far more fluid and responsive to change. The difference is often down to the style of management adopted by senior staff in the organisation. An 'open' and democratic management style often leads to speedy decision-making and innovative thinking in even the biggest organisations. You can learn more about different management styles in unit 6 on page 267.

Communication systems

People working in travel and tourism need to communicate both internally and externally. Internal communication is liaison within an organisation, perhaps between members of staff in different departments or colleagues in different branches of the same company. External communication takes place with people outside the organisation, for example customers, trade bodies, the press, suppliers, regulatory agencies and members of the general public.

WEBLINK

www.ba.com

Check out this website for more information on British Airways..

FOCUS ON INDUSTRY – Communications at British Airways

BA's Corporate Communications Department exists to enhance, protect and manage the global reputation of British Airways and ensures that a wide range of audiences, including staff, customers, shareholders, media and governments, as well as competitors, know about developments and news within the airline. The staff in the department operate on a 24-hour, 7-day a week basis, responding to tens of thousands of media and staff enquiries every year. Staff in the department produce a weekly newspaper which is available to more than 50,000 staff. The team also manages the airline's Intranet, which can be used to communicate to the thousands of flight crew, cabin crew and staff who are working overseas.

BRITISH AIRWAYS

Travel and tourism organisations use a wide variety of verbal, written and electronic communication methods when communicating internally and externally, as the following sections of this unit demonstrate.

Verbal communication

Travel and tourism is a 'people industry' that thrives on verbal communication. Staff working in the industry regularly come into contact with customers, suppliers, professional bodies, regulatory authorities and the like, in the course of their everyday work. They must have good verbal communication skills that can be applied to a variety of work situations, whether it is selling a product or service, handling a complaint on the telephone or making a presentation.

Face-to-face communication is the most common of all types of verbal communication. It can be informal, perhaps a supervisor in a travel agency praising a colleague for a good job done, or more formal, as is the case when making presentations and attending meetings. Meetings fulfil a number of important purposes in organisations, such as:

- Making decisions;
- Exchanging information and ideas;
- Setting budgets;
- Negotiating pay rates and working conditions;
- Agreeing schedules;
- Setting policies.

Communicating by telephone is an essential part of most people's work duties. Staff working in travel and tourism use a wide range of telephone systems, including:

- Mobile 'phones;
- Switchboard-controlled systems;
- Voicemail;
- Telephone conferencing;
- Two-way radios.

Advances in digital technology mean that telephone systems are continually being updated to offer new facilities of a higher quality.

Written communication

There are many types of written communication methods that a travel and tourism organisation uses to liaise with people inside and outside the organisation. The main advantage of written communication is that it provides a permanent record of what took place, which can be stored for future reference. Other advantages of written communication methods are that:

- They enable complex information to be sent, e.g. statistical data;
- They serve as a permanent reminder for the recipient;
- The quality and style of presentation can be altered to appeal to different audiences, e.g. the quality of paper and use of colour;
- They provide evidence of confirmation of previous discussions.

Some of the most common types of written communication methods used in travel and tourism include:

Unit 2

- Letters and memos;
- Fax;
- Brochures and leaflets;
- Reports;
- Documents for meetings;
- Notice boards;
- Annual reports;
- Advertisements;
- Press releases.

Electronic communication

Rapid advances in new technology have opened up countless new methods of electronic communication, such as:

- Email – combines the accuracy of the written word with speed and ease of use, especially when using Broadband technology;
- Internet and Intranet – are used to communicate with the outside world (Internet) or with a closed group (Intranet) such as work colleagues in a department or whole organisation.

You can learn more about communication methods elsewhere in this book, particularly in unit 5 and unit 6.

UNIT SUMMARY

In this unit you have investigated the ownership of a variety of different travel and tourism organisations, from large international firms to small businesses. You have considered the advantages and disadvantages of different types of ownership, finding that sole traders and partnerships have a lot of independence, but whose personal assets are at risk if the business gets into trouble. Owners of limited companies, on the other hand, are cushioned from debts, but have more administrative and legal hurdles to jump. You have seen that effective and efficient financial and administrative systems are an essential component of a successful travel and tourism business, regardless of its size or industry sector. Different management structures have been explored, with a recognition that a non-hierarchical, non-bureaucratic structure, coupled with an open and democratic management style, is most likely to motivate staff and get results for the organisation. Finally, you examined internal and external communication systems used in the travel and tourism industry.

If you have worked methodically, by the end of this unit you should have:

- Investigated different types of travel and tourism organisations, their ownership and the organisations that provide support;
- Examined financial and administrative systems within the travel and tourism industry;
- Explored management structures and communication systems in the travel and tourism industry.

You are now in a position to complete the practice assignment for this unit, under the direction of your tutor. Before you tackle the assignment you may like to have a go at the following questions to help build your knowledge on the business of travel and tourism.

TEST YOUR KNOWLEDGE

1. What is the primary objective of private sector travel and tourism organisations?
2. How does a franchise work and what are the advantages and disadvantages of this type of organisation to somebody wanting to start a travel and tourism business?
3. What is a public-private partnership?
4. What is the role of HM Revenue and Customs?
5. What are the advantages of operating as a partnership rather than a sole trader?
6. What is 'limited liability'?
7. How does a merger differ from a takeover?
8. Why does the government provide finance for a range of organisations that provide support for travel and tourism businesses?
9. How do tourist boards support new and existing businesses?
10. How does being a member of a trade association help a travel and tourism business?
11. What services do banks provide for new business start-ups in travel and tourism?
12. Why does a travel and tourism organisation need effective financial systems?
13. What do 'chip and pin' and 'clearing' mean in the banking world?
14. What type of people might be interested in examining a company's accounts?
15. List the main documents used when a purchase takes place between two companies.

Unit 2

UNIT 2 ASSIGNMENT: The business of travel and tourism

Introduction

This assignment will give you practice in developing the skills and knowledge needed to complete your Integrated Vocational Assignment (IVA).

Just like the IVA, this assignment is made up of a number of tasks which, when successfully completed, are designed to give you practice in producing the sort of evidence needed to meet the Pass (P), Merit (M) and Distinction (D) grading criteria for the unit. If you have carried out the activities and read the case study in this unit, you will already have done a lot of work towards completing the tasks for this assignment.

Scenario

You've been lucky in getting a placement job with Steve Walker, the Tourism Development Manager for Worsetshire County Council. Worsetshire has just received an Objective One grant from the EU amounting to 1.8 million Euros for tourism projects in this coastal county. The money is to be used to help tourism businesses in Worsetshire improve the quality of their facilities and services for visitors. Tourism is seen by the Council as one of the key ways of encouraging economic, social and cultural development.

Part of the grant money is to be used for supporting new start-up tourism businesses and those which have been trading for less than a year. Steve is in charge of this project and wants you to help him with some of the project tasks. The first part of your job is to gather together some information that Steve can use in a series of business start-up fact sheets. The first four in the series cover:

1. Different types of travel and tourism organisations;
2. Financial systems in travel and tourism;
3. Administrative systems in travel and tourism;
4. Communication systems in travel and tourism.

Complete the following four tasks and present the information to Steve as draft fact sheets.

TASK 1

Describe four different types of travel and tourism organisations, including their ownership, and the organisations that provide support to them, explaining their role *(this task will give you practice in providing evidence for unit 2 P1).*

Unit 2

Task 2

Describe the role and purpose of financial systems in the travel and tourism industry *(this task will give you practice in providing evidence for unit 2 P2)*.

Task 3

Describe the role and purpose of administrative systems in the travel and tourism industry *(this task will give you practice in providing evidence for unit 2 P3)*.

Task 4

Describe the different types of communication systems used in the travel and tourism industry *(this task will give you practice in providing evidence for unit 2 P5)*.

The second part of your placement involves a series of visits with Steve to meet a couple who have been awarded a £35,000 grant from the Objective One money to start a new activity holiday centre close to a beautiful stretch of coastline. Steve has been giving them advice on starting a tourism business for the last six months. They are both qualified canoe and abseiling instructors, but have never run a business before. They will lead most of the activities at the centre themselves and be in overall control, but will employ two instructors during the summer season (one senior and one junior) and one during the winter, when they will run off-road cycling weekends and mid-week breaks. They also need a manager to look after the six self-catering log cabins on the site (total capacity 36 guests). Steve thinks that two further part-time staff will be needed, one to help on the domestic side and another to work on reception and act as a clerical/finance assistant.

Steve wants to give you some experience of working with the couple and has asked you to complete the following tasks.

Task 5

Devise an appropriate management structure for the activity holiday centre and produce an organisation chart *(this task will give you practice in providing evidence for unit 2 P4)*.

Explain how the management structure you have developed is appropriate to the needs of the activity holiday centre *(this task will give you practice in providing evidence for unit 2 M3)*.

Task 6

Explain the advantages and disadvantages of different types of ownership for the activity holiday centre and how each type of ownership affects the type of support available for its operation *(this task will give you practice in providing evidence for unit 2 M1).*

Task 7

Select appropriate administrative, financial and communication systems that could be used in the activity holiday centre and explain their operation *(this task will give you practice in providing evidence for unit 2 M2).*

Justify how the administrative, financial and communication systems you have selected meet the needs of the activity holiday centre *(this task will give you practice in providing evidence for unit 2 D1).*

Unit 3

Marketing Travel and Tourism Products and Services

INTRODUCTION TO THE UNIT

Marketing is one of the most important aspects of travel and tourism. It is a dynamic and continuous process that involves identifying customers' needs and then supplying holidays and other travel services to meet these needs. In the highly competitive travel and tourism industry, organisations of all sizes need to take a professional approach to marketing if they are to succeed in business.

This unit introduces you to the principles of marketing in the context of the travel and tourism industry. You will examine different types of market research and see how the marketing mix is applied to travel and tourism. The unit also gives you the chance to apply practical marketing skills.

WHAT YOU WILL STUDY

During the course of this unit you will:

1. Explore **marketing** in the context of the travel and tourism industry;
2. Examine different **methods of market research** and how they are used by the travel and tourism industry;
3. Consider how the **marketing mix** could be applied to a travel and tourism organisation;
4. Apply **practical marketing skills** for the travel and tourism industry.

You will be guided through the main topics in this unit with the help of the latest statistics, industry examples and case studies. You should also check out the weblinks throughout the unit for extra information on particular organisations or topic areas and use the activities to help you learn more.

ASSESSMENT FOR THIS UNIT

This unit is externally assessed, meaning that you will need to complete an Integrated Vocational Assignment (IVA) covering units 2 and 3. This is set by Edexcel and marked by your tutor(s), who will tell you how long you have to complete the assignment and what access you will have to support and resources. A grading scale of pass, merit or distinction is used for the IVA, with higher grades awarded to students who show greater depth in analysis and evaluation. A practice IVA assignment, which covers the grading criteria for this unit, can be found on page 150. Don't forget to visit www.tandtONLine.co.uk for all the latest industry news, developments, statistics and tips to help you with your IVA.

SECTION 1: MARKETING IN TRAVEL AND TOURISM

We see examples of travel and tourism marketing around us every day, such as:

- Window displays in travel agencies;
- Holiday adverts and travel articles in newspapers and magazines;
- Holiday promotions on packets of breakfast cereals and drinks;
- Interviewers asking us about our holiday likes and dislikes;
- Holiday programmes and channels selling holidays on television;
- Flyers posted through our letterboxes;
- Discounts and other special offers on flights and holidays.

These are all part of marketing, which goes far beyond just advertising and promotion, as you will learn when you work through the rest of this unit.

Marketing principles

In this first section we investigate some of the key principles that underpin marketing in travel and tourism, starting with defining just what we mean by the term 'marketing'.

Definition of marketing

A useful 'shorthand' definition of marketing is that it is about getting the right products to the right people in the right place at the right time at the right price using the right promotion. A ferry company, for example, will invest a lot of time and money finding out exactly what its customers want from the company, e.g. when they want to travel, what facilities they would like, which destinations they want to travel to and how much they are willing to pay. It will then try to provide services geared to its customers' needs, using a whole host of ways of letting them know what's on offer, for example through brochures, advertisements, mailshots, posters and via the Internet.

A more formal marketing definition from the Chartered Institute of Marketing (CIM), the UK professional body for marketing professionals, is:

'Marketing is the management process for identifying and satisfying customer needs profitably'.

Unit 3

This definition stresses the importance of marketing as a management process, to be considered along with personnel, finance and human resources in organisations of all sizes. Identifying customer needs is crucial and involves a range of market research techniques that we will investigate later in this unit.

Functions of marketing

Many people think that marketing is just about advertising; this couldn't be further from the truth. In reality, the functions of marketing are much more complex, involving identifying customer needs, developing products and services, promotion and evaluation, as shown in Figure 3.1.

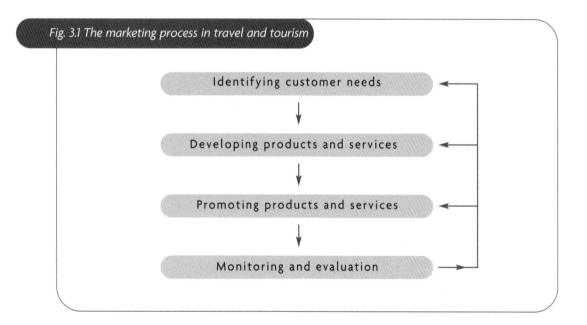

Fig. 3.1 The marketing process in travel and tourism

Identifying customer needs

Developing products and services

Promoting products and services

Monitoring and evaluation

Figure 3.1 demonstrates a number of important points about the functions of marketing:

- The marketing process starts with identifying customer needs. Knowing the facts about your customers, such as whether they like your holidays, how much they are willing to pay, whether they are satisfied with the service you offer, where they live, and so on, provides essential information when marketing decisions are being made. Different types of market research are used to find out this sort of information.
- Once you know your customers it is much easier to develop products and services that they will want to buy. By giving attention to such matters as price, location, access and features, you will be able to give your customers what they want.

Unit 3

- Having developed your products, you must decide the best way of promoting them to your customers, which could include advertising, direct mail, sponsorship or any one of a wide range of techniques that we will investigate later in this unit.
- Evaluation is an important part of the process since marketing is a dynamic activity that must adapt to changes in people's tastes and fashions. It is only by constantly monitoring and evaluating its marketing that a travel and tourism organisation can make best use of its resources.

Market and product orientation

So far, we have stressed the importance of putting customers at the heart of the marketing process in travel and tourism; this is known as 'market orientation' and is the approach that should be adopted to ensure the best chance of marketing success. Companies such as Virgin, British Airways, Disney and Center Parcs, all put customers at the heart of their operations to achieve business success. 'Product orientation' focuses on developing products and services without taking full account of customer needs, an approach that is very likely to fail.

Understanding customer needs and wants

We have already seen that successful marketing must start with understanding customers' needs and wants, adopting a 'market-orientated' or 'customer-focused' approach. In order to be able to put the customer at the hub of all activity, travel and tourism organisations need to have certain basic information on the characteristics of their customers, such as:

- How many are there?
- Where do they live?
- What ages are they?
- Are they male or female?
- What is their income level?
- How much money do they spend?
- How do they make their bookings?
- What do they think of your products and services?

Without this basic data, any travel and tourism organisation, whether it's a city-centre hotel, museum, art gallery, activity centre or visitor attraction, will be basing its management decisions purely on guesswork. Decisions on matters such as pricing, design of promotional material, advertising media used and choice of menus, can only be carried out effectively with accurate knowledge of present and future customers.

Unit 3

It is important to appreciate that customers' needs and expectations are always changing. For example, what was acceptable on a package holiday 10 years ago is unlikely to meet the needs of today's customers. Today, we demand speedy travel to our holiday resorts, fine food, wines and service when we get there, plus a standard of accommodation that is no worse (and sometimes better!) than we have in our own homes. Higher standards of living, greater freedom to travel, advances in technology and transport developments have all combined to raise our expectations of travel and tourism.

ACTIVITY

Working as a member of a small group, carry out a simple survey of a selection of people of different ages. Ask them what they look for when choosing a holiday abroad and how their needs have changed over the years. Record their answers on a sheet and discuss with other members of your group the similarities and differences of the people interviewed.

Market segmentation

Market segmentation is the process of dividing the total market for a product or service (i.e. all the people who could buy it) into different 'segments', each with broadly similar characteristics. Companies carry out segmentation since it allows them to focus more clearly on the needs and wants of particular groups, for example older people, young people wanting activity holidays or high spenders looking for the ultimate in luxury.

Markets can be segmented in a number of ways, for example by:

- Geographical region, e.g. all the people living in a particular postcode area of a city could be sent a holiday company's brochure;
- Age, e.g. designing holidays to meet the needs of the 18-30 age group or people over the age of 55;
- Social class, e.g. targeting all the people in an area in the C2 (skilled working class) social group;
- Gender, e.g. developing holidays for women;
- Life style, e.g. introducing new activity holidays for young people who live adventurous life styles.

Market segmentation is, therefore, a tool that a travel and tourism organisation can use to satisfy the needs of its particular customers. Being concerned with the needs and expectations of customers, however, does mean that segmentation relies heavily on market research to help match the product exactly to the clients' needs.

Unit 3

FOCUS ON INDUSTRY – Market segmentation

Blackpool Pleasure Beach is the UK's most popular tourist attraction with around 6 million visitors every year. The company carries out in-depth market research on its visitors and uses the data to segment its market. The under 15 and 15-25 age groups make up the bulk of customers to the attraction and this is reflected in the products on offer, e.g. the rides and fast-food catering. Around 80 per cent of visitors come from the C1, C2 and D socio-economic groups; the company uses this information to choose where to advertise the attraction.

The marketing mix

The 'marketing mix' applies to all industries, but is particularly important in travel and tourism. It is sometimes called the 4 Ps, 5 Ps or even 7 Ps! The 4 Ps are the cornerstones of the marketing mix – product, price, place and promotion. More recently, planning has been added as another key aspect of marketing (see Figure 3.7 on page 122). Travel and tourism organisations must strike a balance between the 5 Ps of the marketing mix in order to achieve their marketing objectives, e.g. a new company just setting out is likely to spend more on promotion in order to get itself known, while an established business will need to monitor its prices in relation to the competition and make changes as necessary. Just how much effort and budget an organisation gives to each of the 5 parts of the marketing mix will change over time. The marketing mix is covered in greater detail in section 3 of this unit (see page 122).

Marketing communications methods

Travel and tourism organisations use a wide variety of methods to communicate with their customers. Advertising is the most visible, but there are other methods that can be equally as effective, for example brochures and other print items, direct marketing, public relations (PR) work, sales promotion and sponsorship. Communication allows companies to inform customers of products and services, and persuade them to buy. All of these communication methods are looked at in greater detail in section 3 of this unit when we investigate the marketing mix in travel and tourism in greater depth (see page 122).

Constraints and issues

Marketing does not take place in a completely free and unregulated business environment; if it did, customers would have no protection and companies could use all sorts of unwelcome techniques to market their products. There are many constraints on how companies carry out their marketing activities and various issues to be considered, as shown in Figure 3.2.

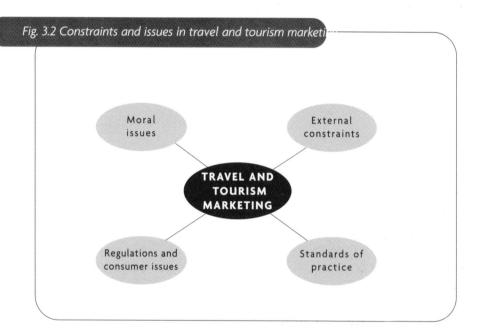

Fig. 3.2 Constraints and issues in travel and tourism marketing

The constraints and issues shown in Figure 3.2 are put in place to protect individuals and society in general from unscrupulous, illegal and unethical marketing activities.

Moral issues

All marketing activity must conform to acceptable moral standards, for example by not showing prejudice against religious, ethnic or other sections of the population and by not being overtly sexual or distasteful in content. Like all companies, travel and tourism firms are expected to show social responsibility and to be ethical in all their marketing activities. A good example of this are companies that adopt the principles of 'green tourism', sometimes called 'sustainable tourism' or 'responsible tourism'; they go out of their way to promote holidays that do not harm the environment or the local people in the holiday destinations they feature.

Unit 3

WEBLINK

www.tourismconcern.org.uk

Check out this website for the latest information on Tourism Concern and its campaigns for fair tourism.

FOCUS ON INDUSTRY – Tourism Concern

Tourism Concern is a campaigning non-governmental organisation (NGO) that highlights injustices in tourism development around the world, particularly in developing countries, and seeks to promote a type of tourism that is fair to all. One of their recent campaigns has been to focus attention on the poor working conditions of Sherpas who work with tourists in the Himalayas.

External constraints

Travel and tourism organisations need to be aware of external constraints on their operations, i.e. factors outside of their direct control. Many use a technique called PEST analysis to examine their external business environment. PEST stands for political, economic, social and technological, the main external factors that can influence organisations. The PEST analysis will vary between different organisations, but is likely to include information on the following influences:

Fig. 3.2 Electronic ticketing (e-ticketing) is being introduced in more airorts to save time at check-ins

- Political – central/local government and European Union policy on travel and tourism, taxation, local authority constraints, regional development, legislation, regulation/deregulation. A good example is the introduction of the latest phase of the Disability Discrimination Act legislation and its impact on access to tourism businesses;
- Economic – disposable incomes, exchange rates, cost of oil, inflation, levels of unemployment. The recent rise in the price of crude oil and its impact on the cost of air travel is a good example of an economic factor;
- Social – demographic trends, lifestyle changes, community involvement, education, changing work practices, holiday entitlement, retirement, environmental awareness. A good example is the ageing of the population and the opportunity it offers holiday companies to sell to a growing market;
- Technological – global communications, the Internet, reservations systems, payment methods, transport developments. The introduction of e-ticketing by airlines is a good example of a technological factor in travel and tourism.

Unit 3

Travel and tourism organisations must also keep abreast of what their competitors are doing in terms of products, pricing and standards of service. This competitor analysis is vital if they are to be successful.

ACTIVITY

Using the examples of PEST factors given above, work with a colleague to identify three more specific examples in each category (political, economic, social and technological). Discuss your ideas with other members of your group when you have completed your list.

Regulations and consumer issues

Travel and tourism organisations must follow a variety of laws and regulations when carrying out their marketing work, including:

- The Consumer Protection Act 1987 – this Act makes it a criminal offence for an organisation or individual to give misleading price information about goods, services, accommodation or facilities they are offering for sale. The Act has special significance for travel and tourism operators who must ensure the accuracy of any price information in their brochures, on the Internet or in other publicity material;
- The Trades Description Act 1968 – one of the original pieces of consumer legislation that aims to protect customers against false descriptions, either verbally or in writing, given by suppliers of goods and services. In the case of travel and tourism, any description of, for example, a hotel or tourist attraction, must be truthful at the time it was written (if circumstances subsequently change, the operator must inform the customer);
- The Data Protection Act (DPA) 1998 – this important legislation, originally introduced in 1984, aims to promote high standards in the handling of personal information by organisations and so protect a person's right to privacy. The DPA applies to firms holding information about individuals in electronic format and, in some cases, on paper. Under the terms of the Act, organisations holding information may need to register and comply with a series of Data Protection Principles, covering such matters as accuracy and security of the information, and its use for lawful purposes.

Companies must also follow contract law when selling their products and services to customers.

Unit 3

Figure 3.3 shows us that market research can be grouped around four key areas – customers, products, promotion and competitors.

Customers

Identifying customer needs, attitudes and values is a key purpose of market research; the more a company knows about its customers the better chance it has of providing products and services that they will buy. As we will see later, there are many techniques that can be used to collect customer data, from face-to-face interviews to self-completed questionnaires.

Market research can also be used to classify customers into different groups, thereby helping with market segmentation. Common classifications used in travel and tourism include:

- Socio-economic;
- Lifestyle;
- Lifecycle;
- Demographic;
- Geographic.

Socio-economic classification

For many years, this classification based on 'social class' was the only one available to marketers. Individuals were placed into one of six categories according to the occupation of the head of the household (see Figure 3.4).

SOCIAL GRADE	SOCIAL CLASS	TYPICAL OCCUPATIONS
A	Upper middle	Higher managerial, admin. and professional (e.g. judges, surgeons)
B	Middle	Intermediate managerial and admin. (e.g. teachers, doctors)
C1	Lower middle	Supervisory, clerical, junior management (e.g. bank clerk, estate agent)
C2	Skilled working	Skilled manual workers (e.g. joiner, welder)
D	Working	Semi- and unskilled manual workers (e.g. driver, porter)
E	Lowest level	Pensioners, casual workers, unemployed people

Fig. 3.4 Socio-economic classification

The underlying principle of the socio-economic classification is that those in each category will have similar interests, display similar patterns of buying behaviour and have similar income levels. It is assumed, also, that those at the top of the scale will have the highest level of disposable income, i.e. money left over when all household and other commitments have been met. Clearly, it is unrealistic to assume that everybody in a

Unit 3

particular category will act in exactly the same way, for example, a surgeon (social grade A) may choose to read The Mirror, a newspaper read mostly by working class people (social grade D). In recent years, this type of classification has been replaced by more sophisticated techniques which analyse what people actually do with their time.

Lifestyle classification

A further refinement of the process of categorising customers came with the introduction in Britain during the 1980s of the concept of lifestyle classification, a technique that had been previously used in North America. One of the first British companies to test the concept was Young and Rubicam, a well-known advertising agency, who developed a lifestyle classification known as the '4 Cs'; four classes of people who were categorised according to their lifestyles, as the following case study shows.

CASE STUDY – Lifestyle classification

Introduction

Classifying customers according to their lifestyles is now commonplace in travel and tourism. As the boundaries between young and old, rich and poor, work and leisure are broken down, it is much more useful to gather information on what people actually do in their leisure time rather than using classifications that generalise about age, income and employment. Young and Rubicam were one of the first advertising agencies to use this type of classification.

The categories

The company developed the following categories according to people's lifestyles:

* Mainstreamers – these are people who are looking for security and who live a conventional lifestyle. They usually buy well-known brands of products, such as Heinz, Birds Eye and Fairy Liquid, rather than 'own brands'. Mainstreamers do not want to 'stick out from the crowd'. They are by far the largest of the four groups, accounting for around 40 per cent of the British population. Their travel preferences are rather conventional, choosing well-known holiday companies, such as Thomson and British Airways Holidays, and familiar overseas destinations, such as Spain and Portugal.

Unit 3

- Aspirers – these are people looking for status and who like to be thought of as being 'at the cutting edge' of society. They buy status symbols such as fast cars and expensive jewellery and generally like 'the good things in life'. They are risk-takers and many aspirers run their own businesses. Holiday interests include adventure activities such as hang-gliding, motor sports, power boating and expensive overseas holidays to long-haul destinations.
- Succeeders – these are people who have already achieved status and who ultimately like to be in control of their lives. They have no need for status symbols but value quality in all that they purchase. Travel interests include gardening, taking short breaks, cultural holidays and playing golf.
- Reformers – these are people who consider that 'quality of life' is more important than status and status symbols. They are the best educated of all four groups and tend to join groups to influence decision-making in society. They buy many natural products and 'own label' products; they are sometimes referred to as 'the Sainsbury shoppers'! Travel is often family-orientated and includes camping, walking and cycling, both in the UK and overseas countries such as France and Holland. They are the group most likely to seek out companies that offer 'green tourism' holidays.

CASE STUDY QUESTIONS

1   Why is this type of lifestyle classification likely to give a travel and tourism company better market research data than the socio-economic classification?
2   Name three holiday destinations that are likely to appeal to aspirers.
3   Name three holiday companies that mainstreamers are likely to use.
4   Name three cities that succeeders may well choose for a short break.

ACTIVITY

Divide your group into four equal teams, each choosing to investigate one of the lifestyle classification categories described in the case study (mainstreamers, aspirers, succeeders or reformers). Working with others in your team, carry out some detailed research on two holidays that you think would appeal to people in your category. Include full details of the holidays (cost, destination, mode of travel, etc.) and explain your reasons for choosing the holidays and why you think they would be of appeal.

Unit 3

Life cycle classification

The life cycle concept puts an individual into one of nine categories which are based, not on income, but on where that person is in his or her life cycle. The categories, with an indication of their likely demand for travel and tourism products, are:

1. Batchelor stage – young single people with few ties and a reasonable level of disposable income. Likely to frequent clubs in the UK and take adventurous holidays abroad;
2. Living together/newly-wed – possibly a higher disposable income with leisure pursuits such as going to the cinema, eating out, going to clubs, taking short breaks and holidays abroad;
3. Full nest 1 – young marrieds/living together with youngest child less than six. Beginnings of family-orientated leisure including visits to the park, tourist attractions and family holidays;
4. Full nest 2 – as above but youngest child over six. Falling disposable income, less spending on travel, but some holidays taken in the UK;
5. Full nest 3 – older couples with dependent children, perhaps still studying. Disposable income low. Leisure centred on the home, with some holidays in the UK and cheaper overseas holiday options;
6. Empty nest 1 – older couples, childless or children all left home. Level of disposable income likely to be restored. Demand for short breaks, overseas travel and active leisure;
7. Empty nest 2 – older couples, chief breadwinner retired. Income again restricted. Avid watchers of the television and listeners to the radio with holidays again centred on the UK;
8. Solitary survivor 1 – single/widowed person in work. Home and garden likely to provide most leisure activity, with few holidays taken;
9. Solitary survivor 2 – as above but retired. Little spare cash for travel. Television, radio and other home entertainment are important leisure activities.

WEBLINK

www.saga.co.uk and
www.soloholidays.co.uk

*Check out these websites
for more information on
Saga Holidays and Solo
Holidays.*

Demographic classification

Another way to classify customers is by using 'demographics', i.e. by looking at the characteristics of the population, such as age, family circumstances, gender and ethnicity. Travel and tourism companies sometimes develop holidays according to certain demographic factors, e.g. Saga Holidays for people over the age of 50 and Solo Holidays for lone-parent families. Britain, along with many other Western countries, has an ageing population, with people generally living longer, healthier lives. This offers travel companies business opportunities in what is a growing market.

Unit 3

Geographic classification

It is sometimes useful to group customers according to where they live or even based on the destinations they choose for their holidays; this is known as geographic classification. A database system called ACORN (a classification of residential neighbourhoods) groups people according to where they live in the UK. The information on the database is drawn from various sources, including the electoral register, and can be used to produce names and addresses in particular postcode areas for marketing campaigns. Travel agents and tour operators hold databases of their clients' destination choices, which can be used to alert the clients to special offers in their favourite resorts.

WEBLINK

www.caci.co.uk

Check out this website for more information on the ACORN system.

FOCUS ON INDUSTRY – Geographic classification

A country house hotel in Wales used the ACORN system to target A, B and C1 individuals in the West Midlands as part of a direct mail campaign to attract more customers. The mailing consisted of a colour brochure of the hotel and a personalised letter from the owner. The campaign was very successful in attracting 30 per cent more customers from the West Midlands in a single year.

Products

Market research has a very important role to play in developing products and services, since it can help to shape product development and raise product awareness amongst customers. For example, if a holiday company finds from its market research that customers are unhappy with the service standards at a particular resort hotel, the company may decide to switch to a different hotel or even a different resort altogether if the problem persists.

A travel and tourism company will also use internal data to monitor sales trends in its products and make adjustments as necessary, e.g. a self-catering cottage agency may decide not to represent particular properties if sales are poor.

FOCUS ON INDUSTRY – Monitoring sales trends

Low-cost airlines such as easyJet, bmibaby, flybe and Ryanair use sophisticated computer software to monitor levels of sales and activity across their route networks, introducing new services where demand exists and closing unpopular routes if demand is low.

Unit 3

Promotion

Travel and tourism organisations use market research to make sure that their promotional work is as effective as possible. A major airline or holiday company, for example, may employ an advertising agency to measure the effectiveness of its advertising campaigns to make sure that the money spent isn't wasted. They do this by holding focus groups (see page 119), interviewing airline passengers and monitoring sales levels. The agency will monitor how much extra business is generated by the advertising and report back to the travel company.

Competitors

Keeping an eye on what the competition is doing is an important activity for any business, not least in the highly competitive travel and tourism industry. Organisations use a variety of methods to monitor competitor activities and employ staff to gather useful 'market intelligence' on their competitors. In the case of a major tour operator, this will include information such as how much competitors are charging for their holidays, when their brochures are launched, where they advertise their holidays, what they include on their Internet sites, which countries they feature in their brochures and which regional airports they use. A company will use information about its competitors to fine tune its own products and services to try and stay ahead of the competition. Gathering information about competitors is such a sensitive area in travel and tourism that when staff leave one company to join another they often have to sign a statement to say that they won't disclose any information about their former employer's products and business practices. This is sometimes called a 'gagging clause'.

Methodology

Once a travel and tourism organisation has identified the need to carry out some market research, it has to decide whether to conduct primary research, secondary research or a mixture of the two. Primary research is collecting new data that is not already available from another source, e.g. a survey of visitors to a theme park. Secondary research is the analysis of data that is already available, either from an organisation's own records or from another source, for example a report from Mintel or a tourist board's annual report. Figure 3.5 shows some of the main market research sources used in travel and tourism.

Unit 3

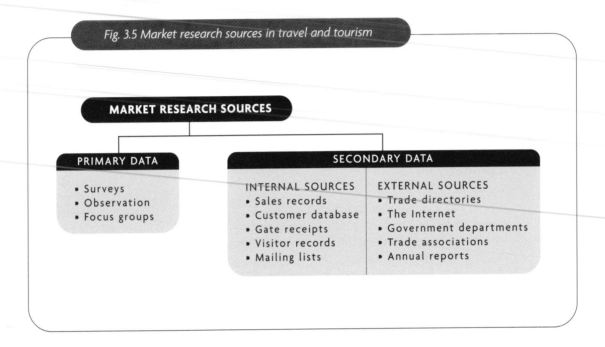

Fig. 3.5 *Market research sources in travel and tourism*

MARKET RESEARCH SOURCES

PRIMARY DATA

- Surveys
- Observation
- Focus groups

SECONDARY DATA

INTERNAL SOURCES
- Sales records
- Customer database
- Gate receipts
- Visitor records
- Mailing lists

EXTERNAL SOURCES
- Trade directories
- The Internet
- Government departments
- Trade associations
- Annual reports

Primary research

There are three common types of primary research used in the travel and tourism industry:

- Surveys using questionnaires;
- Observation;
- Focus groups.

Surveys

By far the most common method of collecting primary data in travel and tourism is by conducting a survey, which involves collecting information and views from a cross-section of people. There are three main types of survey that can be used to collect primary data:

- Face-to-face interview survey;
- Self-completed questionnaire survey;
- Telephone survey.

Unit 3

Face-to-face interviews

A face-to-face interview survey involves an interviewer asking questions of a member of the general public, known as the respondent, and recording his or her answers and comments on a questionnaire. This type of survey is very common in all sectors of the travel and tourism industry, from tourist attractions to holiday resorts. The face-to-face interview is a very good way of obtaining both quantitative and qualitative data (see page 121).

Face-to-face interviews can be carried out in a number of different locations, such as:

1 At the respondent's home — more in-depth interviews tend to be carried out in the comfort and privacy of the home;
2 In the street — busy high street locations are often used to interview a cross-section of the general public on general issues related to holidays and travel;
3 On-site — for example, at a leisure centre, tourist attraction, hotel, resort, airport, fitness centre, etc. On-site surveys have the advantage that customers can be interviewed while they are actually taking part in the activity;
4 *En-route* — for example, at a frontier post, a toll booth, on a ship or at a motorway rest area;
5 At work — organisations wanting information on business and conference tourism may choose to interview respondents at their place of work.

Face-to-face interviews have a number of advantages when compared with other survey methods:

• The interviewer is able to explain difficult questions;
• Visual aids such as photographs can be used;
• The interviewer can prompt the respondent for further detail;
• Initial interest on the part of the respondent is aroused.

The principal disadvantages of the face-to-face interview are that it is expensive, since the interviewers have to be fully trained and the administrative load is high, and that it is time-consuming when compared with other techniques, e.g. telephone interviews. It does, however, continue to be used very widely in travel and tourism as a means of providing valuable information that can be used by management to improve its products and services.

Self-completed questionnaire surveys

A survey that asks respondents to fill in a questionnaire themselves has the benefit of being cheaper than a face-to-face interview survey, since there is no need to recruit and train interviewers. Self-completed questionnaire surveys are used extensively in travel and tourism, as a relatively low-cost method for obtaining both qualitative and quantitative data on customers. Many tour operators carry out a postal survey of returning holidaymakers, asking them to complete a questionnaire related to their holiday experience (see Figure 3.6).

Unit 3

Setting objectives

We all need objectives or targets to work towards to be successful. You may be saving up for driving lessons or perhaps a holiday with friends and have set some targets of your own. The same applies to marketing in travel and tourism organisations. Marketing objectives are the specific aims or goals that an organisation sets itself when deciding on its marketing activity. It is important for all travel and tourism organisations to be clear from the outset what they are trying to achieve from their marketing. Examples of marketing objectives for an expanding holiday company could be to:

- Increase profitability – by improving sales by 10 per cent and reducing costs by 5 per cent in the next 12 months;
- Challenge the opposition – by developing a new range of holidays to Australia to compete with a competitor company;
- Build the company's image – by starting a high-profile advertising and public relations campaign;
- Increase market share – by capturing another 5 per cent of the total sales of holidays to Fiji;
- Enter new markets – by increasing the number of holiday destinations it uses from 8 to 12 within 18 months;
- Combining elements of the marketing mix – by increasing expenditure on promotion and reducing spend on distribution.

Every travel and tourism organisation will have its own specific marketing objectives which will reflect its overall business aims. Private sector operators, such as travel agencies and hotels, operate in the commercial world and will gear their marketing towards maximising their sales. The public and voluntary sectors, including local tourist attractions and the National Trust, will be looking to fulfil their wider community and social objectives by perhaps providing facilities for local people or following a conservation cause.

Whatever marketing objectives an organisation sets itself, they must be SMART, in other words:

- Specific – it's no use having 'woolly' ideas that are not well thought through or clearly defined;
- Measurable – objectives must be capable of being measured so that you know if you have achieved your targets;
- Achievable – setting objectives that are wildly optimistic wastes everybody's time;
- Realistic – objectives must fit in with the organisation's overall business aims;
- Timed – it is important to set time deadlines to review progress.

Remember also that setting objectives is not a 'one off' activity; they must be constantly monitored and updated in the light of changing circumstances.

Unit 3

FOCUS ON INDUSTRY

The management of a new country house hotel in Devon has set itself the following clearly-defined business objectives:

- To achieve a minimum room occupancy of 72 per cent;
- To set up a website within 6 months;
- To achieve a Michelin Star for the restaurant;
- To achieve a tourist board 4* rating for quality;
- Implement customer service training for all staff;
- Achieve Investors in People status.

All management and staff in the hotel work as a team in order to achieve these objectives.

ACTIVITY

Working in small groups, imagine that you are helping a relative to set up a travel and tourism business in your local area. It could be a new travel agency, a cycle hire scheme, a B & B or perhaps a series of guided walks for visitors. Write down a list of the marketing objectives that the company will need to achieve if it is to be a success. Remember that they must be SMART!

Product

Travel and tourism products are very different from many other products that we buy and use. Even using the term 'product' is rather misleading, since travel and tourism is a service industry offering a variety of holiday experiences and travel services, rather than providing consumer goods such as cars, CDs or hi-fi systems. In fact, travel and tourism is often thought of as an industry that succeeds by 'selling dreams', perhaps a Caribbean cruise or a weekend break in Amsterdam - but we still have to pay for it!

Travel and tourism products are sometimes sold separately, for example a return flight from Birmingham to Paris, or they may be combined with other products to make a package, e.g. hotel accommodation, charter flight and coach transfer all combined to make an overseas package holiday.

Below are a few examples of travel and tourism products:

- Short breaks;
- Airline flights;
- Tourist attractions;
- Car hire;
- Coach travel;
- Package holidays;
- Hotel accommodation;
- Cruises.

The range of travel and tourism products offered for sale is very wide, since there are many specialist companies satisfying the needs of a wide variety of customers. In reality, anything that can be sold by a travel and tourism company can be thought of as a product, even a cycling trip in the Himalayas or a balloon flight over the Grand Canyon. The important part is that somebody is willing to pay for the experience and that the company can offer a safe, reliable and efficient standard of service.

The nature and characteristics of travel and tourism products

Unlike many other everyday products that we buy, travel and tourism products are:

- Intangible – for example, you can't touch or see a short-break holiday to Venice or a visit to a tourist attraction in the same way that you can a new car or mobile 'phone. The travel and tourism industry is in the business of selling 'experiences';
- Perishable – a seat on a ferry, ticket for an event or room in a guesthouse that is not sold today can't be stockpiled and sold at a later date and is, therefore, a lost sales opportunity for the company concerned. Discounts, special offers and promotions can be used to generate extra sales;
- Service-related – staff working in travel and tourism are employed to provide a service and they play a crucial role in providing customers with a pleasant experience while on their holiday, short break or day visit.

Branding

A brand is an easily-recognisable name given to a company, product or service in order to raise awareness amongst customers and generate sales. People often buy travel and tourism products from companies with well-known brand names, for example Thomson, National Express, Holiday Inn, Disney and easyJet. These companies spend huge sums of money on promoting their brand, in advertising, public relations work, livery (the colours and logos used on their vehicles, etc.), staff uniforms and corporate stationery. Branding gives a

Unit 3

company or product a clear identity and helps set it apart from its competitors. Many customers show 'brand loyalty', meaning that they will regularly buy a particular company's products above all others. It is not uncommon for clients to book with the same travel agency, airline or holiday company year after year, with the expectation of high standards of service every time.

easyJet has a very clear brand identity

WEBLINK

www.ba.com

Check out this website for full details of BA's business activities.

FOCUS ON INDUSTRY – Branding at British Airways

'British Airways' is the company's primary brand and it is used to create a certain expectation about the products and services that people will experience when travelling with the airline. BA's brand promise is a combination of both emotional and functional benefits, which manifest themselves through the company's customer service operations. In addition to its main brand, BA also has sub-brands that are targeted at particular segments of the market. These sub-brands include First, Club World, World Traveller Plus, World Traveller, Club Europe, Euro Traveller, Domestic and Executive Club.

USPs, niche products and differentiation

Travel and tourism is a very competitive industry and organisations work hard to make their products and services more appealing to potential customers. Some companies try to develop a USP (unique selling proposition), which is a special benefit that one product or

Unit 3

(e) Identify the main marketing objectives of your market research document in task 3(d) and demonstrate that you have applied effective marketing skills by designing and producing a market research document that meets the needs of Center Parcs *(this task, together with task 4(c)) will give you practice in providing evidence for unit 3 M3).*

(f) You should demonstrate that you are able to produce a market research document in task 3(d) to business standard. You should also produce a detailed explanation of how your market research document meets the needs of Center Parcs and your marketing objectives in task 3(e) *(this task, together with task 4(d), will give you practice in providing evidence for unit 3 D2).*

Task 4

(a) In your groups, discuss the range of promotional activities appropriate to and used within the travel and tourism industry.

(b) Individually, produce two different types of promotional material suitable for Center Parcs *(this task will give you practice in providing evidence for unit 3 P4).*

(c) Identify the main marketing objectives of your promotional materials in task 4(b) and demonstrate that you have applied effective marketing skills by designing and producing the promotional materials that meet the needs of Center Parcs *(this task, together with task 3(e), will give you practice in providing evidence for unit 3 M3).*

(d) You should demonstrate that you are able to produce promotional materials in task 4(b) to a business standard. You should also produce a detailed explanation of how your promotional materials meet the needs of Center Parcs and your marketing objectives in task 4(c) *(this task, together with task 3(f), will give you practice in providing evidence for unit 3 D2).*

Unit 4

Tourist Destinations

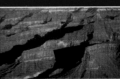

INTRODUCTION TO THE UNIT

Having a good knowledge of popular tourist destinations and what they can offer visitors is essential for many people working, or hoping to work, in the travel and tourism industry. Tourists are becoming more adventurous and are travelling further afield, always looking for new areas to visit and trying out new experiences. Staff in travel and tourism must be able to satisfy this demand for more knowledge about destinations, knowing where to find information for visitors and how to present it to them in a logical manner.

This unit gives you the opportunity to study aspects of tourist destinations, in the UK, continental Europe and worldwide. You will develop your research skills by using a range of atlases, trade directories, brochures, tourist guides and the Internet. You will also explore major transport routes that link tourist-receiving and tourist-generating countries, i.e. the holiday destinations and the home countries of the travellers. The unit also explores the factors that contribute to a destination's appeal and looks at the tourism potential of destinations.

WHAT YOU WILL STUDY

During the course of this unit you will:

1. Use **sources of reference and research skills** to provide a range of information;
2. Examine major **transport routes** that link tourist-generating and receiving areas;
3. Explore the **factors** that contribute towards a destination's appeal;
4. Investigate the **tourism potential** of different locations.

You will be guided through the main topics in this unit with the help of the latest statistics, industry examples and case studies. You should also check out the weblinks throughout the unit for extra information on particular organisations or topic areas and use the activities to help you learn more.

ASSESSMENT FOR THIS UNIT

This unit is internally assessed, meaning that you will be given an assignment (or series of assignments) to complete by your tutor(s) to show that you have fully understood the content of the unit. A grading scale of pass, merit or distinction is used for all internally assessed units, with higher grades awarded to students who show greater depth in analysis and evaluation in their assignments. An assignment for this unit, which covers all the grading criteria, can be found on page 189. Don't forget to visit www.tandtONLine.co.uk for all the latest industry news, developments, statistics and tips to help you with your assignments.

Unit 4

SECTION 1: SOURCES OF REFERENCE AND RESEARCH SKILLS

Working in travel and tourism often calls for a detailed knowledge of destinations and the features that appeal to different types of visitors. Luckily, you are not expected to know everything about every destination in the world the minute you start your job in the industry! Knowledge and experience of destinations grows over time. However, what you will be expected to know very quickly is where to get hold of information, which is the topic we look at first in this unit by examining a range of the most common reference materials used in travel and tourism.

Reference materials

Reference materials used by staff working in travel and tourism will vary depending on the type of job they do. For example, much of the information that travel agency staff need is computer-based, but many still use a variety of atlases, country guides, brochures, travel directories, timetables, maps and manuals in the course of their work, giving information on resorts, hotels, attractions and general travel requirements. People working in 'tourism' jobs, e.g. in a tourist information centre or for a National or Regional Tourist Board, may well use different reference sources, such as hotel guides, data from surveys, e.g. the International Passenger Survey (IPS), and reports from the World Tourism Organisation.

WEBLINK

www.statistics.gov.uk

Check out this website for more information on the International Passenger Survey.

FOCUS ON INDUSTRY – International Passenger Survey (IPS)

The IPS is a survey of a random sample of passengers entering and leaving the UK by air, sea or the Channel Tunnel. Over 250,000 face-to-face interviews are carried out each year. The survey provides valuable information on international travel for the government, public agencies and the travel and tourism industry.

Atlases

Atlases are an excellent starting point for locating countries, continents and popular tourist destinations. They usually have a range of maps at different scales and often include information on weather and climate. The World Travel Atlas published by Columbus Travel Guides is produced specially for people working in travel and tourism. As well as a variety of general and specialist maps, it includes detailed information on world airports (with 3-letter codes), heritage areas, national parks and transport routes.

Unit 4

The World Travel Atlas

Country, area, resort and city guides

Countries that are keen to attract tourists will have a national tourism organisation (NTO) that is responsible for producing guides and brochures on tourist accommodation, attractions and facilities, e.g. the French Government Tourist Office or the Spanish National Tourist Office. These publications often use high quality pictures to tempt people to visit. Smaller tourist areas also develop guides, which may not be as glossy but give very detailed local information. Major resort areas, such as the Costa Blanca in Spain and Brittany in France produce their own guides for visitors, usually working with hoteliers and tourist attraction operators who pay for an entry. City guides offer detailed advice on travel, accommodation and tourist information. You should remember that all of these types of guides are first and foremost sales tools, i.e. they are designed to encourage people to visit the areas being promoted and spend money there! As such, they are written in very glowing terms and may not always give a balanced view of a destination. Commercial destination guides, such as those from Lonely Planet and the *Rough Guides* series, as well as organisations such as Which?, claim to offer a more objective view of what an area offers visitors.

Manuals

WEBLINK

www.oag.com

Check out this website to see the full range of OAG Guides for the travel and tourism industry.

Manuals are aimed at people working in travel and tourism (the 'travel trade') rather than the general public. They provide very detailed information on, for example, destinations, airlines, hotels and rail companies. The *World Travel Guide* from Columbus Press has country-by-country information, including transport to and within areas, passport, visa and health requirements. OAG (formerly Overseas Airways Guides) publishes a range of guides for air and rail services, including the *OAG Rail Guide* and the *OAG Flight Guide*. Trade Associations, e.g. ABTA, the Passenger Shipping Association (PSA), AITO (the Association of Independent Tour Operators) and IATA (the International Air Transport Association) produce specific manuals for the travel trade.

Timetables

WEBLINK

www.nationalrail.co.uk
www.raileurope.co.uk

Check out these websites for planning rail journeys using the National Rail Timetable and Rail Europe

Individual airlines, ferry operators, cruise companies, tour operators, rail companies and coach/bus operators produce their own timetables to help travel agents and members of the public plan journeys. Timetables are available in printed form and many are published on the Internet, e.g. the UK National Rail Timetable. Rail travellers wishing to go further afield can consult the *Thomas Cook European Timetable* and *Thomas Cook Overseas Timetable* to plan their journeys. Rail Europe provides details of train journeys in Europe on its website.

Unit 4

Brochures

Brochures are an essential part of selling holidays and other travel products. A good brochure helps turn an enquiry into a sale. The range of brochures used in travel and tourism is vast, covering everything from holidays abroad, luxury hotels and activity breaks to ferry services, holiday centres and cruises. As well as giving basic information on products and services, brochures often include details of prices or tariffs. Some companies prefer to use their brochures just to create an image, while providing prices and other details on their website; this allows them to change prices without having to reprint their brochures. The cross-Channel ferry companies are a good example of this. Remember that brochures are sales tools, so may not always give an unbiased view of a holiday or travel product.

Brochures are full of useful information

The Internet and CD-roms

The Internet is a particularly good source of information on travel and tourism, but the secret is discovering the really useful websites amongst the millions that search engines tend to find! The secret is to be as specific as possible when using Internet search engines such as Google, MSN Search and Yahoo, e.g. searching for 'self-catering villas with pools in Nice' will give you much more useful information that simply entering 'holidays in the south of France'. CD-roms are useful for storing large amounts of information on travel and tourism, although Internet-based products are becoming more popular.

The following websites are useful starting points for gathering information on tourist destinations:

- www.wtgonline.com;
- www.antor.com;
- www.travelocity.com;
- www.abtanet.com;
- www.aito.co.uk;
- www.lonelyplanet.com;
- www.oag.com;
- www.roughguides.com.

Unit 4

ACTIVITY

To develop your Internet research skills, gather details from each of the eight websites listed above (starting with www.wtgonline.com) and produce information sheets containing useful tourist information for visitors to any two of the following destinations – Pisa, Madrid, Vienna, Stockholm or Prague. Each information sheet should cover no more than 2 pages of A4.

This activity is designed to provide evidence for P1.

The Internet is also useful for finding general information on travel and tourism from a variety of sources, for example:

- Annual reports of the UK tourist boards, i.e. VisitBritain, Northern Ireland Tourist Board, Wales Tourist Board and VisitScotland;
- Consultancy reports from a range of companies, e.g. Mintel, MORI;
- Data from the Office for National Statistics;
- Reports from professional bodies, e.g. the Tourism Society, Institute of Travel and Tourism (ITT), HCIMA (Hotel and Catering International Management Association);
- Annual reports from commercial travel and tourism organisations, e.g. British Airways, Thomas Cook, TUI Thomson, MyTravel Group.

Remember that www.tandtONLine.co.uk has direct links to all the websites featured in this book, so you can get many more details about particular companies, organisations or topics at the click of a mouse!

Gazetteers

Gazetteers are used by travel agents to find independent information on destinations and accommodation in resorts. Two of the most popular are the *Hotel and Travel Index (HTI)* and the Apartment Gazetteer.

Hotel guides

Hotel guides are available from hotel companies themselves, e.g. Best Western, Holiday Inn, Crowne Plaza and Marriott Hotels and Resorts. Again, these are promotional booklets, so are written in a very positive style. Guides from independent publishers, for example the *Good Hotel Guide* and the *Which? Guide to Good Hotels*, claim to offer unbiased advice. Hotel guides produced by tourist boards usually only feature hotels that are registered and meet agreed accommodation standards.

Unit 4

In 2001, road transport represented 51 per cent of the total and air transport 39 per cent. Transport by water accounted for 7 per cent and rail transport 3 per cent. Over time, a clear trend can be seen — a slow but steady increase in air transport at the expense of transport over land (road and rail). From the UK perspective, we saw in Unit 1 that travel by private car is the most popular type of transport used by British people on tourist trips, accounting for 73 per cent of all trips in 2003.

The following sections of this unit look in more detail at the main types of transport used to reach tourist destinations — road transport, travel by rail, air travel and water transport services.

Road transport

Road transport includes travel by private car, bus and coach, taxi, hired car and bicycle. The private car is an important form of travel for tourist purposes, especially for domestic tourism and intra-continental travel. British people use their cars for day trips, short breaks and longer holidays, often travelling great distances to reach their destination. For example, taking a car to France or Spain for a summer holiday or driving to the Alps for skiing or snowboarding is not uncommon. The car offers a degree of flexibility, convenience and value for money that other types of transport find hard to beat, but it does bring with it considerable environmental problems.

Britain has a well-developed motorway and trunk road network, although it can get very congested at times. Unlike in many other European countries UK motorways don't charge tolls, although the recently-opened M6 relief road skirting Birmingham does levy a charge. The London Congestion Charge is now an accepted part of travel in the capital and it is likely that more road-pricing schemes will be introduced in the future to help persuade drivers to leave their cars at home and take public transport instead.

ACTIVITY

Download a blank map of the UK from www.tandtONLine.co.uk and, using an atlas or road map, mark on the main UK motorways and the principal towns/cities they connect.

Unit 4

Coach travel offers a range of services aimed at different customers, particularly young people travelling on a tight budget and older people on organised tours. Scheduled services from National Express link more than 1200 of Britain's cities and main towns, while coaches are used by tour operators for airport transfers and excursions on overseas package holidays.

Coach holidays offer good value for money

WEBLINK

www.nationalexpress.com /eurolines_microsite/index.cfm

Check out this website for more information on Eurolines.

FOCUS ON INDUSTRY – Eurolines

Eurolines (part of the National Express Group) operates low-cost, scheduled coach services from London to more than 25 countries in Europe, including Croatia, France, Morocco, Latvia, Lithuania and Estonia.

Travel by rail

The UK has an extensive rail network linking all major centres of population and many rural areas. It has, however, suffered from lack of investment over a long period of time and is presently undergoing major engineering work and upgrading of rolling stock. The government aims to support and promote a bigger, better and safer railway system, with £60 billion of public/private funding over the next 10 years.

In stark contrast to the situation in the UK, the French government has invested considerable public funds in its rail system, with its 'flagship' TGV (train de grande vitesse) network offering a high-speed service across the country. The French rail system is used extensively for tourist travel and the TGV is regarded as a viable alternative to domestic air services for business travel within the country. A similar situation exists in Japan, where the so-called 'bullet' trains link major centres of population. One notable exception to the poorly developed UK rail network is the Eurostar service linking London with Paris, Brussels and other major European cities via the Channel Tunnel, offering a high-speed service to business and leisure travellers.

Unit 4

WEBLINK

www.raileurope.co.uk/
inter-rail/

*Check out this website
for more information on
the Inter-Rail pass.*

FOCUS ON INDUSTRY – Inter-Rail

Inter-Rail is a travel pass that gives the holder unlimited travel on train services in 29 European countries (including Morocco) for 16 or 22 days, or a full month's travel. The Inter-Rail map of Europe is divided into 8 zones. Travellers can choose to travel in any 1 zone, 2 zones or all 8 zones. Current prices range from £145 for a 16-day pass to be used in 1 zone by somebody under 26 years of age to £405 for a one-month pass for use in all zones by a person over the age of 26. Countries in the scheme include Bulgaria, Ireland, Croatia, Poland, Portugal, Spain and France.

ACTIVITY

Do some more research on the Inter-Rail pass and plan an itinerary for two 19-year old students who want to spend a whole month travelling around Europe this summer. They particularly want to visit Scandinavia and some of the new EU member countries. They would like to start from London and travel on Eurostar for the first part of their journey. Show all travel costs.

Air travel

We saw in unit 1 that air travel is the fastest-growing sector of transport for tourism, driven by increased demand for long-haul travel and the rapid growth of the low-cost airlines. The majority of overseas visitors to Britain arrive by air, particularly those from long-haul destinations such as Australia, the Far East and the USA. Travel by air within the UK has grown dramatically in recent years, the result of cheaper fares and an expanded network of services to and from regional airports. Data from the CAA (Civil

Airport	Terminal passengers ('000s)
Heathrow	63,208
Gatwick	29,893
Manchester	19,520
Stansted	18,716
Birmingham	8,924
Glasgow	8,115
Edinburgh	7,476
Luton	6,786
East Midlands	4,254
Belfast International	3,954
Source: CAA	

Fig. 4.2 Top 10 UK airports 2003

Unit 4

Aviation Authority) indicates that passenger numbers at UK airports have grown steadily in the last 25 years, from 58 million in 1980, up to 102 million in 1990 and peaking at 200 million in 2003. Figure 4.2 shows the busiest UK airports in terms of passenger numbers in 2003.

Much of this growth in air travel is the result of the way low-cost airlines have developed so rapidly. Figures from ABTA show that weekly seats offered by the low-cost carriers rose from 100,000 in 1995 to 1 million in 2002, due in no small part to the growing popularity of the Internet.

WEBLINK

www.thomsonfly.com

Check out this website for the latest information on Thomsonfly.com.

FOCUS ON INDUSTRY – Thomsonfly.com

Thomson, part of the German-owned TUI Group, launched its own low-cost airline Thomsonfly.com in December 2003 and began flights from Coventry Airport in March 2004. The airline currently flies out of 3 bases – Coventry, Robin Hood Airport Doncaster Sheffield and Bournemouth Airport – to a range of European beach, leisure and city destinations, including Alicante, Paris and Malaga. Thomsonfly.com carried its one millionth passenger in February 2005 and, by summer 2005, will be operating with a team of over 450 crew members, a four-fold growth on the airline's original 110 employees.

The growth in demand for air travel has led to new developments in airports and associated infrastructure, e.g. extra car parking, new road and rail access routes, etc. Airport expansion is a controversial topic; it seems that everybody wants cheap and convenient air travel on their doorstep, but not everybody is prepared to put up with the noise and inconvenience that airports and air travel can cause.

ACTIVITY

Visit easyJet's website at www.easyjet.com and find out which destinations the airline flies to. Mark these on an outline map of Europe that you can download from www.tandtONLine.co.uk

Travel by sea and inland waterways

As an island nation, Britain has a variety of ferry services around its coasts. The busiest of these provide links to France, Ireland, Spain, Holland and Scandinavia for passengers and freight. The number of services crossing the English Channel has fallen sharply since the opening of the Channel Tunnel in 1994. In 2004, Eurotunnel carried 2.1 million cars and 63,000 coaches, accounting for half of all cross-Channel traffic, while Eurostar (the train service through the Channel Tunnel) carried 7.2 million passengers. To compete with the Tunnel, ferry companies have introduced faster and more comfortable vessels, enhanced levels of customer service and greater on-board shopping and entertainment facilities.

Unit 4

WEBLINK

www.the-psa.co.uk

*Check out this website
for the latest information
on cruising from the PSA.*

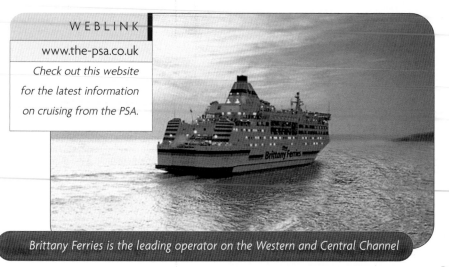

Brittany Ferries is the leading operator on the Western and Central Channel

Cruising is a sector of the travel and tourism industry that is growing steadily and developing new markets. Whereas in the past cruising tended to be the preserve of rich and famous senior citizens, today's cruising industry has products geared to all ages and budgets. The arrival of mass-market tour operators and new generation vessels onto the cruising scene has heralded a new era of packaged cruises at bargain basement prices. For the first time in 2003, one million British travellers took a cruise, according to figures from the Passenger Shipping Association (PSA).

ACTIVITY

Locate the following popular cruise destinations on an outline map of the world (which you can download from www.tandtONLine.co.uk):

Vancouver, San Francisco, Los Angeles, Buenos Aires, Rio de Janiero, Manaus, Bridgetown, San Juan, Miami, Tampa, New Orleans, New York, Tenerife, Funchal, Malaya, Lisbon, Barcelona, Civitavecchia, Naples, Piraeus, Istanbul, Aqaba, Venice, Genoa, Nice, Amsterdam, Hamburg, Copenhagen, Gothenburg, Bombay, Singapore, Tokyo, Hong Kong, Bangkok, Sydney, Auckland.

WEBLINK

www.britishwaterways.co.uk

*Check out this website
for more details of
Britain's inland
waterways.*

The network of inland waterways in the UK offers British and overseas tourists an opportunity to discover some of the remoter parts of the country, while at the same time exploring Britain's industrial heritage. There are approximately 3,200 km of navigable canals and rivers in England, Scotland and Wales, half of which is owned and managed by British Waterways.

Routes

We have seen in this unit that travellers can choose from a wide variety of travel types to get to their destination. The precise route that they take depends on a number of factors, such as:

Unit 4

- Cost – everybody looks for value for money when they are choosing their travel arrangements, whether it is a trip to Edinburgh with a budget airline or an expensive cruise across the Atlantic on the Queen Mary 2 cruise liner. Cost is not always such an important consideration for business travellers, who often have to travel at short notice and on premium services, although many companies try to economise on business travel costs whenever possible. Travellers with limited means will often use the Internet to get the best possible deals on their travel arrangements;

- Journey time – this can be an important factor for people who need to reach their destination as quickly as possible, perhaps to catch an onward flight or make an important business engagement. Other travellers may be quite happy to choose a route that takes them 'off the beaten track';

- Convenience – travel by car is perhaps the most convenient of all types of travel given its 'door-to-door' appeal, although it is impractical for longer journeys. Public transport services worldwide have become far more convenient in recent years, with greater investment in services and facilities for all types of travellers;

- Frequency of services – this may be an important consideration for people who make a lot of journeys to the same destination, or who may be unsure of their exact time of departure or arrival. Not surprisingly, the most popular routes tend to have the highest frequency of travel services, to meet customer demand;

- Range of services provided – people with specific needs, for example access to business facilities or particular food and drink requirements, may choose services with this factor in mind.

If we take the example of a trip from London to Paris, which is served by an array of travel services and routes, a cost-conscious traveller may well choose to take the Eurolines coach from London's Victoria Coach Station to the centre of Paris. A businessman may decide to take the Eurostar rail service from Waterloo to the Gard du Nord in Paris, but come back on a British Airways' flight to Heathrow. A couple on a weekend break may take their own car with them for convenience and use the Channel Tunnel or a ferry, taking the Autoroute to Paris. Whatever route is chosen, all will hope to have a safe and secure journey there and back.

ACTIVITY

Using the above example of a trip to Paris, carry out some detailed research to find the choice of routes and transport services for travellers from London to the following destinations – Milan, Amsterdam, Madrid, Lille and Berlin. Make a note of costs, frequency of services, companies that operate the services and journey times.

This activity is designed to provide evidence for P1 and may contribute towards D1.

Unit 4

Gateways

All destination countries have 'gateways' through which tourists arrive. These can be airports, ports, border crossings or rail stations. Gateways are the focus for transport services, offering travellers convenient entry points with a range of facilities and services provided, e.g. refreshments, currency exchange, shopping, etc. Gateways also allow authorities to control and monitor movements of people in and out of their country, ensuring safety and security for all passengers. Security at international gateways has been tightened up since the 9/11 disaster in 2001 and more recent terrorist attacks.

The number of gateways to a particular country will vary depending on a number of factors, such as its popularity as a tourist destination, its size and transport infrastructure. As an example, the USA currently has 20 international gateway airports spread throughout the country, located in or close to the following cities:

- Atlanta
- Baltimore
- Boston
- Chicago
- Dallas/Fort Worth
- Denver
- Detroit
- Houston
- Los Angeles
- Miami

- Minneapolis/St Paul
- New York/Newark
- Orlando
- Philadelphia
- Phoenix
- San Francisco
- Seattle
- St Louis
- Tampa
- Washington

ACTIVITY

Locate the international airports listed above on an outline map of the USA, including the full name and 3 - letter code of each airport (you can find information on airport codes at www.worldairportguide.com). You can download a blank map of the USA from www.tandtONLine.co.uk

Airports

Airports around the world are expanding to accommodate the rapid growth in global air travel. Preliminary figures from Airports Council International, representing the world's international airports, show the following as the world's busiest airports in 2004 (passenger numbers in brackets in millions):

Unit 4

1. Atlanta   (83.5)
2. Chicago   (75.3)
3. London (Heathrow)   (67.3)
4. Tokyo   (62.3)
5. Los Angeles   (60.7)
6. Dallas/Fort Worth   (59.4)
7. Frankfurt   (51.1)
8. Paris   (50.8)
9. Amsterdam   (42.5)
10. Denver   (42.4)

Ports

Ports are focal points for ferry services and cruise ships. They offer a range of facilities, such as currency exchange, refreshments and travel advice.

ACTIVITY

Make a chart of the main ferry ports in the UK, the ferry companies that operate out of these ports and the destinations they serve. Use the sources of information mentioned at the beginning of this unit (see page 154) as the starting point for your research.

Stations

Stations can be both the start/finish point of a journey and act as interchanges for passengers who need to change trains of change to a different mode of travel. One of the busiest stations in London is the Eurostar terminal at Waterloo.

Eurostar train at Waterloo International Terminal

Unit 4

WEBLINK

www.eurostar.com

Check out this website for more information on Eurostar.

ACTIVITY

Log on to the Eurostar website and compile an information sheet for travellers. Include details on destinations served, typical prices, facilities for travellers, short breaks, etc.

This activity is designed to provide evidence for P1

Hubs and interchange points

Transport routes are often concentrated on hubs or interchange points, to make it more convenient for travellers and more cost-effective for operators. A hub is simply a single point from where a series of transport services start and finish, e.g. Victoria Coach Station in London is one of the hubs for the National Express network of coach services. Airlines often operate a 'hub and spoke' arrangement, with the 'hub' representing the home airport and the 'spokes' being the routes that the airline operates from that airport. British Airways uses Birmingham International Airport as an important hub for many of its European services, as shown in Figure 4.3.

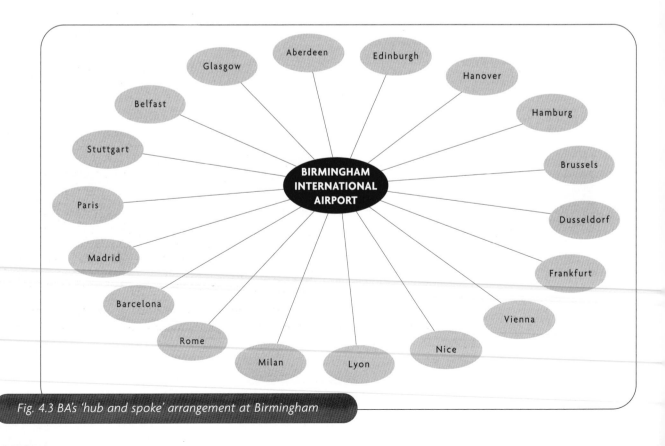

Fig. 4.3 BA's 'hub and spoke' arrangement at Birmingham

Unit 4

Time zones

Greenwich Mean Time (GMT) evolved from an international agreement in 1884 to use the time at Greenwich in London as a base time for all parts of the world. From that time, each area of the world took on a time that was either behind or ahead of GMT. For example, New York is five hours behind GMT and we refer to the time in New York as GMT-5, while South Africa is two hours ahead of GMT, i.e. GMT+2. The same still applies today, although the term GMT was officially replaced in 1979 by UTC (Universal Time Co-ordinate). In the UK and USA, however, GMT is still used. Figure 4.4 shows the world's times zones.

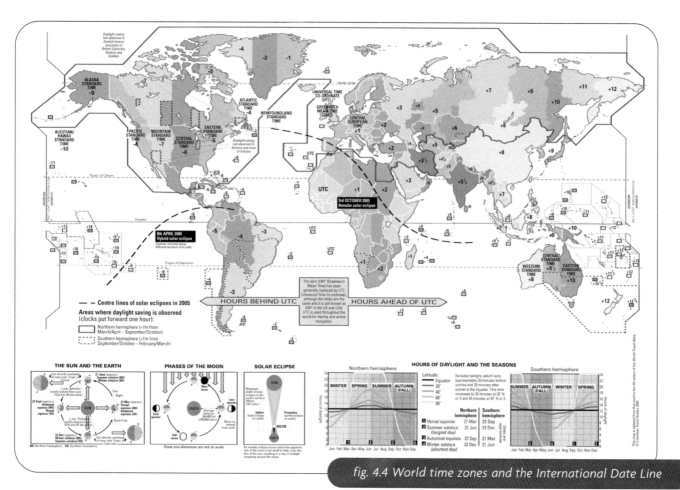

fig. 4.4 World time zones and the International Date Line

Arrival and departure times are always quoted in local time (incorporating any addition or subtraction from GMT), so it is important to be very accurate when working out the actual time taken for a journey.

Daylight-saving time operates in most countries of the world, so as to better synchronise available daylight with most people's work patterns. In the UK daylight-saving is known as British Summer Time (BST); on the last Sunday in March clocks are put forward one hour and put back one hour on the last Sunday in October.

The International Date Line, shown on Figure 4.4, is an imaginary line that loosely follows the 180 degrees line of longitude. The date is put forward a day when crossing the line going west and back a day when travelling east.

ACTIVITY

Using the time zone chart in Figure 4.4, calculate the actual journey time of the following:

(1) A summer flight that leaves London at 0900 hours and arrives in New York at 1300 hours local time.
(2) A flight in April that leaves Stansted at 1440 hours and arrives in Poitiers (France) at 1650 hours.
(3) If it is 5 o'clock in the afternoon in June in India, what time is it in Leeds?

Unit 4

SECTION 3: FACTORS THAT CONTRIBUTE TOWARDS A DESTINATION'S APPEAL

We all have our own reasons for visiting a particular destination, whether in the UK or abroad. It could be to see a spectacular natural feature, such as the Great Barrier Réef or the Victoria Falls, or it may be that we simply want to soak up some sunshine, have fun with friends or take time out from a stressful job. Whatever our choice, there are many factors that contribute towards a destination's appeal, including:

- Access;
- Culture;
- Motivation;
- Geographical features;
- Attractions.

This section of the unit looks at these factors in detail, but first of all considers some of the characteristics of the wide range of 'destinations' that people choose to visit.

Destinations

Destinations are the end points of people's journeys. It is often the destination, its images, tourist facilities and the way it is promoted, that stimulates a person to want to travel. Destinations are of prime importance in travel and tourism, since they are the focus of the many different sectors of the industry, as Figure 4.5 demonstrates.

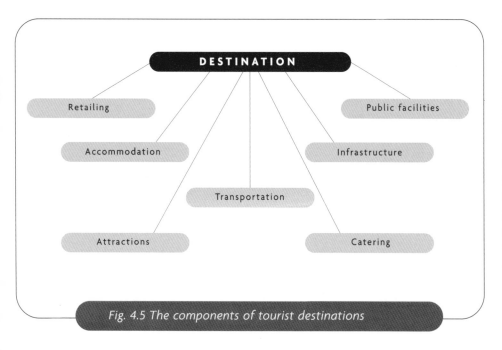

Figure 4.5 indicates that a destination can be thought of as an 'umbrella' under which the different sectors of travel and tourism work in partnership to provide facilities and services for visitors. A typical tourist destination will have a variety of commercial and non-commercial tourism organisations working in tandem. Public bodies will generally supply the infra-structure, planning reg-ulations, tourist information services and destination promotion, while

Fig. 4.5 The components of tourist destinations

Unit 4

private operators provide most of the facilities for visitors, such as accommodation, catering, shops, attractions and entertainment.

The word 'destination' covers a very wide variety of natural and purpose-built areas that are visited by tourists. A destination may be within the UK, for example the historic city of Bath, the Lake District National Park or Isle of Skye; in continental Europe, e.g. the Costa del Sol, Swiss Alps or Italian Riviera; or further afield in the world, for example Bali, Las Vegas or Yosemite National Park. The many different destinations that tourists visit can be grouped under the following types:

- Towns and cities — these destinations have a wide variety of facilities for tourists, including accommodation of all types, attractions, entertainment and tourist information services. They are generally well-served by public transport, such as rail, bus, air, coach and tram services. European cities, such as Amsterdam, Barcelona, Bilbao, Brussels, Prague and Venice, have become popular short-break destinations for UK visitors in recent years;
- Coastal/seaside areas — have been popular with tourists since Victorian times and continue to be so today. The growth of package holidays from the 1960s onwards gave coastal resorts in the Algarve, Costa del Sol, Costa Blanca, Majorca and the Greek Islands a major boost for tourism (see case study on Corfu below). In the UK, seaside resorts continue to be popular with the family market;
- Purpose-built resorts — companies such as Disney, Sandals, Center Parcs and Butlins offer purpose-built facilities for their visitors, where accommodation, entertainment, activities, catering and information are all provided on site;
- Natural and rural areas — have long been a magnet for visitors of all types who want to get away from the stresses and strains of everyday life. National Parks and other protected areas are found in many countries around the world, offering visitors the opportunity of experiencing fresh air and exercise in natural surroundings. Increased interest in activity holidays, such as mountain biking, climbing and walking, is putting many popular rural areas under increased pressure from visitors;
- Historical and cultural areas — 'heritage' is one of the main reasons why overseas visitors come to Britain and visit many other destinations around the world. As many people look beyond the 'sun, sea and sand' destinations for a more enriching experience, historical and cultural destinations such as Normandy, China and India are increasing in popularity;
- Business travel destinations — business people have particular needs when visiting destinations, such as facilities for meetings, conference venues, high quality accommodation and fast transport links.

Unit 4

WEBLINK

www.thomascook.com
/guides/home.asp and
www.gnto.grk

*Check out these websites
to help answer the
questions in this case
study and for more
information on Corfu.*

CASE STUDY – Corfu

Introduction

Corfu is the most northerly of the Ionian Islands just off the west coast of mainland Greece. It is a popular holiday destination for visitors from northern Europe and attracts around half a million British tourists each year. Visitors are attracted by the island's 200km of coastline, rugged terrain and lush interior. Corfu is beginning to change its image from a destination that developed on the back of the package holiday boom of the 1980s and 1990s to a place where more discerning visitors can enjoy the island's peace and tranquillity. Walking and bird watching are growing in popularity, while watersports are on offer in many parts of the island. The capital of the island, Corfu Town with some 40,000 inhabitants, has a rich architectural and cultural heritage, the result of successive years of Venetian, French and British rule.

Holiday areas

Corfu has a range of holiday areas that appeal to a wide variety of visitors. Much of the 'mass tourism' development is clustered immediately north and south of Corfu Town. Resorts such as Dassia, Ipsos, Sidari and Benitses cater well for the family market and feature in many tour operators' brochures. Much of the northern coast is quieter, especially around Kassiopi and Kalami, although Sidari on the north-west tip is one of Corfu's largest resorts. Kavos, on the southern tip of the island, is very popular with young people, boasting many clubs and bars. Corfu has its own waymarked, long-distance footpath, the Corfu Trail, which runs for 220 km from the southerly white cliffs of Arkoudillas to Cape Agia Ekaterini in the north.

Travel and transport

Flight time from the UK is approximately 3 hours 30 minutes, landing at the island's only airport just outside Corfu Town. As well as flights from the UK there are regular charter services from other European countries. Roads are generally good in the built-up areas, but can be a little dangerous off the beaten track. There are regular ferry services in the summer to Italy and other Ionian Islands.

CASE STUDY QUESTIONS

1. Carry out some research and select 3 tour operators that offer holidays to the same resort on Corfu. Compare the prices of the holidays, the markets they are aimed at and how the resorts are portrayed in the different companies' brochures and websites.
2. Why do you think that Corfu is trying to change its image to appeal to a different type of visitor?
3. List some of the main destinations in Europe that Corfu is competing with for holidaymakers.
4. Do some research into the resort of Kavos and try to find out what local people think about the type of tourism this resort caters for.

Unit 4

Access

If a destination is not easily accessible it is unlikely to be popular with large numbers of tourists, although remoteness can add to a destination's appeal for certain people. If we take the example of the UK National Parks, the Peak District, which is easily reached from both Manchester and Sheffield, has up to 20 million visitors per year. In contrast, Northumberland National Park, which is further away from major centres of population, welcomes 1.5 million visitors per year. The popularity of overseas destinations also varies depending on accessibility. According to figures from ABTA, Paris was one of the most popular short-break destinations for British people in 2004. The city has excellent road, rail and air links to many European countries, making it a very accessible city for visitors.

However, the growth in long-haul travel clearly demonstrates that not everybody is happy just to visit places that are easily accessible and close to home. Aircraft can now travel further without the need to refuel, thereby increasing the popularity and affordability of long-haul destinations. Many major tour operators now feature long-haul destinations in their programmes and sell charter flights to faraway places, sometimes with stopovers to break the journey.

FOCUS ON INDUSTRY

Thomson announced in December 2004 that it was introducing weekly flights from Gatwick to Natal in north east Brazil for its 2005-2006 winter long-haul programme. Holidays to Brazil under the company's Faraway Shores brand would also be on offer. Thomson chose to expand its long-haul operations into Brazil because of the excellent accommodation on offer and the country's vibrant culture.

The long-haul market has suffered a period of decline since the tragic events of September 11th 2001. Subsequent acts of terrorism and natural disasters, including the tsunami in December 2004, have exacerbated the problem. However, figures from Mintel show that the long-haul market is on the road to recovery. The UK market for long-haul travel grew by 19 per cent in the first eight months of 2004, as the strong pound and Euro made long-haul destinations good value for money. The latest statistics available from Kuoni, the UK-based and Swiss-owned long-haul operator, show that, for the first time ever, the Maldives was their most popular long-haul destination in 2003. Thailand was knocked into second position and Sri Lanka was third. Thailand's drop to second place is the result of the impact of SARS and the various security issues that affected Asian tourism in 2003.

Unit 4

Destination	No. of visits ('000s)
USA	3,613
Caribbean	817
North Africa	714
Canada	530
Australia	525
Rest of Africa	496
India	494
South Africa	475
Central and South America	444
Middle East (excluding Israel)	439
Source: ABTA	

Fig. 4.6 Top 10 long-haul destinations for UK tourists 2003

Data from ABTA shows that, for 2003, the USA was by far the most popular long-haul destination for UK tourists, followed by the Caribbean and North Africa (see Figure 4.6)

Closer to home, the events surrounding the fall of the Berlin Wall in 1989 and the fragmentation of the former Soviet Union have had an important impact on access to European tourism. People living in former communist countries now have greater freedom to travel to the West, although many lack the money to be able to do so. Western travellers, on the other hand, are visiting the East in ever-increasing numbers, making cities such as Prague and Berlin very popular short break destinations for tourists.

In 2004, the European Union (EU) welcomed a further 10 new members countries, many former Soviet states. The new countries are:

1. Cyprus;
2. Czech Republic;
3. Estonia;
4. Hungary;
5. Latvia;
6. Lithuania;
7. Malta;
8. Poland;
9. Slovakia;
10. Slovenia.

Many of these countries are looking to tourism to help regenerate their economies, moving from heavy industries to 'cleaner' economies based on services.

Paris is a popular short-break destination

Unit 4

ACTIVITY

Locate the 10 new EU member states on an outline map of Europe, together with the existing 15 EU countries. Find out the capital cities of the 25 countries and mark these on your map as well. You can download a blank map from www.tandtONLine.co.uk

Culture

As people become more sophisticated and better educated, many tourists are looking beyond 'sun, sea and sand' destinations for a more rewarding cultural experience, perhaps by learning more about the history of an area or the traditions and way of life of its people.

New Orleans Mardis Gras

This holds true for trips in the UK, to countries in Europe and further afield to long-haul destinations. There is a growing trend for tourists to want to experience a 'sense of place' when in a destination, by taking part in local festivals and events, eating and drinking local produce, and taking time to meet local people. Specialist tour operators cater well for this 'niche market'.

A good example of this 'cultural tourism' is Egypt, the subject of the next destination case study.

Unit 4

WEBLINK

www.wtgonline.com;
www.abtanet.com;
www.aito.co.uk

*Check out these websites
to help with the
questions in this case
study and for more
information on Egypt as a
holiday destination.*

CASE STUDY – Egypt

Introduction

Egypt is located in north Africa, with its northern coast adjacent to the Mediterranean Sea and its west coast fronting the Red Sea. To the south and west it borders Sudan and Libya respectively. The River Nile divides the country in two and is both a mainstay of the economy and a tourist attraction at the same time. Away from the intensively-cultivated regions close to the Nile, the landscape of Egypt is mainly flat, dry desert with little vegetation. The country has a population of approximately 68 million, 7.5 million of whom live in its bustling and vibrant capital Cairo, which is a fusion of African, Oriental and European cultures.

Holiday areas

Many people visit Egypt for its religious and cultural attractions, a cruise on the River Nile or a trip to one of the Red Sea resorts. Culturally, Egypt has some of the most remarkable historical relics to be found anywhere in the world, covering a continuous period of more than 3,000 years. Only China comes anywhere near this in terms of its historical continuity. Egypt's pyramids, the most famous of which are found at Giza and Sakkara, are classed as one of the 'seven wonders of the ancient world'. Examples of Pharaonic and Byzantine art and sculpture can be found in many sites throughout the country. Cruises on the River Nile are also popular, operating from Luxor to Aswan and vice versa. Egypt's Red Sea resorts have become very popular winter-sun destinations in recent years and are particularly popular with divers, who relish the clear waters and abundance of wildlife. One of the most popular resorts on the Red Sea's Sinai Peninsula is Sharm el Sheikh, with El Gouna, Hurghada and Makadi Bay also popular with British visitors.

Travel and transport

Egypt has four main international airports, at Cairo, near Alexandria, further south in Luxor and in the Red Sea resort of Sharm el Sheikh. Flight time from the UK is approximately 5 hours, depending on destination airport. A number of operators offer Nile cruises, with specialist steamers carrying between 50 and 100 passengers. Travel by taxi is the most common way of getting around in Egypt's cities and major towns.

CASE STUDY QUESTIONS

1. Carry out some research and select 6 UK tour operators that offer holidays to Egypt. Make notes on how each company describes the culture of Egypt in its publicity materials and how this is used to sell the destination and its resorts.
2. Select suitable holiday itineraries to Egypt for the following types of visitors – a couple celebrating their golden wedding anniversary; a family with 2 young children; a group of 4 young professionals looking for some entertainment and adventure in Egypt.
3. List some of the main destinations that Egypt is competing with for UK holidaymakers.
4. Why do you think that the Egyptian government is encouraging tourism development and what are they doing to make sure that tourism doesn't harm Egypt's rich cultural and religious heritage?

Unit 4

Motivation

Motivation in travel and tourism is all about why people choose to visit one destination rather than another. As you learned in Unit 1, tourists travel to destinations for a variety of reasons, including:

- Visiting friends and relatives (VFR);
- Taking part in educational trips;
- Conducting business;
- Visiting religious centres;
- Going on holiday or taking a short break;
- Going to a concert;
- Taking part in a sporting event or activity.

Precisely what motivates a person to travel to a particular place and for a specific reason is often difficult to understand. If we start from the standpoint that all individuals have a unique set of characteristics that determines their physical and psychological make-up, then the variety of influences on each person's reasons for travel is immense. Why, for example, will one person choose to visit Australia to visit the outback while another will be happy with a week's camping holiday in Norfolk?

Certain factors that influence destination choice are outside the control of the individual. These factors are often referred to as 'determinants' and include having sufficient time and money to be able to travel, being in good health and living in a part of the world that allows free movement of its citizens. 'Motivators', on the other hand, are the complex influences that shape a person's choice of holiday or destination.

Travel motivators

Even when a person has satisfied the necessary determinants of tourist travel, there are complex psychological influences at work within the individual that will affect their choice of destination. Major travel and tourism organisations invest large sums in market research in order to understand better these motivating factors that influence a tourist's choice, in the hope of improving the products and service they offer their customers. Probably the most widely quoted work on motivation theory is that of Maslow, who developed the 'hierarchy of needs' (see Figure 4.7).

Self - actualisation

Esteem

Belonging and Love

Safety Needs

Physiological needs

Fig. 4.7 Maslow's hierarchy of needs

In Maslow's model shown in Figure 4.7 there are five levels of needs that an individual seeks to satisfy, from physiological needs at the base of the pyramid to self-actualisation at the pinnacle. Maslow argues that individuals must satisfy certain physiological needs, such as shelter, warmth, water and food, and safety needs before moving on to the need for belonging and love, esteem and ultimately self-actualisation. Applying Maslow's hierarchy of needs to tourists' motivation to travel, it is clear that, depending on the particular circumstances of the individual, tourism can satisfy all levels of needs. A holidaymaker, for example, will choose accommodation, hospitality and travel arrangements that meet his or her physiological and safety needs. Holidays can certainly provide opportunities for developing social relationships, thereby contributing towards the need for belonging and love. Tourists sometimes use their travel experiences as a way of boosting their esteem among peers. Particular types of tourism-related experiences may also contribute to a person's achievement of self-actualisation or self-fulfilment, perhaps becoming spiritually enlightened or learning a new language while on holiday.

In attempting to understand the complexities of tourism motivators, it is clear that tourists' choices are influenced by a wide variety of factors, which, leaving aside the determinants of time, money, freedom to travel and health that have already been considered, include:

- Education — has a profound effect on individuals, not least in relation to their demand for travel and tourism, given the tendency for education to broaden the mind and stimulate the desire to travel;
- Stage in the life cycle — tourism demand fluctuates in relation to a wide variety of life cycle characteristics, such as age, family composition and domestic commitments;
- Fashions and fads — destinations and tourist products go in and out of fashion;
- Personal mobility — access to a private motor vehicle can open up greater tourism opportunities;
- Rural/urban residence — people who live in towns and cities may be motivated to seek the peace and solitude of rural areas for tourism, and vice versa;
- Race and gender — cultural surroundings and societal stereotyping can influence the demand for tourism;
- Media and destination image — the techniques used to create a favourable image of a destination and to promote it for tourism, and the methods used to communicate this promotional message to prospective tourists, will influence destination choice.

It is important to stress that none of these factors works in isolation, but rather each is part of a complex, interrelated mechanism that shapes an individual's motivation for travel.

ACTIVITY

Carry out a small-scale survey of people of different ages and ask them about the UK and overseas holidays and day trips they have taken in the last 3 years. Find out where they visited and what motivated them to choose these destinations in particular.

Unit 4

Geographical features

The earth's geographical features play a crucial role in the appeal of destination areas around the world. An area's topography, i.e. the type and variety of natural features that go to make up the appearance of the landscape, is often the main motivator for travel to an area. For example, tourists have long been drawn to the beauty of mountainous areas such as the Alps, the Andes, the Lake District, Ben Nevis and the Himalayas. Coastline, seas, rivers and oceans also play an important part in attracting people, e.g. the popular 'costas' on Spain's Mediterranean coast, the clear waters of the Caribbean and the Red Sea, and the great rivers that run through many of Europe's capital cities are magnets for tourists. Given that the earth's environment is so important in attracting tourists, it is vital that everybody with an interest in the future of the industry supports types of tourism that are respectful of the environment, by signing up to the principles of 'sustainable tourism'.

Climate is arguably the single most important factor that affects the appeal of tourist destinations and 'climate change' is high on the agenda of the world's politicians. The world has a number of climatic zones, i.e. areas with broadly similar climate characteristics, which can be summarised as:

- Polar – very cold and dry all year round, e.g. Greenland;
- Temperate – cold winters and mild summers, e.g. United Kingdom;
- Arid – dry and hot all year, e.g. much of central Australia;
- Tropical – hot and wet all year, e.g. the Amazon basin;
- Mediterranean – mild winters and dry, hot summers, e.g. Italy;
- Tundra (mountains) – very cold all year, e.g. Rocky Mountains.

ACTIVITY

Using an atlas, make a list of major tourist destinations that are found in each of the six climatic zones described above.

There are a number of factors that affect an area's climate, including:

- Latitude – temperature decreases as you move further north and south of the equator;
- Altitude – temperatures decrease with height;
- Wind – winds originating from warm areas will raise temperatures and vice versa;
- Distance from the sea – land heats up and cools down faster than the sea, hence coastal areas have a lower temperature range than inland areas;
- Aspect – in the northern hemisphere, south-facing slopes are usually the warmest as they have most exposure to the sun. The opposite applies in the southern hemisphere, i.e. north-facing slopes are generally the warmest.

Unit 4

It is a feature of modern tourism development that people who live in cool, temperate countries tend to favour areas with warmer climates for their holidays. Spain, for example, is the most popular overseas destination for British holidaymakers, attracting 13.7 million UK visitors in 2003.

Seasonal variations in the weather have direct impacts on travel and tourism. Many tourist resorts in the UK and elsewhere in Europe have a busy peak season when the weather is warm and sunny. Some tourism businesses close altogether in the winter, but the rise in popularity of activity holidays and short breaks, which are not so weather-dependent, has made tourism a year-round activity in a growing number of destinations. The peak season for Europe's ski resorts is, of course, in the winter when the weather is poor, although many Alpine resorts are now very busy all year round, with activities such as walking, mountain-biking and canoeing taking place in the summer months. Some travel and tourism operators get around the problem of bad weather by building wet-weather facilities, e.g. Center Parcs with their undercover, sub-tropical swimming facilities.

Attractions

Attractions play a major role in tempting people to visit a destination. Natural attractions, such as the Grand Canyon, the French Alps or the Victoria Falls, are magnets for millions of tourists every year. Some attractions are built specifically to attract tourists and are commercial ventures, for example Alton Towers, Disneyland Paris and Universal Studios in Florida. Other attractions may not have been built specifically for tourism, but nonetheless attract millions of tourists, e.g. Buckingham Palace, the Taj Mahal and the Vatican in Rome. Events can play an important part in attracting tourists to destinations, particularly sporting and cultural events, for example the Olympic Games, Rio Carnival, Rugby World Cup and European Football Championships.

The Grand Canyon

ACTIVITY

Carry out some research to find information on the most popular free and charging tourist attractions in the UK. Locate the attractions on a blank map of the UK, that you can download from www.tandtONLine.co.uk

Unit 4

SECTION 4: TOURISM POTENTIAL

You have seen in this unit and elsewhere on your course that travel and tourism is a major economic activity across the world. Countries are keen to develop tourism as a way of generating wealth and creating jobs. Many areas that are not yet developed for tourism have the potential to attract visitors, but turning this potential into people sleeping in hotel beds and eating in restaurants is a different matter! Many of the new EU member states that joined in 2004 are good examples of countries that have undoubted tourism potential, but must develop this potential in a commercial, yet sustainable, manner.

Supply and demand

When assessing their tourism potential and the feasibility of developing a healthy tourism industry, destination areas must focus on both supply and demand (see Figure 4.8). The diagram shows that, like all economic activity, travel and tourism is about a variety of 'suppliers' creating tourist facilities in destinations for domestic and international tourists.

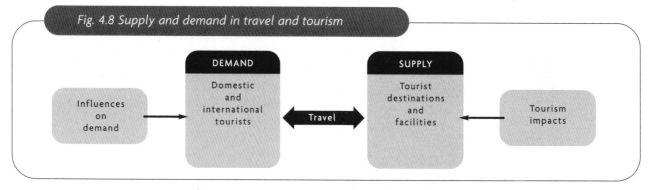

Fig. 4.8 Supply and demand in travel and tourism

The supply side of tourism is concerned with the destination itself and what facilities it can offer tourists. An area that has a favourable climate and attractive scenery already has a head start. If it is accessible to a sizeable catchment area of potential visitors, either as a result of its location or the existence of a good transport network, this too is a positive factor. A variety of attractions, either built or natural, also demonstrates tourism potential.

Exploiting tourism potential

The tourism potential of a region is dependent above all on the relationship between supply and demand. Even the most valuable tourism attractions have no tourism potential if they have no visitors to find them worthy of interest. Tourism potential can be neglected, or partially or fully exploited. To maximise an area's tourism potential there must be a fully researched and costed tourism plan. The plan should set out:

- The aims and objectives of the tourism development;
- Supply-side issues – quality and quantity of accommodation, transport networks, catering facilities, tourist attractions, etc;
- Demand – market research, product development and marketing strategies;
- Finance – sources of local, regional, national and international investment;
- Organisational structure – who will be responsible for implementing the plan;
- Monitoring and evaluation – measures to make sure that the plan is meeting its original purpose.

In addition to these, tourism is affected by factors that cannot easily be controlled by the travel and tourism industry itself, such as the general political and economic situation of the potential tourist destination, trends in tourism and security concerns.

Two key areas for maximising tourism potential are working in partnership and developing sustainable tourism.

Partnerships

It is generally recognised in world tourism that the best way to develop an area's tourism potential is for all concerned to work in partnership to achieve the desired aims and objectives. This means commercial (private sector) and non-commercial (public and voluntary sector) organisations working together on developing and marketing a successful tourism industry in the destination area.

Effective partnerships in tourism offer a number of advantages, including:

- Maximising the economic and social benefits of tourism;
- Helping to minimise tourism's negative environmental and cultural impacts;
- Maximising the use of resources;
- Spreading the risks of tourism development.

Sustainable tourism

We saw earlier in this unit that the natural environment is a key factor in attracting people to tourist destinations. 'Sustainable tourism' is all about ensuring that the environment is not harmed through excessive and unplanned tourism development. An extension of 'green tourism', which has developed out of concern for the environment, sustainable tourism is part of a much wider global debate on sustainable development, highlighted by the Brundtland Report in 1987 and the first Earth Summit in Rio in 1992. Various bodies concerned with travel and tourism have developed policies on sustainable development, including the English Tourist Board (now part of VisitBritain) 'Tourism and the Environment Task Force', whose principles for sustainable tourism developed in 1991 state that:

Unit 5

- Argue of swear in front of customers;
- Lose your temper at work;
- Drink alcohol at work;
- Act in a way that could anybody at risk.

By following these commonsense guidelines you will create a positive first impression with customers and gain pleasure from providing a courteous and professional service.

Personal presentation

Time and again, employers in travel and tourism stress the crucial importance of personal presentation amongst their staff. Matters such as wearing appropriate dress, personal hygiene and adopting a positive attitude are key points to note.

Personal presentation is important

What you wear at work says a lot about you and the organisation that employs you. Wearing 'appropriate dress' does not necessarily mean wearing the smartest clothes that money can buy! 'Appropriate' is the key word. If you were a sales representative for a major holiday company regularly visiting travel agencies, smart formal clothes such as a suit may well be the most appropriate. On the other hand, staff working as camp site couriers would be more appropriately dressed in casual sportswear. Many people working in travel and tourism wear uniforms in order to present a consistent image to the public and help build customer loyalty, for example customer service staff working for train companies, travel agency personnel, air cabin crew and overseas tour representatives.

Uniforms help to create a positive first impression with customers and make staff easily identifiable if customers need help or advice.

WEBLINK	**FOCUS ON INDUSTRY**
www.avis.co.uk	Customer Service Agents working for the Avis car rental firm at Heathrow Airport are key
Check out this website for more information on Avis	people in creating the right first impressions about the company with customers. To project the right image to members of the public, all Customer Service Agents wear the company's corporate uniform and are trained to be attentive and welcoming to customers. Avis looks for conscientious, reliable and flexible people who enjoy helping others and want to be noted for their exceptional support at the company's flagship airport location.

Unit 5

Close contact with customers on a regular basis makes personal hygiene an important matter for travel and tourism staff. This can be a sensitive area, particularly when supervisors and managers have to remind staff about the importance of arriving at work in a clean, hygienic and presentable fashion. All staff working in travel and tourism, but especially those whose work brings them into close contact with customers, must:

- Be generally clean;
- Have hair that is clean and combed;
- Have fresh breath.

Customers will not tolerate staff with poor body odour or bad breath and may well take their custom elsewhere. It is important to remember that the staff are the outward image of an organisation. For example, if you are greeted at a hotel by a doorman who smells of stale cigarettes or whose hair is unkempt, your first impressions of the hotel and of your stay are likely to be negative. If, on the other hand, the doorman is smartly presented, with a pleasant smile and tidy hair, you are much more likely to be impressed with the hotel from the outset.

ACTIVITY

Imagine that you have been asked to help write a job description for a new job of Customer Service Assistant in a busy tourist information centre. List the key points about appropriate dress, personal hygiene, personality and attitude that you think should be included in the job description.

FOCUS ON INDUSTRY

WEBLINK

www.havenholidays.co.uk

Check out this website for details of the holiday parks operated by Haven and British Holidays.

Haven and British Holidays, part of the Bourne Leisure Group, are among Britain's leading leisure companies, with over 35 years of experience. The two sister companies own and operate 35 holiday parks spread across England, Scotland and Wales. All parks have been selected for their location in areas of natural beauty or their proximity to holiday resorts. Staff at the two companies are fully trained in customer service, in particular the importance of having the right attitude towards customers. The customer care programme stresses that employees with the right attitude are:

- Able to create a great first impression;
- Positive in outlook;
- Clean, neat and well groomed;
- Welcoming to customers – use their names if you can and remember that a smile costs nothing;
- Proud of doing their jobs as well as they can;
- Ready to take the initiative;
- Friendly and sincere;
- Willing to act promptly and effectively;
- Ready to take extra trouble and make extra effort to give the customer what they need.

Unit 5

[Handwritten note:]
Teams
- crew of a jet
- travel agency staff.
- tour reps
- a team of students carrying out a survey
- check in staff.
- conference organiser and helpers
- train crew

Communication with customers

There is a saying that dealing with customers is easy, but dealing with them successfully is the difficult bit! The key to effective customer service is good communication, i.e. meeting customers' needs through positive interaction between customer and members of staff. Whatever situation you find yourself in, it is important to recognise the feelings of customers, meet and greet them effectively, and try to treat them as an individual at all times, perhaps by using their first name if appropriate. Customers also respond to fast and accurate service, so don't keep them waiting longer than you have to!

Dealing effectively with complaints

Most of the time, dealing with customers in travel and tourism is very rewarding and interesting. From time to time, however, you may have to deal with customer complaints. In general, British people are rather reluctant to complain. When they do, however, staff in travel and tourism organisations must know how to handle the situation and even turn the complaint to positive advantage. Handled correctly, complaints can be thought of as another type of feedback from customers that gives the organisation a second chance to put things right and satisfy the customer.

[Handwritten note:]
Difficulties
don't know them
don't know how they are feeling
don't know what they want
may not like them
may not agree with them

FOCUS ON INDUSTRY

The Best Western Hotel Consortium has more than 300 member hotels in the UK and over 4000 hotels in 80 countries worldwide, making it the world's largest hotel chain. Best Western stresses to its customer service staff the importance of dealing with complaints successfully. People who complain can become a hotel's best friend!

'It is the goal of the customer service department to turn every complainant into an ambassador for Best Western by providing an effective and professional service to customer complaints and enquiries'.

The key actions to take when dealing effectively with complaints are:

- Listen attentively so that you get the whole story first time;
- Thank the customer for bringing the problem to your attention;
- Apologise in general terms for the inconvenience but do not grovel;
- Provide support for the customer by saying that the complaint will be fully investigated and matters put right as soon as possible;
- Sympathise with the customer and try to see the situation from their point of view;
- Don't justify the circumstances that led up to the complaint and go on the defensive;
- Ask questions if you are not clear on any points of the customer's complaint;
- Find a solution to the problem (by consulting other staff if necessary);
- Agree the solution with the customer;
- Follow through to make sure that what you promised has been done;
- In future, try and anticipate complaints before they happen!

Unit 5

ACTIVITY

Working with other members of your group, role play the following situations sometimes found in travel and tourism:

1. A customer complaining to an overseas tour representative about the poor condition of his hotel room;
2. A couple complaining to a travel agent about the poor food on their recent cruise in the Mediterranean;
3. A traveller complaining to a customer service adviser at a busy railway station about the late running of her train.

You should take it in turns to play the person complaining and the member of staff dealing with the complaint. Members of the group should make notes on how well the 'staff member' handles the complaint, in line with the key points discussed above.

This activity is designed to provide evidence for P3.

Working as part of a team

Staff dealing with customers in travel and tourism will often find that they are working as part of a team, for example:

- A conference organiser and her team of two who organise business conferences and meetings at a country house hotel;
- The crew of a jet flying from Manchester to Palma in Majorca with 190 holidaymakers on board;
- A team of three students carrying out a visitor survey for a local tourist attraction;
- A small independent tour operator with a team of four sales and reservations staff;
- A team responsible for organising a charity event such as a fun-run;
- An English couple who own and run a wine bar in Benidorm;
- A team of representatives working overseas for a tour operator.

Teamwork at BA

Unit 5

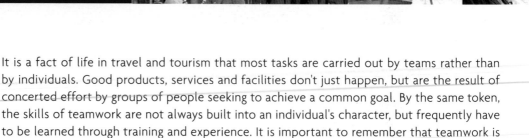

It is a fact of life in travel and tourism that most tasks are carried out by teams rather than by individuals. Good products, services and facilities don't just happen, but are the result of concerted effort by groups of people seeking to achieve a common goal. By the same token, the skills of teamwork are not always built into an individual's character, but frequently have to be learned through training and experience. It is important to remember that teamwork is both a philosophy and a skill; it is one of the roles of the travel and tourism manager to create the organisational culture within which teamwork is encouraged and supported, and to allow staff to develop the skills needed to operate as effective team members.

Customer service charters

Organisations in all walks of life devise customer service charters to inform people what they can expect in terms of standards of service and what the organisation will do in the event of a failure on their part. For example, charters are found in telecommunications companies, high street retailers and mobile 'phone companies, as well as travel and tourism organisations.

WEBLINK

www.virgin.com/trains

Check out this website for more information on Virgin Trains.

FOCUS ON INDUSTRY – Customer service charter

Virgin Trains' Passengers' Charter sets out the company's commitment to give passengers the safe, high quality service that they have a right to expect. Any passenger purchasing a ticket for use on services operated by Virgin Trains should enjoy:

- A reliable and punctual journey;
- Clean and safe trains and stations;
- A Customer Service team member on board every train to be available to provide help if required;
- A refreshment service on most trains;
- A seat if reserved in advance.

All Virgin Trains staff receive full, ongoing training in customer care and related issues and are expected to carry out their duties in a professional manner.

Unit 5

WEBLINK

www.centerparcs.co.uk

Check out this website to help answer the questions in this case study and for more information on Center Parcs.

CASE STUDY – Customer service in Center Parcs

Introduction

Center Parcs is one of the success stories of British tourism in recent years. The company revolutionised the holiday market in Holland more than 30 years ago and did the same in the UK when it opened its first village at Sherwood Forest in 1987, by offering short break holidays on a year-round basis. Three more sites were developed up to the mid-1990s, at Longleat in Wiltshire, Eleveden Forest in Suffolk and Oasis Whinfell Forest in Cumbria. In December 2004, Center Parcs announced its intention to apply for planning permission for a fifth UK village on the Bedford Estate near Woburn. The Center Parcs' concept is based around a high quality holiday that cannot be spoiled by the weather. All UK sites have covered leisure pools with controlled temperature and atmosphere. Accommodation is in fully-equipped villas, apartments and lodges, which are set in forest environments. The villages offer a mix of bars, restaurants and shops, plus a range of indoor and outdoor sports and leisure facilities.

Customer Service

Center Parcs is renowned for its commitment to high standards of customer service. This commitment is built around its mission statement, which is:

'Every day, the perfect break naturally'.

The company considers that 'the guest is king' and states on its website:

- We give guests a unique and positively memorable experience;
- We are obsessed with value, guest satisfaction and quality;
- We are commercial, but not to the extent that we alienate valuable guests or compromise service and safety standards.

Staff are trained to respect and care for guests and treat them individually. Training covers interpersonal skills development, written and oral communication, problem solving, team building, managing people and target setting.

The Center Parcs' formula certainly seems to be working as its villages enjoy occupancy rates of over 90 per cent and repeat bookings or more than 60 per cent within a year.

CASE STUDY QUESTIONS

1. How does Center Parcs ensure the highest standards of customer service?
2. Why does the company invest so much in training its staff in providing excellent customer service?
3. What part does excellence in customer service play in helping the company to achieve its mission and objectives?
4. Why has the Center Parcs' concept been so successful in the UK?

Unit 5

Benefits of customer service

Excellent standards of customer service not only bring benefits to customers, but also to members of staff and the organisation itself. Customers benefit by having their needs met in an efficient and friendly manner, thereby producing an enjoyable experience with less stress! Staff working in the organisation will also reap rewards, with increased job satisfaction, better opportunities for promotion, a better working environment, more training and maybe even financial incentives such as a bonus! The main benefits to the organisation of providing excellent customer service are shown in Figure 5.1

The diagram in Figure 5.1 shows us that the benefits to organisations of offering excellent customer service are part of a cycle, starting with public/press relations activities that create a positive public image; this leads to more repeat business and increased sales; this, in turn, helps to create a better working environment for staff and increased productivity for the organisation.

Other benefits to an organisation of introducing excellence in customer service are likely to include:

- Fewer complaints;
- Improved co-operation between departments;
- Reduced absenteeism by staff;
- Lower turnover of staff;
- Improved security;
- Less waste (of materials, time, money, etc.);
- Improved quality in other aspects of the organisation's work;
- Reduction in advertising spend (through retaining existing customers).

Most of all, following a policy of customer service excellence will help to ensure that the organisation achieves its objectives and that all who have a stake in the business, whether they are owners, shareholders, staff, managers or tax payers, will benefit.

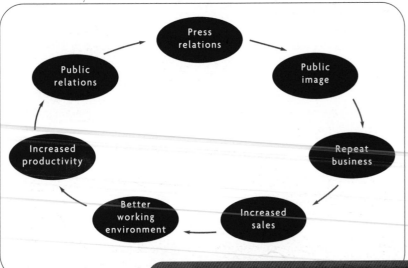

Fig. 5.1 The benefits to organisations of excellent customer service

Unit 5

WEBLINK

www.britishairways.co.uk

Check out this website to help answer the questions on this case study and for further details on British Airways.

CASE STUDY – Customer service at British Airways

Introduction

The British Airways Group consists of British Airways plc and a number of subsidiary companies, in particular British Airways Holidays (tour operations) and British Airways Travel Shops (retail travel). BA is the UK's largest international scheduled airline, flying to more than 550 destinations around the world.

Customer Service

British Airways has a commitment to service excellence and has emphasised this by signing the Airline Passenger Service Commitment. BA states that it is focused on delivering a superior product and service to its customers so that it remains the airline of customers' choice. Safety and security are of the utmost importance to the airline and is never compromised. The company constantly reviews and develops its products, services and policies in the light of changing demands from customers and other external factors.

British Airways is part of the Oneworld alliance which was launched in 1999. It is a network of airlines working in partnership to pool resources, complement each other's services and offer an integrated service to customers. Currently, the following eight airlines form the alliance – Aer Lingus, American Airlines, BA, Cathay Pacific, Finnair, Iberia, LanChile and Qantas. Each of the Oneworld alliance airlines offers a commitment to:

- The belief that the customer is at the heart of the business;
- Outstanding customer service;
- The importance of its people;
- Service standards such as punctuality, check-in, baggage handling and in-flight service – all of which are monitored constantly.

Every six months, all member airlines measure their performance against an established set of performance standards in order to ensure that the level of service to passengers is consistently high across the alliance. Customer queries are resolved by staff of any of the members of the alliance, even if this airline is not responsible for the sector in question.

CASE STUDY QUESTIONS

1. Do you think that BA will be able to maintain its high standards of service in the face of increased competition from the low-cost airlines?
2. Why does the company invest so much time and money in training its staff in providing excellent customer service?
3. What advantages does being part of the Oneworld alliance offer the company and its passengers?
4. Log on to the British Airways' website and find out about the rewards it offers to business and leisure travellers who travel frequently with the airline and with other Oneworld member airlines.

Unit 5

Customers

Travel and tourism products and services are used by people of all ages, types and nationalities, including those with specific needs, such as people with disabilities or with young children. Staff working in travel and tourism must be trained in identifying and meeting the differing needs of a wide variety of customers. Before we begin to consider the different types of customers found in the travel and tourism industry, it is important to spend a little time defining exactly what is meant by the term 'customer'. People sometimes confuse the terms 'customer' and 'consumer'; the consumer is the end-user of a product or service, but not necessarily the person who bought it in the first place (the customer). For example, a mother may treat her son to a package holiday after finishing his exams; the son will be the consumer and the mother the customer.

Many organisations that are working hard to improve their customer service use statements similar to the following to focus their staff:

Customers are:

- The most important people to our organisation;
- Not dependent on us – we are dependent on them;
- Not an interruption of our work – they are the purpose of it;
- Not people to argue with or match wits against;
- Not statistics but human beings with feelings and emotions;
- The people who bring us their needs – it is our job to handle these profitably for them and for ourselves;
- Always right!

Everybody working in a travel and tourism organisation has 'customers', whether or not they deal face-to-face with the general public. 'Internal customers' are people working in the same organisation as you, for example clerical staff, maintenance staff, receptionists, etc., who you come across in the normal daily course of events and who provide you with services and support. Good customer service requires a team approach and a recognition that it is not just the customers 'on the other side of the counter' who need respect and consideration, but that colleagues within the organisation need to be dealt with in the same supportive manner.

WEBLINK	FOCUS ON INDUSTRY – The Tower Bridge Exhibition
www.towerbridge.org.uk *Check out this website for further details of the Tower Bridge Exhibition.*	Managers at The Tower Bridge Exhibition, one of London's best-known tourist attractions, believe that each section of the attraction plays a unique part in ensuring customer satisfaction. The exhibition, ticketing, retail and guiding staff who, together with security, are in daily face-to-face contact with the public, as well as the technical, finance, marketing, education and office staff, are all part of the same team behind the attraction, dedicated to providing the highest standards of service to customers.

Unit 5

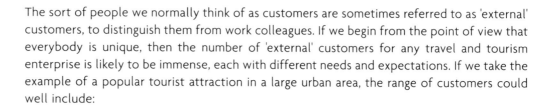

The sort of people we normally think of as customers are sometimes referred to as 'external' customers, to distinguish them from work colleagues. If we begin from the point of view that everybody is unique, then the number of 'external' customers for any travel and tourism enterprise is likely to be immense, each with different needs and expectations. If we take the example of a popular tourist attraction in a large urban area, the range of customers could well include:

- Individuals;
- Groups;
- People with special needs, for example those needing wheelchair access, people with sensory disabilities, on special diets and those with young children;
- People from different cultures;
- People of different ages;
- Non-English speakers.

Providing high standards of customer service to such a wide range of people with very different needs requires commitment and enthusiasm on the part of the staff involved and the correct training provided by a supportive management team.

ACTIVITY

Choose two contrasting travel and tourism enterprises with which you are familiar and list the different types of customers each serves. For each type of customer, write down statements about their particular needs.

This activity is designed to provide evidence for P1 and M1.

WEBLINK

www.britishairways.com

Check out this website for full details of British Airways' special meals to meet individual customer needs.

FOCUS ON INDUSTRY – British Airways

British Airways offers its customers a variety of special meals to meet both religious and dietary needs on the majority of its routes. These include Asian vegetarian, vegan vegetarian, Hindu, Muslim, Kosher, diabetic, gluten-free, low cholesterol and non-lactose. Meals must be ordered at least 24 hours in advance of flying.

Meeting the needs of individuals

As you know, people come in all shapes and sizes! We all have different leisure needs and, in the context of travel and tourism, are looking to friendly and efficient staff to meet these needs. Meeting the needs of individuals is all about building a one-to-one relationship. Customers like to feel that they are special and, in a one-to-one situation, want to be put at ease and have the full attention of the member of staff serving them. Staff should not become distracted when dealing with individuals and should be trained in prioritising requests for their time and attention.

Unit 5

Tackling ineffective customer service

Many of the problems associated with poor standards of customer service in travel and tourism are the result of a lack of training. Staff must be trained in the skills needed to provide an excellent service to customers, not just when they start a job but throughout their working life. Managers need to:

- Discover any underlying problems that are causing the customer service problems;
- Arrange staff training sessions to help deal with the problems;
- Provide a supportive environment in which staff can flourish;
- Involve all staff in customer service improvement.

One of the most successful customer service training schemes in the UK is Welcome to Excellence (Formerly Welcome Host).

WEBLINK

www.welcometoexcellence.co.uk

Check out this website for more details of the Welcome to Excellence training programmes

Welcome
to Excellence

FOCUS ON INDUSTRY – Welcome to Excellence Training Programmes

The Welcome to Excellence series of training programmes, offered through Regional and National Tourist Boards in the UK, has trained more than 240,000 staff since first introduced to the UK by the Wales Tourist Board as Welcome Host in 1991. Companies taking part range from small accommodation providers to larger organisations such as Bourne Leisure, English Heritage, YHA, Center Parcs and many public sector organisations.

There are now seven one-day courses, which provide front-line customer service staff and managers with the skills they need to provide high standards of customer service:

- Welcome Host – the original course designed to highlight the importance of excellent customer service;
- Welcome Host Plus – building on Welcome Host, this course covers advanced customer service skills;
- Welcome International – designed to give people working in travel and tourism greater confidence when meeting and greeting international visitors in another language;
- Welcome All – offers practical advice on service to customers with disabilities and special needs (includes information on the Disability Discrimination Act);
- Welcome Management – designed to assist managers and supervisors who set the standard of customer service in their businesses;
- Welcome Line – concentrates on improving telephone-based customer service skills and techniques;
- Welcome E-business – provides an insight into the world of electronic commerce (e-commerce) for customer service staff and managers.

In addition there are sector-specific customer service courses, which include Welcoming Walkers and Cyclists, Welcome to Health and Welcome Host for Transport.

Unit 5

ACTIVITY

Carry out a small-scale survey of a mixture of people to find out their recent experiences of good and bad service in travel and tourism facilities (e.g. airports, hotels, tourist attractions, travel agencies, ferry terminals, villa complexes, tourist information centres, etc.). Record their responses and analyse the results with the rest of your group. Suggest how the examples of poor customer service standards could be put right.

This activity is designed to provide evidence for P2.

Fig. 5.3 Implications for high quality customer service

Implications

Figure 5.3 highlights four key implications concerned with providing high quality customer service in travel and tourism – legal, customer-related, organisational and employee-related. All have a bearing on providing high quality customer service and must be addressed by managers and supervisors in a planned manner.

Legal

All travel and tourism organisations must work within the law of the land, by following standard business regulations and providing a safe and secure environment for staff to work in and visitors to enjoy; customer service staff play a key role in this and must be trained accordingly. Organisations that fail to comply with the various health and safety, consumer protection and company laws can face serious consequences when problems arise.

There are a number of laws and regulations that lay down how organisations must deal with customers, including:

- The Data Protection Act (DPA) 1998 – this important legislation, originally introduced in 1984, aims to promote high standards in the handling of personal information by organisations and so protect a person's right to privacy. The DPA applies to firms holding information about individuals in electronic format and, in some cases, on paper. Under the terms of the Act, organisations holding information may need to register and comply with a series of Data Protection Principles, covering such matters as accuracy and security of the information, and its use for lawful purposes.

Unit 5

WEBLINK

www.informationcommissioner.gov.uk

Check out this website for more information about the Data Protection Act and the new Freedom of Information Act.

- The Consumer Protection Act 1987 – this Act makes it a criminal offence for an organisation or individual to give misleading price information about goods, services, accommodation or facilities they are offering for sale. The Act has special significance for travel and tourism operators who must ensure the accuracy of any price information in their brochures, on the Internet or in other publicity material;

- The Supply of Goods and Services Act 1982 – this states that the seller of a holiday or travel product should use "reasonable care and skill", e.g. a tour operator or travel agent should make sure that they carry out a booking correctly, the product itself should be of a generally satisfactory standard, and it should comply with any descriptions.

- The Package Travel Regulations 1992 – these regulations stem from a European Union Directive whose main aim is to give people buying package holidays greater protection in law and access to compensation when things go wrong. The Regulations place a number of duties on package holiday organisers to provide, for example, clear contract terms, emergency telephone numbers, compensation options if the agreed services are not supplied and proof of the organiser's security against insolvency;

- The Trades Description Act 1968 – one of the original pieces of consumer legislation that aims to protect customers against false descriptions, either verbally or in writing, given by suppliers of goods and services. In the case of travel and tourism, any description of, for example, a hotel or tourist attraction, must be truthful at the time it was written (if circumstances subsequently change, the operator must inform the customer);

Customer

Not surprisingly, the people who gain most from high standards of customer service are the customers themselves! Their holiday or travel experience can be made extra special with the help of attentive and professional customer service staff. By the same token, if service standards are poor, it is the customers who suffer first.

Any customer service operation should be built around giving the customer complete satisfaction at all times. Failure to offer a consistent and reliable standard of customer service can result in a less than enjoyable experience for the customer and could lose the company business in the long run, as this research from the US Office of Consumer Affairs demonstrates:

- 96 per cent of dissatisfied customers never complain;
- But 90 per cent of them will not return in the future;
- One unhappy customer will tell at least nine others.

One way that travel and tourism companies try to maximise their customers' experience is by offering a customer satisfaction guarantee. For example, train companies often agree to pay compensation to travellers if their train is delayed by a certain amount of time.

Unit 5

Travel and tourism companies also try hard to keep the customers they already have by building customer loyalty. This could be via regular mailings about special offers, discounted deals or more complex customer loyalty programmes as the next example demonstrates.

WEBLINK

www.virgin-atlantic.com

Check out this website for more details about Virgin Atlantic's frequent flyer programme.

FOCUS ON INDUSTRY – Improving customer loyalty

Flying Club is Virgin Atlantic's frequent flyer programme. Travellers taking a qualifying flight with the company or one of its partner airlines earns one Flying Club mile for every mile travelled in the air. The miles earned can be exchanged for flights, hotel stays, car rental and other Virgin Group products and services.

Organisation

Most travel and tourism organisations are private-sector companies looking to maximise their profits. In an increasingly competitive business environment, high customer service standards can make a real difference to a company's 'bottom line', i.e. their profit margin, by encouraging repeat business and by 'word of mouth' from satisfied customers. Giving excellent customer service can also give a company a competitive advantage over other businesses in the same sector; for example, two restaurants in the same street in a holiday resort could offer very different standards of customer service, with low standards leading to less customers and lower profits. With so many companies competing for tourists' spending, the way that staff treat customers can make the difference between success and failure for a company. Also, organisations that treat their customers well tend to treat their staff in the same way, thereby attracting high calibre employees, keeping staff turnover to a minimum and creating a positive impression with customers.

Employee

As well as the implications faced by organisations when providing customer service, employees also have a critical role to play. Staff working for a company that places a high value on giving excellent customer service can reap a variety of rewards and benefits. To begin with, they are likely to enjoy job security from knowing that their employer is among the best in the sector for customer service. Through planned and co-ordinated training programmes, staff will also advance their personal and professional development. There are, of course, costs associated with recruiting and training the best staff available, but in the long run this is often a very good investment for both employer and employee.

Unit 5

SECTION 3: CUSTOMER SERVICE SKILLS

Developing excellence in customer service is one of the most important skills any employee in travel and tourism can learn. Staff play such a vital role in the customers' holiday experience and are often the first person they meet from the organisation they booked with. Hence, developing skills such as listening, meeting customers' needs, providing advice and handling complaints, is crucial to the success of the customers' experience and, ultimately, the profitability of the company.

Customer service methods

There are three main methods in dealing with customers:

- In writing;
- Face-to-face;
- By telephone.

The following sections deal with each of these in detail.

ACTIVITY

Under the direction of your tutor, brainstorm all of the ways in which staff in (1) a travel agency and (2) a major theme park come into direct and indirect contact with customers. Identify the customer needs for each situation you have listed, how these should be met and what skills are needed by different members of staff.

Written communication

With the many developments in telephone and Internet systems, it would be easy to think that customer service staff no longer need to communicate in writing, but it does still happen! In fact, there are many types of written communication used in the travel and tourism industry, for example:

- Letters, faxes and email;
- Memos;
- Brochures and leaflets;
- Reports;
- Documents for meetings;
- Notice boards;
- Posters and advertisements;

Unit 5

- Press releases and articles;
- Annual reports;
- Timetables and manifests (lists of travellers).

Written communication may be formal, for example a reply from a hotel manager to a customer's letter of complaint, or informal, such as a hand-written telephone message from one member of staff to another. Remember too that written communication may be targeted at external customers, for example a poster or advertisement, or circulated to internal customers in an organisation, for example a staff newsletter.

Whatever type of written communication is used, there are certain important rules that should be followed, including:

- Make sure that there are no mistakes in spelling, grammar and punctuation;
- The intended message should be conveyed effectively and accurately;
- In the case of messages, it should be made clear who it is to, who it is from, when it was received and if any action has been taken or needs to be taken;
- The written communication should be clearly legible and pleasing to the eye, whether it is a professional business letter, a company report or a memo;
- The language used should be appropriate for the intended audience.

ACTIVITY

Design and write a memo to be sent by the Marketing Director of a specialist ski tour operator to all members of staff in the organisation, inviting them to the launch party of the new winter season brochure in two week's time at a nearby venue of your choice.

This activity is designed to provide evidence for P3.

Face-to-face communication

We mentioned at the beginning of this unit that travel and tourism is a 'people industry' and, as such, there are many occasions when staff deal directly with customers face-to-face, either individually or in a group situation, e.g. tourist information centre staff directing a party of overseas visitors to nearby attractions, a hotel receptionist welcoming a guest or a travel agent advising a client on the benefits of a particular holiday.

Dealing with customers face-to-face

Unit 5

Establish customer needs

The aim of this stage of the selling process is to help the customer to state his or her needs clearly, so that the salesperson has the best chance of presenting a product or service that the customer will want to buy. Again, it is helpful to ask 'open' questions, rather than those that call for yes/no replies, to give the customer more opportunity to express a preference and to help the conversation to continue. It is important, also, not to assume that you know a customer's needs and that the process of investigating customer requirements is a two-way affair, with the salesperson acting in a supportive role.

In the case of a travel agency, the following are the types of questions that will help the salesperson build up a picture of the client's needs:

- What is the size of the party travelling?
- Are there any children and, if so, what ages are they?
- When do you want to travel and for how long?
- Where do you want to go?
- Is there a particular company you prefer to travel with?
- How do you want to travel?
- How much do you expect to pay?
- Does anybody in the party have any special requirements?

Customers will not necessarily know the answers to all the questions a salesperson may be asking them, so it is important to start with easy questions to which they can give an immediate answer and go into more depth as the sales conversation continues.

Select customer requirements

Having determined the customer's needs, the next stage of the sales process is to present the product to the customer based on their individual requirements. Presenting a travel and tourism product to a customer is rather more difficult than, say, showing him an electric iron or toaster in a shop! The intangible nature of travel and tourism products (the fact that you can't see or touch them) means that sales staff are often showing the customer brochures and other publicity material to help them make a decision. This indicates the crucial importance of well-designed promotional items to achieve sales in travel and tourism.

The key to success in this stage of the sales process is to concentrate on three types of statements during the product presentation, namely:

- Features statement – involves highlighting the features of a particular product or service to the customer, for example the number of rooms in a hotel or the facilities on offer in a holiday centre. Often the customer's reaction is one of indifference at this stage;

Unit 5

- Advantages statement – indicates what the product or service can do in general for the customer. For example, the fact that a departure time of 15.30hrs for a flight means that the client will not have to get up early to get to the airport. Again the reaction may be that the customer needs a little more specific information and persuasion;

- Benefits statement – expresses specifically what the product can do for the individual customer. The information is selected on the basis of the customer's needs and is seen to be entirely relevant and easier to absorb.

Product knowledge is crucial to the success or otherwise of this part of the selling process. Staff must familiarise themselves with the features of particular products and take every opportunity to experience the products and facilities for themselves, in order to be able to speak with authority and confidence.

WEBLINK
www.superbreak.com
Check out this website for more information on Supbreak.

FOCUS ON INDUSTRY

Customer service staff at Superbreak, one of the UK's leading short break operators, use the following top ten sales tips to generate extra business:

UK SHORT BREAK SALES - TOP 10 SALES TIPS

1. TARGET YOUR EXISTING CUSTOMERS
- 40% of your customers will take a UK break. 50% will take more than one per year
- 40-60 age group – high spenders, faraway, cruise customers
- Ask them the question…"Have you thought of a UK short break this year?"
- Welcome home letters, direct mailings, quote a short break offer

2. THE ALTERNATIVE WINDOW CARD
- Offers from Viewdata. Place alongside late availability offers. A customer looking for a holiday in Corfu or the States may also be interested in a theatre break!

3. KEY SELLING OPPORTUNITIES
- Fathers Day/Mothers Day, Valentines Day, Bank Holidays, sporting events (London Marathon, soccer matches).. we all have birthdays and anniversaries. Look to promote 3 to 4 weeks prior to the event

4. CHILD REDUCTIONS
- Free or 50% - all year round including Bank and school holidays plus free or reduced rail travel

5. GROUP BOOKINGS
- Contact local amateur dramatic societies, place theatre break offers in rehearsal rooms
- Sports clubs, special interest groups
- Contact our groups department for a quote on any group idea or activity

Unit 5

6. PEOPLE COMING TO STAY IN YOUR AREA

- Family and friends attending a wedding often need hotel accommodation. Don't let them book direct, check out our availability and prices. Earn money on your own doorstep!

7. AIRPORT HOTEL ADD-ONS

- Offer your customer the comfort of a night's stay before flying off on their two weeks in the sun (or when flying back!). Sell in the free car parking facilities too.

8. VIEWDATA

- Use as a sales tool. Sit the customer down and check out the availability search. Close the sale.

9. THEATRE/EVENT BREAKS

- Best seats, theatre dinners, London and provincial shows – check out our separate brochure.
- Concerts, shows, sports from the British Grand Prix to the Chelsea Flower Show, including accommodation, breakfast, coach transfers between hotel/venue and most importantly the ticket to the event.

10. RACKING

- Vital to tempt the sale.
- Similar to buying a chocolate bar at the supermarket (they are always placed to tempt you near the check out!). A UK short break is an impulse purchase, so try racking our programmes near your door

Closing the sale

'Closing the sale' is all about persuading the customer to make a commitment. Throughout all the sequences of the sales process, sales staff use their product knowledge and communication skills to match customer needs with identified products and services. Rapport is established and the benefits of a selection of products are highlighted. However, none of these actions commits the customer to buy the product or service, or do anything at all. Helping the customer to move from 'I'd like' to 'I'll buy' is what this part of the sales process is all about. It may also be possible to 'switch sell' at this point; this involves getting customers to buy extra products in addition to their main purchase, e.g. buying travel insurance and foreign currency when booking their overseas holiday. Staff are sometimes encouraged to 'sell up' when closing the sale, i.e. persuading customers to buy a higher priced product than the one they originally intended, e.g. booking a more expensive outside cabin on a cruise holiday.

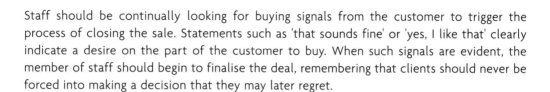

Unit 5

Staff should be continually looking for buying signals from the customer to trigger the process of closing the sale. Statements such as 'that sounds fine' or 'yes, I like that' clearly indicate a desire on the part of the customer to buy. When such signals are evident, the member of staff should begin to finalise the deal, remembering that clients should never be forced into making a decision that they may later regret.

One aspect of the sales process that often occurs at this stage is the need to overcome objections from the customer. These may be genuine, perhaps based on price or availability of services, or they may be the result of a customer being offered insufficient choice by the salesperson. Alternatively, there may be an additional need not already identified to the member of sales staff. Whatever the reason, it is important to respect the wishes of the customer and perhaps investigate further in order to fully match the product to their particular requirements.

Not every sales conversation will necessarily end in a sale; what is important from the organisation's point of view is to end up with the best possible outcome to the process. For large purchases, customers may wish to consider the benefits in greater detail or discuss the sale with other people, before making a commitment to buy. In this situation, all sales staff can do is to ensure that the customer has been given excellent customer service throughout, thus increasing the chances of an eventual positive sales outcome.

After-sales service

It is important for all organisations and staff involved in selling to remember that the process doesn't end when the customer has parted with his or her money. Just as we expect an after-sales service for consumer and household items we buy, the sellers of travel and tourism products too must offer this service to their customers. Adding a new customer's details to an existing database should be the first step in developing a long-term relationship that will hopefully benefit both the organisation and the customer.

ACTIVITY

Working with a partner, role play the situation of a member of the public being sold a package holiday to Majorca. Ask another member of your group to evaluate how the 'seller' performed in relation to each of the key stages of the sales process. Finally, evaluate your own performance, explaining where improvements could be made.

This activity is designed to provide evidence for P4, M3 and D2.

Unit 5

Selling methods

We saw earlier in this unit that customer service staff use a variety of written, face-to-face and telephone methods to carry out their jobs. The same applies to selling skills, which, in reality, are very closely tied in with customer service; the goal is that excellent customer service skills will lead to increased sales.

Brochures are important in generating sales

Written selling methods include brochures, point-of-sale (POS) materials, flyers, Internet sites and direct mail letters.

Face-to-face is by far the most interactive and persuasive selling method used in travel and tourism, and takes place in a variety of settings, e.g. over the counter in a travel agency, on-board a cruise ship and in hotels.

Telephone selling direct to customers is now big business in travel and tourism. Many of the major holiday companies have telephone sales operations, sometimes in purpose-built call centres. Telephone selling complements their other sales activities, such as direct mailing of brochures, holiday hypermarkets and high street travel shops.

The AIDA technique is commonly used in travel and tourism marketing (see unit 3), and can be applied to selling methods as well, for example:

- Attracting ATTENTION by creating imaginative point-of-sale and window displays and by having enthusiastic staff;
- Maintaining customer INTEREST by asking 'open' questions and using a range of visual 'triggers', e.g. brochures and web images;
- Creating a DESIRE on the part of the customer to buy, perhaps by 'selling up', e.g. offering a 5-star rather than 4-star hotel room for only a small extra cost;
- Stimulating ACTION by customers, by using the sales techniques described on page 142 to move them from 'I'd like' to 'I'll buy'.

ACTIVITY

Design a letter to be sent out to all existing clients of a travel agency giving details of special offers and a forthcoming evening event to launch a new range of activity holidays to Portugal. Follow the AIDA technique when designing your letter.

Unit 5

UNIT SUMMARY

This unit has looked in detail at the vital role that high quality customer service plays in today's travel and tourism industry. For organisations to succeed, it is no longer possible to ignore the importance of well-trained and motivated customer service staff. You have seen that many travel and tourism companies offer very similar products and services, and it is often the quality of their customer service that sets one apart from its competitors. Throughout the unit you have been shown examples of good practice in customer service from many sectors of the travel and tourism industry. The case studies on Center Parcs and British Airways serve to highlight how two of Britain's best-known travel and tourism businesses strive to achieve and maintain excellence in customer service.

If you have worked methodically, by the end of this unit you should have:

- Explored how customer service is provided and the benefits it brings to the travel and tourism industry;
- Examined the issues and implications of delivering quality customer service;
- Used customer service skills to deal with customer situations;
- Demonstrated selling skills within travel and tourism contexts.

You are now in a position to complete the assignment for the unit, under the direction of your tutor. Before you tackle the assignment you may like to have a go at the following questions to help build your knowledge on customer service in travel and tourism.

Test your knowledge

1. Why are first impressions so important when staff meet customers?
2. Why do so many travel and tourism companies issue their staff with uniforms?
3. List the key actions to take when dealing with a complaint.
4. What is a customer service charter?
5. List the key benefits to organisations of offering excellent customer service.
6. What is the difference between a 'customer' and a 'consumer'?
7. What are 'internal customers' and 'external customers'?
8. Why was the Disability Discrimination Act introduced?
9. What is 'product knowledge' and why is it important for customer service staff to have good knowledge of the products and services they are selling?
10. What is the main aim of the Data Protection Act?
11. What are the important 'ground rules' when dealing face-to-face with customers?
12. Travel and tourism products are 'intangible' – what does this mean?
13. List the key stages of the sales process in travel and tourism.
14. What does 'closing the sale' mean?
15. What do the letters AIDA mean?

Unit 5

UNIT 5 ASSIGNMENT: Customer service in travel and tourism

Introduction

This assignment is made up of a number of tasks which, when successfully completed, are designed to give you sufficient evidence to meet the Pass (P), Merit (M) and Distinction (D) grading criteria for the unit. If you have carried out the activities and read the case studies throughout this unit, you will already have done a lot of work towards completing the tasks for this assignment.

Scenario

In your first job since finishing your travel and tourism course, you are working for Gemma Foulds, a customer service specialist who advises some of the biggest UK travel and tourism companies on how to get the best out of their staff.

She has been called in by a major airline to help re-launch its customer service plan, following lots of complaints from customers.

Task 1

Gemma has asked you to investigate how customer service is provided in two different travel and tourism organisations. She will use the information you find in a presentation to senior managers of the airline. With advice from your tutor, you could carry out any of the following to help with this task:

- A 'mystery shopper' exercise, where you visit nearby travel and tourism facilities and observe customer service in action. This could be a travel agency, tourist information centre, leisure centre, tourist attraction, hotel, etc;
- Your own experience of working in travel and tourism in a part-time job or work placement;
- By carrying out research on companies on the Internet and in the trade press;
- Watching videos on customer service.

Present the information you find as a short report for Gemma, comparing and contrasting customer service in the two organisations. This should highlight how customer service is provided, examine good and bad points about the companies' approaches, and discuss the benefits that high quality customer service brings to each organisation.

Unit 5

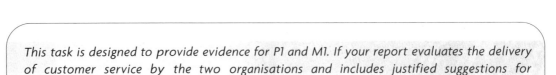

This task is designed to provide evidence for P1 and M1. If your report evaluates the delivery of customer service by the two organisations and includes justified suggestions for improvement, this will provide evidence for D1.

Task 2

Gemma wants to stress to the airline's customer service staff the issues and implications of delivering good (and bad) customer service; senior managers are certain that not all staff are aware of this at the moment. She has asked you to compile a staff handbook, which should describe the issues and implications of delivering high quality customer service for customers, employees and the organisation, as well as addressing legal aspects of dealing with customers.

This task is designed to provide evidence for P2. If your staff handbook includes an analysis of the implications of providing ineffective customer service to the organisation, its employees and customers, this will provide evidence for M2.

Task 3

Gemma wants to show the senior managers of the airline how customer service should be delivered in a practical sense and has asked you to be a 'guinea pig' by demonstrating effective customer service and selling skills in action. This could be through simulated role plays or in real-life situations; you should agree this with your tutor.

This task is designed to provide evidence for P3 and P4. Projecting a professional image and communicating confidently when carrying out these tasks will provide evidence for M3. If you evaluate your own performance when carrying out customer service and selling skills, explaining where improvements are required, this will provide evidence for D2.

Unit 6

Further and higher education courses

Taking a further education (FE) college course in travel and tourism is usually the first step towards a qualification and possible career in the industry. You are presently studying for a BTEC National qualification at Award, Certificate or Diploma level. Other travel and tourism qualifications taken in FE colleges include the BTEC First, AS/A2 in Travel and Tourism, and OCR Nationals.

If you wish to continue developing a career in the travel and tourism industry when you finish your BTEC course you will have two choices:

1. Take a job in the industry and continue with on- and off-the-job training opportunities (as described in the previous sections of this unit);
2. Enrol on a higher education (HE) course – this is an important decision and you should be absolutely sure that you want to spend another 3+ years studying before you go down this route.

Higher education opportunities in travel and tourism

There are currently more than 1200 HE courses in travel and tourism listed on the UCAS website (www.ucas.ac.uk), so there's plenty of choice! These are Degree, HNDs (Higher National Diplomas), other diplomas and Foundation Degrees in a variety of travel and tourism subjects, such as tourism management, adventure tourism, heritage tourism and international tourism. HE courses are also offered by some FE colleges giving you the chance to study in a familiar environment closer to home. Entry requirements for the courses vary enormously, so check carefully by going to the HE institution's own website to get the most up-to-date information. Studying for a HE qualification not only gives you knowledge and skills for a career in travel and tourism, but also provides the opportunity for you to grow as a person, make lasting friendships and widen your horizons.

ACTIVITY

Carry out a search on the UCAS website (www.ucas.ac.uk) and find six travel and tourism courses that appeal to you, either because of the course name, content or where it's offered. Gather together as many details on the courses as possible and present what you find as a set of information sheets that you and others on your course can use for future reference.

Unit 6

The recruitment and selection process

Good employees are the backbone of any organisation in the service sector, and particularly in travel and tourism where they are an integral part of the 'experience' that the customers are buying. But how can you be sure of getting the best people for the job? A systematic approach to recruitment and selection, paying attention to detail and allowing enough time to see the process through to its completion, will pay dividends to the organisation, and in particular will go a long way towards reducing the high levels of staff turnover that are found in some sectors of travel and tourism. Management time spent on recruitment should be seen as a wise investment for the future; all too often, more time and attention is given to choosing a new computer system than to selecting the most important resource that the organisation has – its staff!

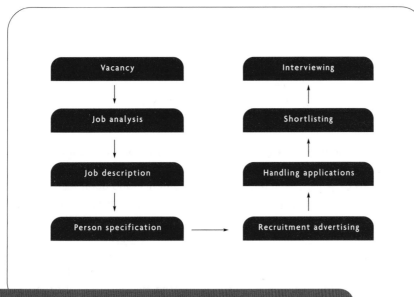

Fig. 6.1 The recruitment and selection process in travel and tourism

The recruitment and selection process is shown in Figure 6.1. Once the need for a new member of staff has been identified, the chart shows that the recruitment and selection process consists of seven interrelated stages, which we look at in more detail in the following sections of this unit.

Job analysis

Whenever a vacancy arises, whether it is to replace a member of staff who is leaving or to fill a new post, it is a good time for an organisation to identify its staffing needs. It does this by carrying out a thorough analysis of what the job entails. If it is an existing post to be filled, simply finding a set of old job details and reproducing them without considering if they are still relevant, is not good enough. The dynamic nature of the travel and tourism industry means that an approach of this sort will not achieve the desired result of getting the best person for the job. Information to be included in the job analysis can be obtained from the existing postholder, previous records, other members of staff, competitor organisations and by direct observation of members of staff.

Unit 6

22 Salop Road
Newtown
DG45 8DS
Tel: 90643 352771

Mr H Brown
Tourism Officer
Runnymore Borough Council
Council Offices
Runnymore
RT23 8RS

22 May 2005

Dear Mr Brown

Post of Tourist Information Centre Assistant

Further to our recent telephone conversation please find enclosed my CV for your consideration. As explained, I have been working in tourism in Australia for the past 12 months, helping to run an activity centre for overseas visitors.

I completed a BTEC National Diploma in Travel and Tourism in 2004 and worked in retail prior to starting on the course. I am fluent in German and have a good grasp of the French language. During my BTEC course I successfully completed Welcome Host training.

I am available for interview at any time that is convenient to you and look forward to hearing back.

Your sincerely

Amy Sparks

Fig. 6.6 A typical business letter

Memos are largely being replaced by email as a way of sending information quickly to staff, but they are used on occasions to remind staff of important meetings and events (see Figure 6.7).

Using fax and email

Fax and email are commonly used in all sectors of the travel and tourism industry. Sending a fax is a relatively simple process and you should always remember to fill in a header sheet to accompany the fax with your full details and the number of pages sent in case of query.

Email is used for communication within a business, between businesses (B2B) and between businesses and customers (B2C). It is a very fast way of communicating text, images and documents. Always remember to keep a copy of the emails you send should you need to refer back to them if a problem arises.

Telephone skills

Using the telephone is an important aspect of working in travel and tourism, so it's important to know how to do it effectively. Staff use 'phones to keep in touch with each other, while many customers' requests for information, advice or to make a booking are now handled over the 'phone. From the customers' point of view, using the telephone is fast, convenient and relatively cheap, as well as enabling instant feedback.

HERITAGE ACTIVITY TOURS

Memorandum

To: All staff
From;   Jenny Bridge, Assistant Manager
Date: 29 July 2005
Subject: Brochure launch

There will be a briefing for all staff on the new brochure launch at 2pm on 3 August 2005 in the board room.

All staff are expected to attend

Fig. 6.7 An example of a memo

Unit 6

Disadvantages include the fact that the callers cannot see each other (non-verbal communication is not possible) and there is no written record of what was said, although it is now common for many organisations to record telephone calls for security and as a staff training aid.

There are a number of important points to bear in mind when dealing with incoming telephone calls, for example:

- Answer all calls quickly – leaving a call for more than 5 rings is considered inefficient;
- Greet the caller with your name and/or your organisation and ask how you can help;
- Smile while you are talking! This may sound crazy, but it really does help you to project a welcoming tone to the customer;
- Listen carefully to what the caller is saying;
- Always speak clearly and use language appropriate to the caller;
- Take notes if there is a message for another member of staff;
- Transfer calls to another appropriate member of staff if you cannot deal with the customer yourself;
- If you promise to call a customer later, make sure you do it!

Similar rules apply if you are telephoning a customer, except that you will be paying for the call!

ACTIVITY

Working with another member of your group, role play a variety of situations in travel and tourism where you make and receive telephone calls (ask your tutor for a practice telephone set). Situations could include a customer complaining about her holiday when she returns, a call you have to make to let a client know that his flight time has been changed or making a booking by 'phone with a hotel for one of your business clients. Use the guidelines on telephone technique above when completing this activity.

This activity is designed to provide evidence for P4.

Making presentations

You could be called upon to make a presentation as part of a job interview or when working in travel and tourism, e.g. a tour rep hosting a welcome meeting for new guests. Important points to remember include:

- Speak clearly and slowly, making sure that everybody can hear you;
- Follow a logical sequence;

Unit 6

- Start with an overview and end with a summary of the presentation;
- Maintain eye contact with your audience;
- Use prompt cards rather than reading from notes;
- Use visual aids as appropriate.

Using a package such as PowerPoint can add a touch of professionalism to a presentation.

Time management

Time management involves prioritising, organising and scheduling your work so as to meet deadlines and complete all tasks. Some people are much better than others at managing their time well, but anybody can be trained to be an effective time manager.

Organisation skills

Good organisation skills often go hand-in-hand with good time management skills. Being an effective organiser is all about setting up systems to manage work processes and tasks, such as ordering brochures, taking and processing bookings, handling cash and non-cash sales, producing itineraries and programming flight schedules.

Working with others

The importance of teamwork and how to work best as a member of a team are covered in detail on page 266 of this unit.

Unit 6

SECTION 4: CREATING AN EFFECTIVE WORKPLACE

Members of staff function best when they are provided with a well-designed and well-equipped working environment. The nature of many travel and tourism organisations means that the 'workplace' for staff is actually the facility itself, e.g. a hotel, museum, aircraft or outdoor activity centre. In attempting to create an effective workplace, managers and owners must consider a range of issues, such as working relationships, performance management, teamwork, legal/ethical responsibilities and training/staff development.

Working relationships

It goes without saying that staff who are happy in their work are an asset to a company, since they are likely to be more effective in their duties. Developing good working relationships between colleagues is an important part of making staff content in the workplace. Managers and supervisors should try to encourage open yet professional working relationships between staff and also develop the same sort of relationships with suppliers as well. Staff who deal with customers should be instructed in the correct procedures and approach to take as part of their training.

Performance management

Managers and supervisors are keen to get the best out of their employees in the workplace. One of the ways they do this is by measuring the performance of staff. This is done informally and formally, using methods such as appraisals and target setting, which can result in staff incentives like performance-related pay.

Appraisals

The main function of staff appraisal, sometimes referred to as staff development review, is to give an employee and his or her immediate superior the opportunity to discuss current performance and to agree a working plan for the future, in relation to specific targets and objectives. The appraisal, usually taking the form of an interview between the two parties, is also likely to highlight training needs for the individual that will have time and cost implications for management.

In order to be of maximum benefit to any travel and tourism organisation, whether it is in the private or public sector, an effective system of staff appraisal needs:

Unit 7

Thomson has the most travel agency branches

Miniple travel agents

'Miniple' travel agents are companies with small numbers of branches, often in a particular geographical area. They pride themselves on being able to give independent advice on holiday choices and a personal service to their clients. Having a branch network gives miniples the chance to negotiate more favourable terms with principals. Galaxy Travel in East Anglia, Lets Go in the South West and Bath Travel are three examples of successful miniples.

WEBLINK
www.bathtravel.com
Check out this website for more information on Bath Travel

FOCUS ON INDUSTRY – Bath Travel

Founded in 1924, Bath Travel is an independent company with a network of 68 travel agencies along the south coast of England. With its head office in Bournemouth, the company sells a variety of holiday and travel products from a wide range of operators. Bath Travel also has its own tour operating business, Palmair, flying out of Bournemouth Airport to destinations as diverse as St Petersburg, Marrakech and Luxor. The company also makes bookings on behalf of clients with the low-cost airlines, including Ryanair, easyJet and flybe, on a fee basis.

Independent travel agents

These are single, independent businesses that are not part of a chain and are often managed by the owner and a small team of staff. Unlike multiple agents that have links with their own tour operating companies, independent travel agents are free to offer their clients a wide range of holiday companies. Independents trade on their ability to give their clients a very personal service and they rely on word-of-mouth recommendation from satisfied customers for extra business.

Independent agents, who may not be able to justify the high rent and rates of town centre locations, will nonetheless want to be in a position that is not too far away from the main shopping thoroughfares. Given the particular nature of the products many independent agents sell, their clients are usually more than willing to travel a little further for their specialist advice. Agents located on the outskirts of towns or in city suburbs may have the

advantage of easier parking, when compared with high street agencies, a factor of particular importance if older or disabled clients are important customers.

Many independent agents join consortia such as Advantage Travel, Worldchoice, Mid Consort or the Campaign for Real Travel Agents (CARTA) in order to have their views heard, benefit from supplier discounts and make useful business contacts.

ACTIVITY

Carry out some research to find out how many independent travel agents there are in your local area. For each one you discover, try to find out if the agency is a member of a trade association or agents' consortium.

This activity is designed to provide evidence for P1.

e-agents

WEBLINK

www.lastminute.com;
www.expedia.co.uk;
www.ebookers.com;
www.travelocity.co.uk

*Check out these websites
to see how e-agents
operate.*

The growth in the use of the Internet has led to the development of e-agents (where e stands for electronic). These are a kind of 'virtual travel agent' as they have no branches and usually operate from a single base with the latest IT systems and equipment. Examples of e-agents include lastminute.com, ebookers, Travelocity and Expedia. E-agents benefit from the speed and flexibility of the Internet, but must generate high sales volumes to remain profitable. E-agents are also tour operators since their websites allow the packaging of accommodation and flights. In fact, Civil Aviation Authority (CAA) figures for 2004 show that e-agents were the fastest-growing sector carrying passengers under ATOLs (Air Travel Organisers' Licences), with Expedia growing by 169 per cent on 2003 and the Destination Group (part of lastminute.com) showing a 120 per cent rise in customers carried.

Holiday hypermarkets

These are large-scale travel agencies offering customers a wide choice of holidays and travel products in a single, convenient, themed setting. First Choice has pioneered the development of travel hypermarkets in the UK since it acquired the Holiday Hypermarkets company in 2000. First Choice now has 38 out-of-town outlets, typically covering 10,000 to 12,000 sq feet, and often located in large retail parks such as the Trafford Centre in Manchester and Bluewater in Kent.

Unit 7

Retail travel environment

Retail travel is a dynamic, fast-moving business environment where companies of all sizes are constantly trying to keep costs to a minimum, maximise their revenues and increase their share of the travel and tourism market. Topics such as vertical integration, co-operative marketing, racking policies and membership of trade associations are all key issues for the sector. These are dealt with in the following sections of this unit, together with the implications for the future of travel services distribution.

Vertical integration

Vertical integration occurs in the retail travel sector when a company controls more than one level of the distribution chain for products and services, in order to gain a competitive advantage. For example, each of the 'big four' multiple travel agency companies mentioned earlier in this unit are part of much larger travel groups, as follows:

- Thomas Cook retail travel shops are part of Thomas Cook AG;
- Thomson travel agencies are owned by TUI AG;
- Going Places retail outlets are part of the MyTravel Group;
- First Choice shops and Holiday Hypermarkets are owned by the First Choice Group.

All four have their own tour operating companies under many different brand names and operate their own charter airlines. Vertical integration of this sort, when a tour operator controls the sales policy of its own travel agencies, is thought by some people to be against the public interest, since it could lead to a company selling its own products above all others in a travel agency, a process known as 'directional selling'. Also, customers may not always realise that there is a commercial link between a travel agent and a tour operator. In certain circumstances, the Competition Commission (formerly the Monopolies and Mergers Commission) can be asked to investigate if the public are indeed being disadvantaged. This sometimes happens when a major airline or holiday company tries to take over one of its competitors. Since 2000, all vertically-integrated travel companies

Thomson is a vertically-integrated company

Unit 7

have been obliged to make their links to other travel companies clear by, for example, having notices in their travel agencies and printed in brochures.

Co-operative marketing

It makes sense for travel agencies to co-operate with other businesses outside the travel sector as a way of increasing customer awareness and stimulating extra sales. It is common for the large multiple agencies to run promotions with national and regional newspapers and magazines. Local, independent agents close to the English south coast ports often have promotions with ferry companies to generate business out of the peak season, using discount coupons and offers in local newspapers. Banks sometimes team up with travel retailers to include offers in mailings to their customers.

Racking policies

'Racking' is the practice of deciding which brochures a travel agency will put on its shelves. An agent's racking policy is crucial to the holiday companies and other principals looking to sell their products and services; if their brochure is not on the shelves, sales are likely to be low. The decisions on racking taken by the 'big four' travel agency chains are particularly important. Thomas Cook, Thomson, Going Places and First Choice have nearly 2,350 branches throughout the UK, representing more than 37 per cent of all agencies. A company whose brochures are racked by these agencies has excellent exposure to customers and can expect to generate substantial sales volumes. As we discussed earlier in this unit, vertical integration means that the racking policies of the 'big four' will tend to favour their own holiday companies' products. Independent agents, on the other hand, are free to rack a wide range of companies' brochures, although miniples will often have racking policies dictated by their head office. Although more people are using the Internet to search for holidays and travel products, brochures still have an important role to play in customers' holiday choices.

Trade associations

ABTA is the principal trade association representing UK travel agents and tour operators (see case study on page 310). Its members are responsible for the sale of some 85 per cent of all holidays sold in the UK. As well as being members of ABTA, travel agencies sometimes decide to join other trade bodies, known as consortia. Often, these are groupings of independent agents that come together to increase their influence and buying power, and join forces to compete with the 'big four' multiple agency chains. Being a member of a consortium allows a travel agency to retain its independence while at the same time reaping the benefits of the extra buying power that a consortium can offer. There are a number of consortia in the retail travel sector, including:

- Freedom Travel Group;
- Global Travel Group;
- Worldchoice;
- Travel Trust Association;
- Travelsavers;
- Advantage;
- Midconsort.

WEBLINK

www.midconsort.com;
www.advantage4travel.com

*Check out these websites
to find out more about
Midconsort and Advantage
Travel Centres.*

Advantage, also known as the National Association of Independent Travel Agents (NAITA), is the biggest travel retail consortium in the UK, representing some 860 independent agents. Worldchoice has more than 600 member companies.

An Advantage Travel Centre in the Cotswolds

Unit 7

WEBLINK

www.worldchoice.co.uk

Check out this website to help answer the questions in this case study and for more information on the Worldchoice travel agents' consortium.

CASE STUDY – Worldchoice

Introduction

Established in 1976, Worldchoice was one of the first travel agents' consortia. Today, it has over 600 travel agency members, making it one of the largest travel groups in the UK. The group considers its independence to be its biggest asset and its combined strength gives the consortium the negotiating power to command the best possible products and prices in retail travel. Uniquely among travel agency consortia, Worldchoice member shareholders jointly own Worldchoice Travel. To date, the consortium has acquired 13 travel agencies throughout the UK and has delivered its first share dividend to its investors.

Aims of the consortium

Advantage's mission is *'to be the most effective force in the independent travel agency sector and to provide the highest levels of profitability for our shareholders and members'.*

Advantage trades on four key principles for customers:

1. Quality;
2. Value;
3. Service;
4. Choice.

Members of the consortium are independent agents who are not tied to any of the multiple chains, thereby having the flexibility to offer customers a wide range of holidays and other travel products. In addition to the usual big holiday companies, Worldchoice agents sell more AITO (Association of Independent Tour Operators) holidays than any other travel agency group. Its members represent over 65 per cent of CARTA membership (Campaign for Real Travel Agents), organised by AITO to recognise those agents selling a wide range of specialist travel products. Research shows that an average Worldchoice agent has access to between 400 and 800 different holiday brochures.

Services and benefits for members

Worldchoice offers its members a range of services, including the best commercial rates of any travel consortium in the UK (according to data from Price Waterhouse Coopers). The consortium negotiates commercial terms with over 140 business partners every year on behalf of its members. The combined strength of over 600 agencies with an annual turnover in excess of £1 billion helps ensure attractive discounts to members. Worldchoice has its own automatic credit accounting system (ACAS), which can help members reduce administrative costs and bank charges, as well as improving cash flow.

Unit 7

The Worldchoice 'brand' is recognised nationally as a reputable and trustworthy organisation. Many of the consortium's members choose to promote and use the brand on their shop front and in-store. Working with the National Passport Office, Worldchoice members can offer their customers a unique service dealing with passport applications. The service provides an additional revenue stream for members and a convenient and valuable service for clients.

The consortium estimates that a typical travel agency with an annual turnover of £1 million could make savings of more than £40,000 by joining, in the following areas:

- Bank charges   £350
- ABTA Bond ART   £750
- Marketing material   £1,750
- Marketing support   £3,000
- Commercial terms   £20,000
- Foreign exchange service   £10,000
- Membership services   £600
- Training   £500
- Legal advice   £1,500
- Shop branding (optional)   £1,250

Sales and marketing activities

Worldchoice offers its members a broad range of sales and marketing activities and support services to help communication with customers. These include:

- Posters – specific seasonal poster campaigns are sent to members every month;
- Late availability window cards;
- Over-branded brochures – Worldchoice branded brochures to provide consistency of message;
- Shop branding;
- Escape magazine – distributed twice per year to every member's client database;
- Bespoke marketing campaigns – to take advantage of specific market conditions, e.g. war, terrorism, disease, weather, natural disasters, exchange rates, etc;
- Public relations – regular PR campaigns to keep the Worldchoice brand in the public domain.

CASE STUDY QUESTIONS

1. What services and benefits does Worldchoice offer to travel agency members?
2. How does it help with marketing support?
3. In what ways is Worldchoice different to other travel agency consortia, such as Mid Consort or Advantage Travel Centres?
4. What impacts will the growth in the use of the Internet have on the Worldchoice consortium?

Unit 7

Future developments in travel services

The biggest threat to retail travel agents is the growing trend towards direct booking of holidays and other travel products via the Internet, call centres and travel channels on TV. A 2002 MORI survey commissioned by ABTA showed that the historic gap between the number of bookings made through travel agents compared with tour operators was closing rapidly. In 2000, 40 per cent of respondents said that they were likely to book direct with a tour operator. The figure for 2002 showed that this had increased to 47 per cent. In 2000, only 6 per cent of respondents had actually bought a package holiday over the Internet. By 2002, this figure had increased to 19 per cent.

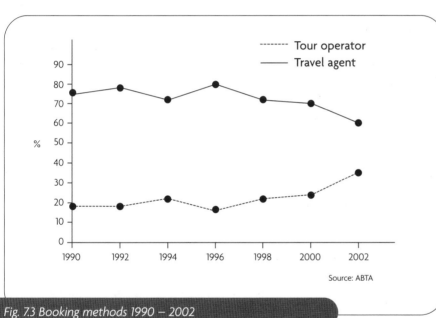

Source: ABTA

Fig. 7.3 Booking methods 1990 – 2002

ABTA has been monitoring trends in booking methods since 1990, as shown in Figure 7.3. The graph indicates that the number of respondents booking their holiday through a travel agent fell by 18 per cent between 1990 and 2002. Conversely, the number booking directly with a tour operator increased by 19 per cent over the same time period. It is likely that this trend will accelerate in years to come, leaving travel agents with an even harder challenge to face.

Another major issue for travel retailers is the capping and even scrapping of commissions by airlines. In 2004, British Airways cut its commission to agents to just 1 per cent, while the low-cost airlines offer no commission at all to travel agents. As a result, more agents are charging their clients a fee for their time, information and expertise. Research from ABTA indicates that the proportion of agents surveyed who said they charged a fee increased from 38 per cent in 2000 to 70 per cent in 2002. The survey also suggested that those agents who had introduced service fees spent less time with people who were unlikely to make a booking.

Travel agents are also trying to meet these, and other, challenges by introducing new web-based technologies to offer customers a more 'tailor made' experience, known as 'dynamic packaging', as the following example quoted in the *Travel Trade Gazette* demonstrates.

Unit 7

WEBLINK

www.club18-30.com

Check out this website for more information on Club 18-30.

FOCUS ON INDUSTRY – Dynamic packaging at Club 18-30

Club 18-30 is breaking away from the traditional seven and 14-night holiday durations to attract DIY packagers. The Thomas Cook brand is using new technology to allow travellers to 'pick and mix' elements of their holiday package. Club 18-30 customers will now be able to book three or 4-night stays with added flexibility. The technology used is the same as that employed by Thomas Cook's mainstream dynamic packaging tool, flexibletrips.com.

The recent decision by lastminute.com to offer its dynamic packaging technology to retail travel agents is further proof that there is as much potential online for agents as for consumers.

ACTIVITY

Carry out some research into 'dynamic packaging' to find out exactly what it involves, which travel companies use it and what type of technology it uses.

This activity is designed to provide evidence for P1.

Unit 7

SECTION 2: COMPETITIVE ADVANTAGE IN RETAIL TRAVEL

Retail travel is an extremely competitive sector of the travel and tourism industry. Running a travel agency is all about maximising profits, by offering a wide range of travel products and services, while at the same time providing excellent standards of customer service. Independent businesses and large, multiple chains are always looking at ways of gaining competitive advantage, i.e. using a variety of techniques to persuade customers to buy their products over and above those of their competitors.

Why do retail travel organisations seek to gain competitive advantage?

It stands to reason that if one aim of a travel agency is to maximise its profits, it will need to compete with other retailers for business; sitting back and waiting for customers to come through the door is not an option! This could be competition with similar types of local travel agencies or alternative types of travel retailers, for example the e-agents that we discussed earlier in this unit. Ultimately, a travel agency will seek to gain competitive advantage to:

- Increase its income from sales;
- Generate revenue to re-invest in the business;
- Attract more customers;
- Increase its share of the market;
- Provide a return for any shareholders it may have.

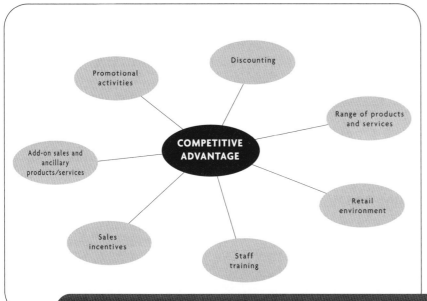

Gaining competitive advantage makes sense for everybody who has an interest in a travel agency business, whether they are owners, managers or staff.

How do retail travel organisations gain competitive advantage?

Travel agents use a variety of methods to try and stay one step ahead of their competitors, including those shown in Figure 7.4.

Fig. 7.4 Methods used to gain competitive advantage in retail travel

Unit 7

Promotional activities

Promotional activities can help an agency to gain competitive advantage by making more people aware of its existence and persuading customers to buy its products and services. Activities range from advertising in national, regional and local newspapers and magazines, creating effective window displays, arranging evening presentations in conjunction with travel principals, sending out press releases to the media and distributing mailshots and newsletters to clients. The multiple travel agency chains use advertising agencies and sales promotion specialists to create a consistent message across all their branches.

Fig. 7.5
Discounting is
common practice
in retail travel

SHORT BREAK VOUCHER

Save up to £105.00* per night

PARAMOUNT
GROUP OF HOTELS

Why not treat yourself and your family to a half price leisure break at one of 16 four and five star luxurious Paramount Hotels located throughout the UK.

If you're planning to treat yourself to a city break or a getaway in beautiful surroundings, your Co-operative Bank credit card can cut the cost of luxury accommodation in half.

It's a genuine half price offer
50% off the standard cost of a twin or double room for two adults, when you stay between two and six nights, with no obligation to dine.

*Terms and conditions apply – see reverse for details

Discounting

It's often said that everybody loves a bargain and people who buy holidays and other travel services from travel agents are no different. Discounting the brochure prices of holidays, flights, cruises and car hire, to name but a few, is now common practice in retail travel (see Figure 7.5). The multiple agents have the greatest buying power and often secure the best prices with principals, but agencies that are members of consortia, such as Mid Consort, Advantage and Worldchoice, offer customers very competitive deals.

Range of products and services

By offering a wider range of products and services than its competitors, a travel agency can attract extra custom, thereby gaining a competitive advantage. Multiple travel agency chains have strict guidelines on which products they promote and sell. Independent agents have more freedom to promote a wider range of specialist holidays and travel products. Some independent agents offer their own escorted tours as a way of increasing income and gaining an edge over the competition.

Retail environment

The external appearance and internal layout of a travel agency play an important part in attracting customers. From the outside,

a travel agency should look inviting to the prospective customer, whether it is in a town centre high street location, a city suburb or a small country town. Inside, the agency should feel warm and inviting, with well-stocked brochure racks and smiling faces. A well-planned internal layout of a travel agency can do a lot to help achieve the agency's principal aim of selling holidays and other travel products profitably. It will offer staff an efficient environment within which to perform their selling skills, give them greater job satisfaction and allow them to maximise sales opportunities. From the customers' point of view, it will encourage them to consult staff, examine brochures and, hopefully, stimulate them to make a purchase.

Certain aspects of the external appearance of a travel agency will be 'fixed', for example the size of the overall shop frontage, its position in relation to adjacent shops and any 'street furniture', i.e. lamp posts, fire hydrants, litter bins, etc. Within these constraints, the possibilities for alterations to its external design are limited only by the imagination and the budget of the travel agent, plus any restrictions imposed by local planning authorities or landlords in the case of leased property. Two areas where the agency staff and management have some control over the external appearance of the premises are:

1. Fascia   2. Window displays

In an effort to convey a single corporate identity and brand image, the multiple travel agency chains adopt the same style of fascia outside all their branches. Independent agents have greater freedom to design a fascia board that says something about the agency and its products. Either way, an effective fascia board is a very important advertising tool for the agent, visible from a long way away.

Window displays are a good way of changing the external appearance of an agency for a short period of time, thereby giving prominence to a particular product or concentrating on different seasons of the year, e.g. city breaks in the autumn and winter, summer sun holidays at the beginning of the main booking season and winter ski scenes. Changing a window display regularly will also generate more interest from passing customers, who may be tempted inside to ask for brochures and information. All travel principals will supply point-of-sale (POS) materials for window and shop displays, often in conjunction with brochure launches. What should be avoided at all costs are hand-drawn or hand-written signs, which give a window display an unprofessional look and do little to enhance the image of the travel agent.

ACTIVITY

Carry out some research into the external appearance of the travel agencies in your local area, noting positive features that attract attention and those that detract from the overall external appearance. Suggest ways that the negative features could be improved.

This activity is designed to produce evidence for M1.

Unit 7

Staff training

There is little doubt that a well-trained workforce is any travel agency's greatest asset. Training in selling and customer service skills are particularly important in helping to secure competitive advantage. Training can play a vital part in gaining an advantage over the competition by:

- Increasing efficiency and profitability;
- Improving customer service;
- Reducing absenteeism and staff turnover;
- Increasing staff flexibility;
- Triggering innovation and new ideas;
- Reducing business costs.

A survey carried out for ABTA in 2002 showed a direct link between training and profitability in travel agencies, as shown in Figure 7.6 Those agents that spent over £500 per employee on training were rewarded with higher than average turnover and profits per employee.

	More than £500 spent on training	Survey average	less than £200 spent on training
Profit per employee	£6,928	£5,311	£4.897
Turnover per employee	£332,000	£313,000	£307,000

Fig. 7.6 Link between training and profitability in travel agencies

ACTIVITY

Investigate the training opportunities that are on offer locally and nationally for people wanting to work in retail travel. This should include courses offered by colleges and those on offer from training providers such as TTC Training (www.ttctraining.co.uk). Present your findings as an information leaflet that could be used by young people interested in a career in the retail travel sector.

This activity is designed to provide evidence for M1.

Unit 7

Call centre staff can take advantage of generous sales incentives

Sales incentives

Incentives are widely used in retail travel to encourage staff to achieve general sales targets or sell a travel product from a particular company, thereby earning their travel agency extra commission. They range from extra commission and discounted holidays to high street shop vouchers and travel goods. Representatives (reps) from the travel principals and other suppliers visit agencies on a regular basis, particularly targeting those that have the highest sales volumes. Principals, including tour operators, ferry companies, car hire firms and airlines, sometimes provide training sessions for staff to increase their 'product knowledge'. This also has the added benefit for the principal of generating extra sales. Agency staff can also take advantage of free or heavily-discounted familiarisation ('fam') trips to sample holidays and travel products first hand. This increases their confidence when dealing with clients back in the agency.

Add-on sales and ancillary products and services.

As profit margins on the sale of holidays can be very low, travel agents are always keen to give clients the chance of buying add-ons to their holiday and ancillary products and services, such as travellers' cheques, airport car parking, travel insurance and car hire. Percentage commission on these products is often much higher than for package holidays, so staff are encouraged to offer them to clients.

WEBLINK	FOCUS ON INDUSTRY – Holiday Extras

WEBLINK

www.holidayextras.co.uk

Check out this website for more information on Holiday Extras.

FOCUS ON INDUSTRY – Holiday Extras

Holiday Extras was the first company to offer UK travel agents an airport hotels and car parking service back in 1983. Today, the company is the market leader in holiday extras – airport hotels, car parking, travel accessories, car hire, travel insurance, etc. It makes arrangements for around 2.5 million passengers per year from its call centre and website. The company is used extensively by travel agents who earn commission on sales and extra incentives such as prize draws and high street shop vouchers. It is still independently owned by its founder Gerry Pack.

Unit 7

We discussed in the first section of this unit three particular ways that retail travel organisations try to gain competitive advantage, namely:

1. Vertical integration;
2. Joining a trade association;
3. Using new technology.

The following case study on Lincoln Travel is a good example of all three of these methods of competitive advantage in retail travel.

WEBLINK

www.lincolntravel.co.uk

Check out this website to help answer these questions and for more information on Lincoln Travel

CASE STUDY – Lincoln Travel

Lincoln Travel is part of TUI UK, the vertically-integrated company that includes Thomson travel agencies and Thomson tour operations. Established in 1984, Lincoln Travel specialises in selling its holidays and travel products on TV and via the Internet. The company advertises nationally on Teletext on ITV, where it has its own sections on many pages within the travel section. Teletext Holidays is also available on the Internet. Lincoln can also be found on 5Text on Channel 5, Skytext on Sky One and Intelfax on Bravo, Discovery, UK Gold, Challenge TV, UK Living, Trouble TV, Live TV and Discovery Home & Leisure.

Lincoln Travel's Internet sites, latedeals.com and skydeals.com, offer a range of holidays and flights around the world departing from the UK. Customers can search for holidays by date, destination, departure airport, duration, budget and accommodation basis, search the late availability database or look for special offers that are updated throughout the day.

Lincoln Travel acts as a retail agent for all the UK's leading tour operators, including the brands that are owned by its parent company TUI UK (part of the World of TUI organisation). Lincoln is a member of the Association of British Travel Agents (ABTA), is fully bonded and only deals with ATOL-protected tour operators.

CASE STUDY QUESTIONS

1. Explain how being part of a vertically-integrated company helps Lincoln Travel gain a competitive advantage.
2. How can new technology give companies such as Lincoln Travel an advantage over high street travel agents?
3. Carry out some research to find out if the other major vertically-integrated travel companies offer the same kind of TV and Internet distribution channels.
4. How does being a member of ABTA and an agent for ATOL-protected tour operators help give Lincoln Travel a competitive advantage?

Unit 7

SECTION 3: WORKING PRACTICES AND LEGISLATION

No two travel agencies are the same and the way that an agency organises its working practices on a day-to-day basis will depend on a number of factors, such as how many staff it has, their levels of experience, the type of IT systems used and management style. There are, however, some basic aspects of working practices and legislation that are common to all and which we will cover in the following sections of this unit.

Legislation

In common with many other industries, travel and tourism organisations are required to comply with a wide range of laws, regulations and agreements in the course of their activities. They may also enter into voluntary codes of conduct as part of membership of a trade body such as ABTA or AITO. Much UK legislation now starts as Directives from the European Union, e.g. the Package Travel Regulations, Distance Selling Regulations and other types of consumer protection legislation.

Agency agreements

All of the business conducted by travel agents on behalf of principals is strictly controlled by individual agency agreements. These contractual arrangements set out the obligations of each party to the agreement, the terms of trade and remuneration details. The most common agency agreement is that between the travel agent and a tour operator, where the agent undertakes to sell the tour operator's products in return for a commission on sales. Other agreements may be made with coach operators, holiday centres, hotel groups, ferry companies, rail companies, National Express, car hire firms and a range of other travel and tourism companies. A standard written agency agreement between a travel agent and a tour operator includes details under a number of clauses, including:

- Accounting procedures for deposits and balances;
- Commission rates and arrangements for payment to the agent;
- Procedures for issuing tickets, vouchers and other travel documentation;
- Policy on refunds and cancellation of holidays by the client or tour operator;
- Handling of complaints made to the agent about the operator's products;
- Racking responsibilities of the agent in respect of the operator's brochures;
- Training and promotional support offered by the tour operator.

Such agreements are generally on a non-exclusive basis, i.e. many other travel agents will be selling the same products. It is only in the case of very specialised products that an agent may enter into an exclusive arrangement with an operator, although exclusive agreements in a particular geographical area are not uncommon.

Unit 7

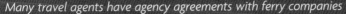

Many travel agents have agency agreements with ferry companies

Contract law

Contrary to popular belief, most contracts do not need to be in writing. From a lawyer's standpoint, a contract is any agreement that the law will enforce, whether in writing, verbal or implied, i.e. assumed from the conduct of the parties. Contracts range from the very simple, e.g. buying a drink at a resort complex, to the very complex, e.g. building a cruise ship. The law of contract is principally concerned with promises that constitute part of an agreed exchange. It governs such questions as which agreements the law will enforce, what obligations are imposed by the agreement and what will happen if the obligations are not carried out.

The following conditions must be satisfied if a contract is to be legally enforceable:

1. There must have been agreement between the parties on all material aspects of the contract;
2. The parties must have intended to create a legally binding contract;
3. There must be at least two parties to the contract.

It is an essential requirement of English law that, for a contract to be legally binding, each party must have agreed to provide something of value to the other. For example, when a customer books a package holiday, but the booking has yet to be confirmed, the contract between the customer and the tour operator may still be legally binding even where he or she has not yet paid for it. The important point is that the customer has promised to pay the price for the holiday when required to do so. The tour operator, by the same token, promises that the holiday is available.

It is important to remember that when a holidaymaker books a package holiday through a travel agent, the contract is between the customer and the tour operator, with the travel agent merely acting as an intermediary. It is against the tour operator that the customer must seek legal redress in the event of a breach of contract, although the travel agent may be liable for any other extras that are not part of the brochure holiday, such as currency exchange, airport car parking, travel insurance, etc.

Unit 7

Fair trading charters

Many of the large travel agency chains produce fair trading charters as a way of demonstrating commitment to their customers. They are often divided into two sections – 'our commitment to you' and 'your commitment to us'. Trade associations such as ABTA and AITO also publish charters for their members to adopt.

WEBLINK

www.gambia.co.uk

Check out this website for more information on the Gambia Experience.

FOCUS ON INDUSTRY – The Gambia Experience's fair trading charter

The Gambia Experience is a specialist UK travel company offering holidays and flights to the Gambia. Its fair trading charter forms the basis of the contract between its customers and the company. Under 'our commitment to you', the charter covers the following aspects of the contractual arrangement – provision of the holiday, reservation, prices and surcharges, flight, changes to holidays, cancellation of holidays, complaints and personal injury. The 'your commitment to us' section of the charter includes information on – booking form and payment, travel insurance, changes to bookings, cancellation of bookings, complaints, ticket conditions, holiday participation, consumer protection and data protection. The company is a member of ABTA and holds an ATOL (Air Travel Organisers' Licence) from the CAA for further consumer protection.

Trade Descriptions Act

This Act protects consumers against false descriptions made knowingly or recklessly by anybody selling products and services, including holidays and other travel products. Any description of, for example, a hotel or resort must be truthful at the time it was written (if circumstances change, then the company must inform the customer of the nature of the changes). The Act places a duty on owners and operators of travel and tourism facilities to produce brochures, websites and other promotional materials that are not intended to deceive customers.

Unfair Contract Terms Act

This law allows customers to challenge any terms in a contract that they consider to be unfair or unreasonable, unfairly weighted against them, or that are ambiguous. Standard contract terms should be written in clear, understandable language. It is illegal to have a contract term that attempts to restrict the customers' statutory rights or avoids responsibility for death or personal injury. In certain cases, the Office of Fair Trading (OFT) may be able to prevent a company from using an unfair contract term in the future.

Unit 7

Package Travel Regulations

The main aim of the Package Travel, Package Holidays and Package Tour Regulations 1992 is to give people buying package holidays more protection and access to compensation when things go wrong, while at the same time harmonising the rules covering packages operated throughout European Union countries. In the normal course of events, travel agents are not bound by the requirements of the Regulations, since they are not the 'organiser' of the package, but the 'retailer'. The Regulations define these terms as follows:

- Organiser – the person who, other than occasionally, organises packages and sells or offers them for sale, whether directly or through a retailer;
- Retailer – the person who sells of offers for sale the package put together by the organiser.

In the UK travel and tourism industry the organiser will normally be a tour operator and the retailer a travel agent. There may, however, be occasions when a travel retailer does fall within the scope of the Regulations. This will certainly be the case when the travel agent escorts his or her own tours for clients, since the contract for the holiday is between the agent and the customer, with no tour operator involved. Similarly, a travel agent who uses a range of reference materials to assemble a package for a client is likely to fall within the requirements of the Regulations. It is only when the customer enters into a contract directly with the tour operator, or other principal, that the travel agent will not be the 'organiser' as defined by the Regulations. Happily for travel agents, this is the normal situation, and most agents are unlikely to become entangled in the complexity of the Package Travel Regulations. To make sure that the position is clear, the agent should ensure that the customer signs the tour operator's booking form and receives an unaltered confirmation invoice from that party. Travel agents must be careful to ensure that correct documentation is passed from the principal, normally a tour operator, to the client. Unit 11 on Tour Operations has more detailed information on the Package Travel Regulations.

Trade association regulations and codes of conduct

Trade associations are found in all sectors of the travel and tourism industry, from transport operators to hotels. They are set up to represent the interests of companies operating in a particular sector and to make sure that their voice is heard. Many trade associations draw up codes of conduct that lay down the minimum standards under which member companies are expected to conduct their everyday business with customers and suppliers. The principal trade association for retail travel agents in the UK is ABTA, the Association of British Travel Agents (see case study in on page 310)

Companies that are granted membership of ABTA are required to adhere to strict rules governing their business practice. These are contained in ABTA's Code of Conduct, which regulates all aspects of tour operators' and travel agents' relationships with their customers

Unit 7

and which have been drawn up in conjunction with the Office of Fair Trading (OFT). The Code of Conduct is designed to regulate the activities of:

- Members dealing with customers;
- Members dealing with other ABTA members;
- Members dealing with principals and agents who are not members of ABTA.

The aims of the Code of Conduct are to:

- Ensure that the public receive the best possible service from ABTA members;
- Maintain and enhance the reputation, standing and good name of the Association and its membership;
- Encourage initiative and enterprise in the belief that properly regulated competitive trading by and between members will best serve the public interest and the wellbeing of the travel industry.

The Travel Agents' Code of Conduct regulates all aspects of travel agents' relationships with their customers, covering their responsibility with regard to the standard of service they provide and the information they give to clients. It also lays down rules concerning travel agents' trading relationships with tour operators. In addition, members of ABTA are required to adhere to precise financial specifications, overseen by ABTA's Financial Services Department, which checks all members' accounts at least once a year.

WEBLINK

www.abtanet.com/currentcode.pdf

Check out this website for full details of the ABTA Code of Conduct for travel agents and tour operators.

Unit 7

WEBLINK

www.abtanet.com

Check out this website to help answer the questions in this case study and for more information on ABTA and its operations.

CASE STUDY – ABTA (the Association of British Travel Agents)

Introduction

Founded in 1950, ABTA is the UK's premier trade association for travel agents and tour operators. Its current number of 1052 tour operator and 6310 travel agency offices are responsible for the sale of some 85 per cent of all holidays sold in the UK. ABTA members had a combined sales turnover of £26 billion in 2004.

ABTA's aims

ABTA's main aims are to maintain the high standards of service among its members, as well as creating as favourable a business climate as possible for the industry. Specific objectives of the Association are to:

1. Establish an organisation which is fully representative of travel agents and tour operators in the UK;
2. Promote and develop the general interests of all members of ABTA;
3. Establish and maintain Codes of Conduct between members and the general public, with the object that membership of the Association will be recognised as a guarantee of integrity, competence and high standards of service;
4. Discourage unfair competition without in any way interfering with initiative and enterprise based on fair trading;
5. Promote friendly relations with others in the travel industry;
6. Provide means for negotiations and liaison with other bodies concerned with the development of travel both in the UK and abroad.

Membership of ABTA

Although it is not compulsory for a UK travel agent to become a member of ABTA, membership does confer a range of benefits, including:

- Commercial – use of the ABTA logo, bonding schemes, independent arbitration service, etc.;
- Representation – lobbying at Westminster and Brussels, plus regular dialogue with other important interest groups;
- Member services – an information bureau giving advice to members, legal advisory service, legal seminars, annual receipt of the ABTA Members' Handbook and ABTA List of Members, monthly issues of ABTA News, regional meetings of the Association, annual ABTA Convention, etc;

- Training – ABTA works with TTC Training, which offers a range of courses for staff and management, including the ABTA Travel Agents' Certificate (ABTAC);
- Charity – ABTA administers its own benevolent fund for members who need financial assistance.

How ABTA works

The Association is a self-regulatory body run by its membership. A network of Councils and Committees, appointed by member travel agents and tour operators, make up the policy-making and enforcing machinery of the Association and help to ensure that ABTA remains in close contact with the whole of its membership. The Association has an education and training function which is carried out by TTC Training, which works closely with City & Guilds on developing the ABTA Travel Agents' Certificate (ABTAC) and ABTA Tour Operators' Certificate (ABTOC).

Up until the end of 1993, ABTA legally operated a type of 'closed shop' arrangement known as the 'stabiliser', which stated that ABTA travel agents could only sell package holidays from tour operators who were themselves members of ABTA, and vice versa. The stabiliser was introduced 20 years ago to safeguard the public against unscrupulous agents and operators. The arrangement was dismantled in 1993, since it was considered to be a restrictive practice and also because, in theory at least, the introduction of the EC Package Travel Directive rendered the stabiliser obsolete.

Protection and redress for the travelling public

In addition to its Codes of Conduct, ABTA seeks to protect the interests of travellers through its Consumer Affairs Department and its own Arbitration Scheme. Staff in the Consumer Affairs Department offer a service for clients who have booked with an ABTA-registered travel agent or tour operator and who have reason to complain about some aspect of the service they have received. ABTA will look into the complaint and seek to redress the situation without recourse to law. If the dispute cannot be resolved through conciliation, the client may pursue the claim through ABTA's Arbitration Scheme, for which a fee is charged depending on the amount of the claim. The ABTA Arbitration Scheme, administered by the Chartered Institute of Arbitrators, gives the client the opportunity for redress without incurring high legal costs.

Tour operator and travel agent members of ABTA are required to provide bonds to protect their customers in the event of financial failure. ABTA currently holds bonds valued at £201 million for travel agents and £170 million for tour operators. The bond can take a number of forms, but is often an insurance policy for the amount required by ABTA, or a bank

Unit 7

guarantee. The financial protection offered by the bonding system enables ABTA, in the event of a member's financial failure, to:

- Arrange for clients whose holidays are in progress at the time of the failure to continue their holidays, as far as possible as originally planned, and in any event to make certain that customers abroad are returned to the UK;
- Reimburse customers whose holidays have not started, the money they paid for their holidays or to make alternative arrangements for the holidays to proceed.

CASE STUDY QUESTIONS

1. How does ABTA help to protect the travelling public?
2. What advantages does ABTA membership offer to travel agencies?
3. What is the ABTA Code of Conduct?
4. Why do ABTA travel agencies and tour operators have to provide the Association with a bond?

Working practices in travel agencies

Front and back office

Dealing with customers is an important front office function

It is common for travel and tourism organisations to divide their business functions into 'front office' and 'back office', developing systems in support of each. In simple terms, the 'front office' (sometimes referred to as 'front of house') refers to the reception area of any travel and tourism facility, the point at which the customer first makes contact with the organisation. The 'back office' (also known as 'back of house') refers to the organisation's functions that take place behind the scenes, for example accounting, maintenance, training and stock control.

The concept of front and back office is widespread in the retail travel sector. The division into front and back office allows management to focus resources on particular functions and train staff in these areas. The selection and training of staff to work in the

Unit 7

FRONT OFFICE FUNCTIONS	BACK OFFICE FUNCTIONS
Welcoming customers	Cash and credit control
Taking bookings	Accounting
Selling services	Client databases
Providing information	Brochure stock control
Handling cash, cheques and cards	Maintenance
Controlling entry	Marketing and publicity
Promoting products and services	Analysis of management data
Answering enquiries	Staff training
Maintaining records	Personnel/human resources
Passing information to back office	Health and safety

Fig. 7.7 Travel agency front and back office functions

'front office' is particularly important, since it provides the visitor with his or her first impressions of the organisation. Staff with an understanding of customer needs and expectations and who are committed to providing excellence in customer service should be chosen to work in this high profile area. The environment in which the 'front office' is positioned also needs to be carefully planned, and should provide a clean, warm, efficient, welcoming and friendly atmosphere.

There must always be a strong link between front and back offices for the organisation's business systems to truly effective; for example, when a client books a holiday in a travel agency, information must be passed to a variety of 'back office' systems, e.g. accounting and credit control. Examples of the different functions carried out by front and back office staff in retail travel agencies are shown in Figure 7.7.

ACTIVITY

While on work experience or in a part-time job, list the front office and back office functions that take place in the organisation. Explain the linkages between the two.

Procedures and documentation for selling travel services

The starting point for the sale of any holiday or travel product is when a client makes contact with a travel agent, either in person, by telephone or email. Figure 7.8 shows each stage of the process in booking a typical package holiday.

Unit 7

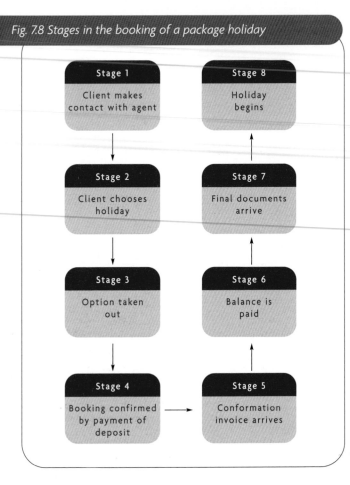

Fig. 7.8 Stages in the booking of a package holiday

Stage 1
Client makes contact with agent

Stage 2
Client chooses holiday

Stage 3
Option taken out

Stage 4
Booking confirmed by payment of deposit

Stage 5
Conformation invoice arrives

Stage 6
Balance is paid

Stage 7
Final documents arrive

Stage 8
Holiday begins

If the client has a definite departure date, holiday company and resort in mind, the agent will quickly be able to check availability on their computer system. If there is availability, the booking can proceed. If not, or if the client is unsure about which resort to choose, some further advice and help will be needed from the agent. The tour operators' central reservation systems (CRS) are designed to be able to search by date, resort, hotel, type of holiday, etc., so the client's needs should be satisfied eventually. Once the holiday is chosen, the agent takes out an option, giving the client the chance to think about the choice before committing himself or herself. The option will be entered on the screen and normally lasts for 24 hours, after which time it lapses and the holiday is put on sale again. If the client makes contact within the 24 hours and pays a deposit, then the booking is confirmed. The client will be issued with a receipt for the deposit payment and a new file is started by the agent.

Normally within two weeks of making the booking, a written confirmation invoice will be sent from the tour operator, giving precise details of the clients travelling, the booked holiday and travel details. The balance is normally paid eight weeks before departure, but if the holiday is booked within eight weeks of departure the full amount must be paid. Two to three weeks before the holiday starts, final tickets and documentation are received by the agent and passed to the client. This is a good point at which to try some 'cross selling' by asking clients if they need any foreign currency or travellers' cheques for their holiday.

FOCUS ON INDUSTRY – Computer systems in travel agencies

Traditionally, travel agents have used Viewdata systems to access tour operators' and other principals' computer systems to check availability and make bookings on behalf of clients. With the rapid developments in Internet use, many agents are switching to more advanced web-based systems that offer 24-hour access and 'real time' searching facilities. One of the most widely-used systems is EasySell from Comtec, which enables travel agents to search for package holidays and flights in real time. The company has also developed TravelCat, an integrated agency management system that links front and back office functions.

Unit 7

Out and About Travel   Tel: (014) 682595

Client details

Names	Address	Tel. No.
1.		
2.		
3.		
4.		
5.		
6.		

Holiday details

Holiday company	Thomson	MyTravel	First Choice	Other
Booking ref:	Holiday no:	Option expiry date:	Date confirmed:	Agency ref:
Resort:	Dep. Date:	Duration:	Dep. airport:	Insurance Y/N
Hotel/Self-catering	Accomm. Details:	Special requests		

Flight details		Airline		Ref:		
	Date	From	To	Flight no.	Dep. time	Arr. Time
Outward						
Return						

Other travel requirements

Notes/costing		Agency ref:
		Taken by:
		Date of booking:

Fig. 7.9 Example of a travel agent's enquiry form

Documentation used in package holiday bookings

One of the most important documents used in travel agencies is the form that records the details of an initial enquiry from a customer. This may be called the enquiry form, office booking form or option form and it becomes the first item of a client's office file, to which other documentation is added later if the booking progresses. Whether the customer makes contact by telephone, email or in person, the enquiry form gives a travel agent the opportunity to record basic client information and holiday details in a logical manner. This will be invaluable when the client wishes to proceed with the booking or the agent needs to contact the client to seek clarification. The form also acts as a reminder to staff, ensuring that the necessary information is obtained and recorded correctly. Figure 7.9 gives an example of the type of information included on an enquiry form.

The enquiry form shown in Figure 7.9 gives a member of staff the opportunity to record client information, such as name, address and telephone numbers, plus details of their chosen holiday or other travel arrangements. There is space at the bottom for the agent to make some price calculations on behalf of the client. With developments in new technology, this sort of information can often be entered on to a computer system.

Unit 7

Confirmation invoice

Once a holiday has been booked, the first document the client receives is a confirmation invoice giving precise holiday details, including:

- Holiday reference/booking number;
- Inclusive dates of the holiday;
- Name and address of lead person;
- Names of all clients travelling (including ages of children and infants);
- Details of travel arrangements for the outward and return journeys;
- Details of the accommodation booked;
- Details of other items booked, e.g. car hire;
- Full holiday costing.

The confirmation invoice will also indicate when any balance of money is due for payment and the date by which it must be paid. Any discrepancies on the invoice noticed by the client or agent should be rectified at this stage. An example of a package holiday confirmation invoice is shown in Figure 7.10.

Two to three weeks before the holiday begins, the clients will receive their final travel details and documents. This will include their travel tickets, accommodation vouchers, insurance details, car hire details (if applicable), baggage labels, customer satisfaction questionnaire and a printed travel information form that duplicates some of the details on the original confirmation invoice. These are the documents that the clients will need to take with them on holiday as proof of purchase when boarding their flights and checking in to the accommodation.

Payment timetable

Every client has a unique booking reference and associated payment schedule. It is standard practice for a client to pay a deposit on booking a holiday, with the balance being due 8 weeks before departure. If a client books within 8 weeks of starting their holiday the full amount is taken at the time of booking. Payments to tour operators and other principals are usually made monthly, less the travel agent's agreed commission.

Client files

Staff in travel agencies must be able to respond quickly to enquires, whether they are from a client, a tour operator or another principal. This calls for an efficient system for filing client documentation and other information, such as country fact sheets and file copies of brochures, timetables, etc. Most agencies still operate manual filing systems, but the

Back Out Tours

Tel: 018 759 28762
Fax: 018 759 28763

Booking details

Booking no:	12345
Issue date:	17/05/05
Sales adviser:	Jim
Holiday type:	Villa inclusive
Party size:	2Ad 2Ch 0Inf

Holiday Details COSTA BLANCA
Provisional Travel Details – subject to alteration – local timings

Sunday 14 August 05	Birmingham – Alicante	1415/1745	Monarch ZB824
Sunday 28 August 05	Alicante – Birmingham	1125/1300	Monarch ZB823

Accommodation

Property: Villa Paella   Sunday 14 Aug 05 to Sunday 28 Aug 05 (14 nights)
                      3-bedroom villa for up to 6. Own pool.

Car & Boat Hire, Motorail, Hotel, etc

Group A car   14 Aug 05 Airport   28 Aug 05 Airport

CONFIRMATION & INVOICE TO
Mr J Brown
10 High Street
Anytown
AN1 7HQ

We have pleasure in confirming your holiday arrangements. Please check the details carefully and notify us by return if there are any discrepancies. Where special requests have been made, details are shown on this form. We will endeavour to fulfil them, but no guarantee can be given. If you have any queries or require further information, please do not hesitate to contact us.

Message

Holiday Costing

	1	2	3
Basic holiday cost	389.00	344.00	0.00
Airport supplement	0.00	0.00	0.00
Seasonal supplement	15.00	15.00	0.00
Insurance	25.00	12.50	0.00
Cost per person	429.00	371.50	0.00
Number of clients	2	2	0
Total columns 1 & 2		1,601.00	

Other

Property deposit	100.00
Car hire (2 x 111)	222.00
Reductions (1 free week car hire)	111.00
TOTAL	£1,812
Payment received	£1,812
Balance due	0

Passenger Details

		Age	Sex	Ins			Age	Sex	Ins
1	Mr Brown		M	Y	2	Mrs Brown		F	Y
3	Miss Brown	13	F	Y	4	Mstr Brown	6	M	Y

Registered in England No. 1234567890

Fig. 7.10 Package holiday confirmation invoice

Unit 7

popularity of computerised filing systems based on database software is growing rapidly. A filing system can be arranged alphabetically, numerically or in date order. Information on countries, office copies of brochures, timetables, etc. are best filed alphabetically. Numerical filing is favoured by some agencies for clients' bookings, each being assigned a unique reference number and filed accordingly. The majority of agents, however, prefer to organise their client files in date order based on the date of departure. One drawback of this method is that the peak travel months of July and August generate a great deal of paperwork, making it necessary to devote extra space to these months. Filing by date of departure is, nonetheless, preferred by most travel agencies.

Some agencies further refine their client filing system according to the status of the booking, with separate sections for:

- Initial enquiries – a record of a client's first contact;
- Options – details of a client who has taken out an option on a booking;
- Confirmations – clients who have paid a deposit;
- Final payments – bookings on which the balance has been paid;
- Awaiting tickets – clients who are awaiting their tickets and vouchers;
- Refunds due – any clients who are due a refund on their payments.

With this system, clients' files are moved from one section to another according to their current status. This way, a member of staff can see at any one time the progress of a client's booking. Client files are normally kept for up to two years, although HM Revenue and Customs' rules on income tax insist on longer periods of time. Files that are no longer current are referred to as 'dead files' or 'closed files' and are stored in an archive in case they are needed for any claims that may be made.

Brochure handling

Brochures play a vital role in the promotion and sale of holidays and other travel products sold in agencies. The brochure is one of the travel agent's prime sales tools and is the mechanism by which a customer's enquiry is, hopefully, turned into a sale. The high costs of designing, printing and distributing brochures, means that tour operators and other principals keep firm control on which agencies receive brochure stocks and in what quantities. The agencies with the best track record of selling a company's products will receive regular bulk supplies and command special treatment, including extra incentives for travel agency staff and management to encourage even more sales. Agencies with smaller sales volumes will still be sent brochure stocks, but on a smaller scale. In all cases, the tour operator will ensure that the agency has a file copy of the latest brochure as soon as possible after printing in advance of the bulk supplies being delivered.

WEBLINK

www.bptravelmarketing.co.uk

Check out this website for more information on BP Travel Marketing Services.

Bulk supplies of brochures are sent to agents in a variety of ways. The mass market tour operators generally have their own distribution departments and networks, whereas smaller operators may use specialist distribution firms, such as BP Travel Marketing Services. Brochure distribution is sometimes graded on a regional basis, where agencies close to airports used by a tour operator are handled separately.

When bulk brochure supplies arrive at the agency, there is often a problem in deciding where to store them. All agencies have an area set aside for storage, but at certain times of the year this may be overloaded. An alternative 'overflow' area should be identified, bearing in mind the safety of staff and customers. Either way, there should be a workable method of storing the brochures, using an alphabetical system that will enable staff to locate a particular brochure when required. Brochures should never be left in piles on the floor of the main selling area of the travel agency. Apart from looking very untidy, there are clear issues concerning fire regulations and health and safety.

Agencies sometimes delegate the task of brochure stock control and re-ordering to a specific member of staff, in order to minimise the chances of running out of supplies. Agencies should, without fail, always keep an office copy of every brochure they sell so that, should the bulk supplies run out, staff will at least have one copy for reference.

Merchandising and displays

Merchandising and point-of-sale (POS) materials, such as window displays, free-standing displays in the main body of a travel agency and brochures, play an important role in promoting holidays and other travel products. They should be changed on a regular basis to provide customers with a new 'focal point' and as a way of alerting clients to new products, late deals and special offers. Displays should, at all times, look professional and tidy. The use of hand written signs and posters should be avoided, since they do little to enhance the image of the product being sold or the agency as a whole.

ACTIVITY

Working in a small group, make a display on a particular theme to do with holidays, e.g., UK holidays, European city breaks, long-haul destinations, etc. Use a range of posters, images and POS materials.

This activity is designed to provide evidence for P3

Unit 7

Sales targets, commission rates and incentive commission

Branches of the multiple travel agents have their sales targets set by head office, and sometimes monitored by a regional manager. Owners and managers of independent agencies agree targets with staff on an individual basis, with variations depending on a member of staff's experience and whether they work full- or part-time.

Commission is the payment that a travel agent receives from a principal for selling that company's products and services. Commission rates vary enormously between companies and different holiday products. Average commission rates are in the region of:

• Package holidays	10%
• Airline tickets	0 - 9%
• Ferry bookings	9%
• Travellers' cheques	1%
• Travel insurance	25% - 40%
• Coach holidays	10%
• Cruises	9% - 15%

These figures should only be taken as a rough guide, since commission levels fluctuate daily in response to competitor activity. Most principals offer incentive commission to generate more sales, where the amount paid to the agent increases as the sales volume rises. It's important to remember that commission is not the same as profit. Out of the commissions that an agent receives, he or she has to pay all the costs associated with running the agency, including staffing, heating, rent and rates, telephone, postage, insurance, etc. Industry sources estimate that a typical high street travel agency will make only 1 per cent net profit over the course of a year's trading. In other words, the profit for an agency that has a sales turnover of £1 million will be £10,000.

Unit 7

Package holidays

At its simplest, a package holiday is an arrangement that includes transport to a destination, accommodation, transfer arrangements and the services of a representative for an all-inclusive price. Tour operators assemble these different components into a saleable product that meets the needs and expectations of the customer. They are sold though travel agents and increasingly via less traditional distribution channels, such as the Internet, TV and call centres. There are literally thousands of UK-based tour operators, from large travel groups such as TUI/Thomson, Thomas Cook, MyTravel and First Choice, to small companies specialising in a particular destination or activity. The range and variety of tour operators' brochures is vast, covering summer sun, winter sun, winter sports, city breaks, themed tours, holiday centres, camping, cruises, etc.

All package holidays differ in their make-up, but we can identify three distinct components:

1. Accommodation;
2. Transportation;
3. Other travel services, e.g. car hire, transfers and the services of a representative.

Accommodation

The accommodation component of a package holiday can be either serviced or self-catering. Serviced accommodation is usually in a hotel that can offer a range of meal arrangements, including:

- Full board;
- Half board;
- All inclusive;
- Room only;
- Self-catering;
- Bed and breakfast.

Hotels in some parts of the world do not include any meals in their standard room rates, an arrangement sometimes known as European Plan. This is common in certain parts of Europe, the USA and the Far East. Customers can usually request a room with extra facilities or a particular aspect for the payment of a supplement, e.g. a room with a sea view or a ground floor room.

Unit 7

Self-catering can be in a wide range of accommodation, such as:

- Studios;
- Villas;
- Apartments;
- Cottages;
- Tents;
- Caravans/mobile homes;
- Boats.

Self-catering accommodation usually comes complete with cooking facilities and utensils, although many people often choose to eat out and avoid household chores while on holiday. Some self-catering accommodation includes a maid service, either included in the price or on payment of a supplement.

Benidorm is a popular package holiday destination

Transportation

The transport element of a package holiday can be travel by:

- Air;
- Coach;
- Rail;
- Ship;
- Self-drive car.

Whichever type of transport is used, tour operators are offered preferential, discounted rates, known as inclusive tour (IT) rates. Depending on the volume of business generated by the tour operator, a ferry company, for example, can offer IT rates that may be discounted by as much as 50 per cent of their standard tariff.

The vast majority of all package holidays sold in the UK use air travel to transport clients to their chosen destinations. These are known as 'air inclusive tours' (AITs) and use either chartered or scheduled flights. Package holidays that use seats on charter aircraft are known as inclusive tours by charter (ITC), while those based on scheduled services are referred to as inclusive tours by excursion (ITX). Aircraft may be chartered for specific flights or for blocks of time, usually a whole year or for the duration of a season. This is known as time

Unit 7

series charter and is financially more attractive than 'ad hoc' arrangements. Many tour operators charter their aircraft on a 'flight series' basis, contracting with the airline for the same time and destination each week. By using flight series charters and setting very high load factors (the number of seats that needs to be filled on a flight before any profit is made), tour operators have been able to keep prices down and stimulate demand. It is not uncommon for an operator to set a break-even load factor as high as 85-90 per cent.

One disadvantage of flight series charters is that there will inevitably be an empty flight home at the beginning of the season and an empty flight out at the end of the season. These flights are referred to as 'empty legs'. In order to maximise capacity, some travel companies operate a 'bus stop' arrangement, whereby an aircraft will take off from one UK airport, say Manchester, but stop at another, perhaps Birmingham International, to pick up passengers, before flying on to its final destination airport. If bookings from one particular regional airport are low, the tour operator may decide to consolidate, i.e. cancel the flight altogether and transfer the passengers by coach to another departure airport.

Other travel services

Apart from accommodation and transport, package holidays usually include other services such as:

- Transfers to and from accommodation in the resort;
- The services of a representative (rep);
- Car hire;
- Excursions;
- Equipment hire, e.g. skis, hammocks, bicycles, etc.

Depending on the number of passengers involved, transfers are by coach, taxi or minibus. Tour operators schedule flight arrivals so that maximum use can be made of coaches, without undue delay being caused to clients.

Resort representatives ('reps') provide information and support services for their clients, deal with any emergencies, arrange excursions and generally ensure the smooth running of the holiday while the clients are in the resort. Many reps are only employed for the duration of the season, either summer or winter, with some returning to work at head office in the UK out of season.

Unit 7

ACTIVITY

Research a range of package holiday brochures and find a suitable holiday for a family of four (2 adults and 2 teenage children) who want to go to a lively Mediterranean resort during the last two weeks in July. They would like to fly from their home airport of Cardiff and be away for 10 nights in total. They are looking for self-catering accommodation with 2 separate bedrooms. Their total budget is £2,250. Produce a costed itinerary and complete a booking form for the family.

This activity is designed to provide evidence for P5.

Reps are an important part of package holidays

Tailor-made services

We discussed earlier in this unit that travel agents were facing a big challenge from the development of the Internet and the growing trend for DIY packaging of holidays and other travel products by customers, which bypasses retail travel agents altogether. It is now quite common for people to put together their own 'unpackaged holiday' by using the Internet to book flights, accommodation, car hire, etc. separately This is having an effect on the sales of traditional package holidays, which have been falling in recent years; Mintel's Travel Trends report showed, for the first time, that package holidays made up less than half of all overseas holidays sold to British people in 2003.

One solution to these problems is for travel agents to offer their customers a more 'tailor-made' experience, rather than selling them just standard package holidays. Many travel agents would say that they do this already, especially the independent agents, who pride themselves on their personal service and high standards of customer care. Creating tailor-made travel arrangements for clients is more time-consuming for the travel agent, but new technology systems such as www.onlinetravel.com (part of the lastminute.com group) make it easier for agents to offer clients a more personalised holiday that meets their requirements. The example of Club 18-30 on page 298 suggests that companies are breaking away from the traditional seven and 14-night holiday durations to attract DIY packagers.

This process of agents drawing together separate components such as hotels, flights and add-ons to create a holiday is known as 'dynamic packaging'. Many industry insiders consider that it will be the most important trend in retail travel in the next few years. The recent decision by lastminute.com to offer its dynamic packaging technology to the trade is further proof that there is as much potential online for agents as there is for consumers.

Unit 7

ACTIVITY

Using www.onlinetravel.com draw up a costed itinerary for a couple who want to go on a 3-night European city break within the next month. They live in London and would like to fly to their destination and stay in a modest 3-star hotel in the centre of the city. They would like you to find the cheapest deal available.

This activity is designed to produce evidence for P5.

Ancillary products and services

Earlier in this unit we discussed the part that sales of add-ons and ancillary products and services can play in helping retail travel agents gain a business advantage over their competitors. Sales of products such as airport accommodation and parking, car hire, passport and visa services, travel insurance and foreign currency provide agents with much-needed revenue at a time when commission payments are being squeezed by principals.

ACTIVITY

Make a list of the add-ons and ancillary products and services that could be offered to the following clients by their travel agent:

- A couple celebrating their honeymoon in the Bahamas at a 5-star resort hotel;
- A family of four taking their car on a camping trip around Europe;
- Two couples flying to the French Alps for a 10-day skiing trip;
- A group of college students taking part in a week-long study tour to Paris;
- Two young backpackers setting off on a 3-month trip to Australia and the Far East.

Unit 7

UNIT SUMMARY

In this unit we have examined many different aspects of the retail travel environment. It is a very competitive sector of the travel and tourism industry, and one which is going through a period of rapid change. The Internet and other new technologies are changing the way that people buy their holidays and other travel products. You have seen why and how travel agents gain competitive advantage over their rivals, e.g. by discounting, increasing their product range or investing in staff training. You have investigated the main legislation affecting the retail travel sector and explored working practices in travel agencies, including procedures and documentation for selling travel services. Finally, you have looked in detail at packaged and tailor-made travel services, and developed your practical skills by arranging a variety of travel itineraries.

If you have worked methodically, by the end of this unit you should have:

- Examined the retail travel environment
- Investigated how organisations in the retail travel environment seek to gain competitive advantage;
- Examined working practices and legislation in retail travel operations;
- Selected and processed a range of packaged and tailor-made travel services to meet the needs of customers.

You are now in a position to complete the assignment for the unit, under the direction of your tutor. Before you tackle the assignment you may like to have a go at the following questions to help build your knowledge of retail travel operations.

Test your knowledge

1. Why is 'directional selling'?
2. Why do so many travel and tourism companies issue their staff with uniforms?
3. List the key actions to take when dealing with a complaint.
4. Explain what is meant by 'vertical integration' and why it is sometimes considered to be against the public interest.
5. List the key benefits to organisations of offering excellent customer service.
6. What is the difference between a 'customer' and a 'consumer'?
7. What are 'internal customers' and 'external customers'?
8. Why was the Disability Discrimination Act introduced?
9. What is 'product knowledge' and why is it important for customer service staff to have good knowledge of the products and services they are selling?
10. What is the main aim of the Data Protection Act?
11. What are the important 'ground rules' when dealing face-to-face with customers?
12. Travel and tourism products are 'intangible' – what does this mean?
13. List the key stages of the sales process in travel and tourism.
14. What does 'closing the sale' mean?
15. What do the letters AIDA mean?

Unit 7

UNIT 7 ASSIGNMENT: Retail travel operations

Introduction

This assignment is made up of a number of tasks which, when successfully completed, are designed to give you sufficient evidence to meet the Pass (P), Merit (M) and Distinction (D) grading criteria for the unit. If you have carried out the activities and read the case studies throughout this unit, you will already have done a lot of work towards completing the tasks for this assignment.

Scenario

You've been lucky enough to secure a summer placement with Lucy Green, a freelance travel agency training specialist who used to be a training manager for one of the UK's leading travel agency chains. Lucy has just won a 12-month contract to deliver training to 100 new travel apprentices to be recruited by a major 'miniple' agency in the south of England. She would like you to help her prepare some of the materials that she will use when training the recruits in the company's head office in Reading.

Task 1

Lucy is going to start the training sessions with a presentation on the travel agency sector in the UK and would like you to produce a PowerPoint presentation which includes:

(a) A description of the current retail travel environment, which should concentrate on the different types of retailers and the environment in which they operate;

(b) An explanation of why organisations in the retail travel environment seek to gain competitive advantage;

(c) An explanation of how organisations in the retail travel environment can gain competitive advantage, giving examples of good practice.

These tasks are designed to produce evidence for P1, P2 and M1.

Task 2

Many of the new apprentices know very little about the travel and tourism industry, so Lucy thinks it is important to give them an overview of working practices in retail travel and key legislation/regulations that affect the sector. She would like you to produce a handbook for the new recruits that:

Unit 7

(a) Describes the working practices of retail travel operations;

(b) Summarises key legislation and regulations that affect retail travel operations;

(c) Explains how legislation and regulations affect working practices in retail travel operations.

Your handbook should not try to cover every detail of working practices and legislation/regulations, but should be a summary of key points presented in a lively fashion.

These tasks are designed to produce evidence for P3, P4 and M2.

Task 3

As part of her 12-month contract, Lucy has been asked by the managing director of the company to hold a training event for the managers of the agency's 48 branches at the Reading head office. The theme of the event is 'gaining competitive advantage in retail travel' and Lucy would like you to do some preliminary research and provide her with:

(a) An analysis of the impact of integration, trade associations and other developments in gaining competitive advantage in the UK retail travel environment;

(b) An analysis of the impact of legislation, regulations and working practices on the operation and competitive advantage of organisations in the retail travel environment.

Your research should be presented as Word documents so that Lucy can cut and paste relevant parts into her PowerPoint presentation for the managers.

These tasks are designed to produce evidence for D1 and D2.

Task 4

Lucy wants to give the new apprentices some practice in processing package holidays and tailor-made travel services before they start their jobs in the agencies. She has produced the following 4 typical travel agency scenarios for the new recruits to work out, but would like you to attempt them first to come up with some example answers that she could use.

For each scenario you are asked to select and process an appropriate travel product that meets the needs of the customers. Lucy suggests that you present your findings as costed

itineraries with relevant supporting materials, e.g. extracts from brochures, the Internet, gazetteers, etc. You must complete the appropriate documentation for each scenario and you must make it clear how your choice of product meets the needs of the customers concerned.

These tasks are designed to produce evidence for P5 and M3.

Scenario 1

The Brown family from Birmingham have £1,800 to spend on a much-needed, two-week summer holiday. Mr and Mrs Brown have 2 children – Debbie aged 6 and Darren 4. They are looking for self-catering accommodation in a fairly quiet Mediterranean resort with lots of facilities for the children, including a swimming pool. They want to travel in the last 2 weeks of July using their local airport for convenience. Find a package holiday that meets their requirements and complete all the necessary documentation.

Scenario 2

John and Betty Swinton have always dreamed of a cruising holiday and now have the time and money to be able to enjoy one, having both just retired from the civil service. They like the idea of a Mediterranean cruise, but don't want to be away from their London home for more than two weeks. A traditional cruise with plenty of entertainment and like-minded people would suit them best. They are fairly flexible on timing and could go away any time in May/June or September/October. They have a total budget of £6,000 between them to cover all costs and want the best double cabin within this budget. They are happy to consider an ex-UK cruise or a fly-cruise using a London airport. Find a cruise package that meets their requirements and complete all the necessary documentation.

Scenario 3

The Quarry Valley Rugby Club have been selected to play in a prestigious rugby sevens tournament in Madrid. The party will consist of 10 players, their manager and a physiotherapist. The tournament is over 4 days in the last week of May and they plan to be away for 7 nights in all, departing on a Saturday and returning the following Saturday. All the players live within a short drive of Nottingham and would like to fly from an airport in the Midlands or London. They are looking for budget accommodation in a hostel or cheap hotel in the centre of Madrid and don't mind sharing with each other. Each player has set aside £500 for all travel and accommodation costs, but the club has said that it could offer each player an extra £200 if it was needed. They will need to hire a minibus for 4 days during the tournament. Produce a suitable, costed itinerary that meets the group's needs.

SECTION 1: UK TOUR OPERATIONS

Tour operations is a dynamic sector of travel and tourism, offering a range of career opportunities in the UK and overseas. In this section we investigate the structure of tour operations, examine different categories of tour operator and discuss the products/services they sell.

Structure of UK tour operations

The tour operations' sector has a complex structure, since tour operators have to deal with so many other organisations when carrying out their business, as the next section of this unit explains.

Links with other organisations

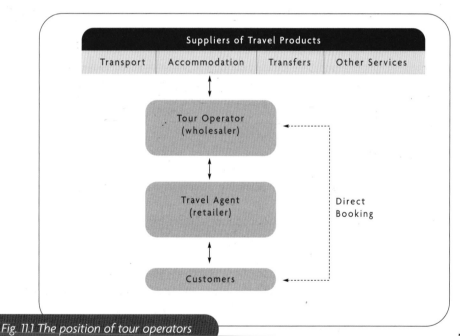

Fig. 11.1 The position of tour operators

Unlike travel agents, who sell holidays and a range of other travel products, tour operators actually assemble the different parts of a holiday, i.e. the type of travel, accom-modation, facilities, transfers, excursions and other services. If we consider that travel agents are the retail arm of the travel business, then tour operators are the 'whole-salers', since they buy in bulk from the providers of travel services, such as the hoteliers and airlines, break the bulk into manageable packages and offer the finished product, the package holiday (or inclusive tour), for sale via a travel agent or direct to the public. The package is sold for an all-inclusive price, which is generally lower than if the different parts of the holiday had been booked individually by the holidaymaker. Figure 11.1 shows the position of tour operators as intermediaries between the suppliers of travel products and travel agents.

Unit 11

There is a growing trend for people to book direct with tour operators rather than booking through a travel agent. Figures from ABTA (the Association of British Travel Agents) show that between 1990 and 2002, the number of people booking their holiday through their travel agent fell by 18 per cent, while the number booking direct with a tour operator increased by 19 per cent. This trend is set to continue and gather pace as the popularity of the Internet and interactive TV grows.

In working with other sectors of the travel and tourism industry, tour operators develop working relationships and links with a wide range of organisations, including:

- Airlines – negotiating and agreeing contracts with charter and scheduled airlines to supply seats on aircraft for holidaymakers;
- Hotels and other accommodation providers – negotiating allocations of bed spaces that form the accommodation element of the holiday;
- Ancillary service providers – contracting with companies to supply representative services, transfers, 'meet and greet' arrangements, car hire, activities, etc;
- Travel agents – using agents as a sales outlet for the tour operator's holidays and agreeing commission payments and booking procedures.

Even the large, vertically-integrated travel groups (see next section) have to liaise on different functions within their own organisations, since individual parts of the group are usually separate companies in their own right, e.g. staff from Something Special Holidays, part of the Thomson/TUI Group, would negotiate with Thomson's own airline Thomsonfly to agree seat allocations for a season.

Horizontal and vertical integration

As competition in the travel and tourism industry has intensified, tour operators have taken over or merged with other travel and tourism businesses as a way of maintaining or increasing their market share and maximising their profits. This is most noticeable in the tour operator/travel agent relationship, where:

- TUI UK owns Thomson tour operating businesses and the Thomson travel agency chain (TUI UK is itself controlled by the German company TUI AG);
- The MyTravel Group owns Airtours and other tour operators as well Going Places travel agencies;
- First Choice Holidays and First Choice Travel Shops are part of the same group;
- Thomas Cook AG (a German group) owns the Thomas Cook tour operating companies and the Thomas Cook chain of travel agencies.

Unit 11

These 'big four' travel groups dominate the sale of package holidays in the UK, accounting for just under 50 per cent of all sales. These are all examples of vertical integration in the travel industry, which is when a company has control over other companies that are at different levels in the chain of distribution or in different sectors. Some of the largest tour operators also own their own airlines, giving even greater control over the component parts of package holidays. Figure 11.2 shows the structure of the 'big four' vertically-integrated travel companies in the UK, showing exactly who owns what.

	TUI UK Ltd.	**MyTravel**	**Thomas Cook**	**First Choice**
Tour Operations	Thomson brands Jetsave Portland Budget Travel Skytours Club Freestyle Just Crystal OSL Headwater Holidays Chez Nous Something Special Holiday Cottages Group Austravel Magic Travel Group American Holidays Tropical Places Spanish Harbour Holidays	Airtours Bridge Travel Cresta Tradewinds Manos Panorama Direct Holidays Escapades Aspro	Thomas Cook JMC Sunset Thomas Cook Signature Latitude Club 18-30 Flexibletrips Neilson Thomascook.com Style Holidays	First Choice Unijet 2wentys Sunquest Sovereign Falcon JWT Holidays Sunstart Hays & Jarvis Meon Villas Exodus Flexiski Citalia Sunsail
Travel Agencies	Thomson Callers-Pegasus Travel House Team Lincoln Travel House Sibbald Travel Latedeals.com	Going Places Travelworld Holidayline MyTravel.com LateEscapes.com	Thomas Cook	First Choice Travel Shops First Choice Holiday Hypermarkets
Airlines	Thomsonfly	MyTravel, MyTravel Lite	Thomas Cook Airways	First Choice Airways

Fig. 11.2 The 'big four' integrated travel companies

WEBLINK

www.mytravel.com;
www.thomsonholidays.co.uk;
www.thomascook.com;
www.firstchoice.co.uk

Check out these websites for more information on each of the 'big four' vertically-integrated travel companies.

Figure 11.2 indicates that the 'big four' have control over the wholesale (tour operations), retail (travel agencies) and airline sectors of the package holiday business. The position is further complicated since the companies are also developing new sales outlets such as via the Internet and digital TV stations, e.g. Thomas Cook TV.

Vertical integration makes sense for the travel companies since they benefit from bulk discounts and make savings by using their own companies as suppliers. However, there is concern that vertical integration of this sort may not always be in the public's interest, since it can reduce the number of companies and give customers less choice. Also, customers may not know that a tour operator is owned by the travel agency that is selling their holiday. Since 2000, all vertically-integrated travel companies have been obliged to make their links to other travel companies clear by, for example, having notices in their travel agencies and printed in brochures.

Horizontal integration is when a company owns or has control over a number of companies at the same level in the distribution chain or the same industry sector. For example, many of the tour operating businesses shown in Figure 11.2 were originally independent companies before being taken over by one of the 'big four', e.g. Neilson and Club 18-30 (now part of the Thomas Cook Group), and Something Special and the Holiday Cottages Group (now merged with Thomson). Large travel companies take over smaller independents as a way or reducing competition in the marketplace, but this is not always a benefit for customers who may have less choice.

FOCUS ON INDUSTRY – Disclosure of industry links

Travel businesses must comply with the following regulations concerning their links with other companies:

- Travel agents must display a prominent notice in the front window of each shop outlining its ownership links;
- A notice must be displayed on the front cover of every in-house tour operator's brochure explaining its links with the agency;
- The name of every tour operator that is part of the same group must be listed inside the shop;
- All company stationery must outline ownership links of the agent;
- All joint advertisements between a tour operator and an in-house agent must spell out the link between the two. This includes Internet and Teletext pages that direct customers to book through a sister company, e.g. a Thomson-owned site that refers people to a Thomson travel agency must explain the connection.

Trade associations and regulatory bodies

Trade associations are established to represent the interests of companies in a particular industry sector. ABTA (the Association of British Travel Agents) is the main trade association for both travel agents and tour operators in the UK (see case study in unit 7 on page 310). There are currently 1052 tour operator office members of ABTA, from large vertically-integrated, mass-market companies to small, specialist tour operators.

AITO (the Association of Independent Tour Operators) is a trade organisation representing around 160 of Britain's specialist tour operators. Its members are independent companies, most of them owner-managed, specialising in particular destinations or types of holiday (see case study in unit 1 on page 28).

UKinbound (formerly BITOA – the British Incoming Tour Operators' Association) is a trade association representing the interests of companies specialising in inbound tourism to the UK.

Unit 11

WEBLINK

www.bitoa.co.uk

Check out this website for more information on the work of UKinbound.

FOCUS ON INDUSTRY – UKinbound

UKinbound was founded in 1977 as BITOA to represent the commercial interests of British tour operators specialising in providing tours and tourism services to overseas visitors to Britain. The primary aim of the association is to help its members manage successful, profitable businesses that are part of a vibrant and sustainable inbound tourism industry. It does this by focusing on three key areas:

- Advocacy – to champion the interests of UKinbound members with government;
- Professionalism – to promote best practice and encourage lifelong learning through training and staff development;
- Networking – to provide opportunities for its members to develop relationships with suppliers, buyers and partners in the UK and overseas.

WEBLINK

www.etoa.org

Check out this website for more information on the European Tour Operators' Association.

The European Tour Operators' Association (ETOA) was founded in 1989 as a direct result of the introduction of the EU Package Travel Directive, which made tour operators aware of the power the European institutions had to influence policy and legislation affecting tour operators. ETOA now has 110 tour operator members and has established a track record of influencing travel and tourism legislation at both national and European levels. It promotes greater awareness of the benefits provided by the travel industry in Europe, particularly the increased income and employment.

The International Federation of Tour Operators (IFTO) is a grouping of trade associations representing tour operators' interests in the various regions of the world. Its vision is to *'ensure the continued long-term success of the organised holiday by influencing legislators and civil servants in the EU, originating and destination countries, as well as other opinion formers, on the benefits to consumers and other public and private stakeholders of organised holidays'.* The secretariat for IFTO is provided by the UK-based Federation of Tour Operators (FTO), one of the most influential of all trade associations in the UK tour operations sector and the subject of the following case study.

WEBLINK

www.fto.co.uk

Check out this website to help answer the questions in this case study and for more information on the FTO.

CASE STUDY – The Federation of Tour Operators (FTO)

INTRODUCTION

The Federation of Tour Operators (FTO) works on behalf of its members to ensure the continued, long-term success of the air-inclusive holiday business. It does this by influencing governments and opinion formers on the benefits to consumers and other stakeholders of air-inclusive holidays compared to other forms of holiday arrangements.

FTO's activities

The following is a brief overview of the activities FTO undertakes:

- Bring about change and improvement in all areas affecting overseas holidays;
- The point of contact for government (UK, EU and destinations) on all UK-outbound tour operating issues;
- Co-ordinate members' activities in key areas of operational delivery – crisis handling, health and safety, sustainable tourism, operational issues, and establishing best practice;
- Co-operation and co-ordination with other trade associations and interested parties;
- Lobby to ensure that the tax burden on holidaymakers is as low as possible;
- Promote the professional and positive image of the industry;
- Provide public relations support;
- Currently acts as a regulator of financial protection on behalf of its members in relation to their non-ATOL business;
- Represent its members at meetings of the International Federation of Tour Operators (IFTO), the European trade association for tour operators.

FTO membership

Full membership is by invitation and subject to the agreement of all existing FTO members. Prospective members must sign up to a set of 'core values':

1. Able to recognise the benefit of working with others in the industry to achieve common objectives, which are of a non-competitive nature, and willing to give appropriate attention and resource to achieving those objectives;
2. Customer-focused – will aim to prioritise product quality and service delivery;
3. A responsible business with effective implemented standards of health and safety, and a balanced approach to environmental issues;
4. Trades in a way that attempts to ensure long-term financial stability.

Unit 11

FTO member companies account for over 70 per cent of all package holidays sold in the UK. Current (March 2005) members include some of the best-known names in the travel and tourism industry, including:

- British Airways Holidays – a fully-owned subsidiary of British Airways plc;
- Cosmos – an independent UK tour operator;
- First Choice – tour operator and high street travel retailer;
- Inghams – tour operator offering skiing, lakes and mountains, and city holidays and short breaks;
- Kosmar – UK tour operator to Greece;
- Kuoni – a market leader in long-haul travel;
- Libra Holidays – tour operator offering holidays, flights and hotels to Cyprus, Greece, Spain, Egypt and Turkey;
- MyTravel – air-inclusive holidays and leisure travel services;
- RCI Travel – serving the timeshare vacation market;
- Thomas Cook – tour operator and high street travel retailer;
- Thomas Cook Signature – tailor-made holiday solutions' company;
- TUI UK – the UK's largest holiday company;
- Virgin Holidays – long-haul and ski tour operator.

FTO and responsible tourism

Responsible tourism is about making a positive difference when we travel, by:

- Enjoying ourselves and taking responsibility for our actions, respecting local cultures and the natural environment;
- Giving fair economic returns to local people, helping to spread the benefit of our visit to those who need it most;
- Recognising that water and energy are precious resources that we need to use carefully;
- Protecting endangered wildlife and preserving the natural and cultural heritage of the places we visit for the future enjoyment of visitors and the people who live there.

Members of the FTO are becoming increasingly aware of the socio-cultural, environmental and economic impacts of their products and services. In 2003, they formed a Responsible Tourism Committee and are developing a series of initiatives to assist tour operators to integrate responsible tourism practices into their core business.

Unit 11

CASE STUDY QUESTIONS

1. What are the 'core values' that prospective FTO members must agree to adhere to?
2. Outline the work that the FTO does in the area of health and safety in the air-inclusive tour operating sector;
3. How is the FTO structured and funded?
4. What is 'responsible tourism' and what activities do the FTO and its members undertake to promote this type of approach to tourism?

Regulatory bodies

WEBLINK

www.caa.co.uk;
www.hse.gov.uk;
www.fco.gov.uk

Check out these websites for more information on the work of the CAA, HSE and FCO

Regulatory bodies exist to make sure that tour operating companies operate in a fair, honest, efficient, safe and secure manner, for the good of the companies, their customers, suppliers and society at large. There are many regulatory bodies whose rules and regulations must be followed by all companies, including tour operators, e.g. HM Revenue and Customs and Companies House. Specific regulatory authorities concerned with tour operating include:

- The Civil Aviation Authority (CAA) – the UK's independent aviation regulator and controller of air traffic services. It manages the UK's largest system of consumer protection for travellers, the Air Travel Organisers' Licence (ATOL) used by tour operators;
- The Health and Safety Executive (HSE) – responsible for many aspects of the safe operation of tour operators' products and services;
- Trading Standards Officers – enforce the Package Travel Regulations (see page 360);
- The Foreign and Commonwealth Office (FCO) – advises on travel to and from all parts of the world, including those seen as a risk to UK travellers.

Categories of tour operator

Tour operators come in all shapes and sizes! Most people are familiar with the big, well-known holiday companies that sell millions of holidays abroad every year, e.g. MyTravel and Thomson. Not so well-known are the many specialist operators that provide packaged and tailor-made holidays to meet particular needs and the domestic operators that sell holidays and short breaks in this country. Incoming/inbound tour operators service the needs of overseas visitors to Britain.

Unit 11

There are many ways of categorising tour operators. They can be:

- Mass-market or specialist – mass-market tour operators sell large numbers of package holidays to a wide variety of popular holiday destinations, while specialist operators offer a more tailor-made service to their clients;
- Independent of part of a large, integrated company – independent tour operators are not part of bigger companies and are free to trade with whichever companies they choose, whereas large, integrated travel businesses have stricter policies on which suppliers they can use;
- Incoming/inbound or outgoing/outbound – incoming/inbound operators service tourists coming to the UK, while outgoing/outbound companies focus on holiday products for British people travelling abroad;
- Domestic or international – domestic tour operators develop and sell holidays in Britain, whereas international operators offer overseas holidays.

ACTIVITY

Find out some detailed information on ONE tour operating company in each of the following categories:

1. Mass-market;
2. Specialist;
3. Independent;
4. Part of an integrated company;
5. Incoming/inbound;
6. Outgoing/outbound;
7. Domestic;
8. International.

Produce a fact sheet on each company that includes details of its history, company structure, range of products, destinations served, membership of trade association, etc.

This activity is designed to provide evidence for P1.

A common way to categorise tour operators is to group them under the following four types:

1. Mass-market operators
2. Specialist operators;
3. Domestic operators;
4. Inbound tour operators.

Figure 11.3 shows a breakdown of these four main categories of UK-based tour operators, with examples of the wide variety of products they sell.

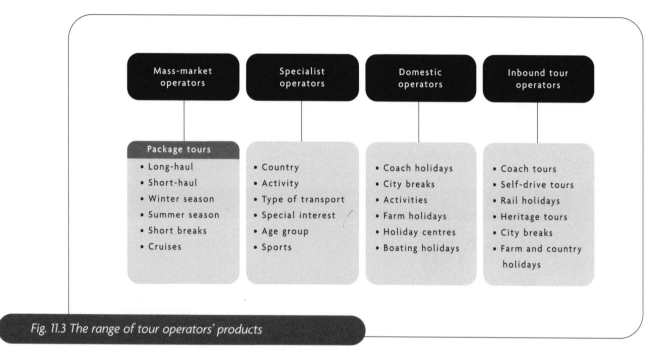

Mass-market operators	Specialist operators	Domestic operators	Inbound tour operators
Package tours			
• Long-haul	• Country	• Coach holidays	• Coach tours
• Short-haul	• Activity	• City breaks	• Self-drive tours
• Winter season	• Type of transport	• Activities	• Rail holidays
• Summer season	• Special interest	• Farm holidays	• Heritage tours
• Short breaks	• Age group	• Holiday centres	• City breaks
• Cruises	• Sports	• Boating holidays	• Farm and country holidays

Fig. 11.3 The range of tour operators' products

Mass-market tour operators

These operators are amongst the best-known names in the travel and tourism industry, courtesy of their big advertising budgets! In many respects they are the 'supermarkets' of the travel industry, since they sell large volumes of value-for-money holidays to millions of customers every year. Data from the Civil Aviation Authority (CAA) shows that the 'big four' mass-market operators in terms of passengers carried in 2004 were:

1. TUI UK/Thomson	4,825,849
2. First Choice	2,773,429
3. MyTravel	2,598,514
4. Thomas Cook	2,462,928

Between them, these four tour operators organised package holidays and flights for around 12.6 million UK travellers in 2004, accounting for 45 per cent of all such products sold. As well as offering popular Mediterranean holiday destinations, tour operators are selling more packages to long-haul destinations, such as Florida, the Caribbean, Australia, New Zealand and the Far East, as travellers seek out new destinations and experiences.

Unit 11

In recent years there has been a gradual move away from traditional package holidays and an increase in demand for more individualised, tailor-made holidays as people become more sophisticated and discerning. This is reflected in the numbers of passengers carried by the mass-market operators – between 2003 and 2004, passenger numbers fell in seven out of the top ten tour operators.

Another trend is the rise in popularity of Internet-based tour operators (e-operators), which offer 24/7 access for customers and the chance for people to put together their own holidays. Leading operators in this field are lastminute.com, Expedia and ebookers. Tour operators are also developing new sales outlets for their products, such as interactive TV and telephone call centres. These trends are making the distinction between tour operators and travel agents less clear.

WEBLINK

www.tui-uk.co.uk

Check out this website to help answer the questions in this case study and for more information on TUI UK

CASE STUDY – TUI UK

Introduction

TUI UK is the UK's largest holiday company and part of the World of TUI, the largest tourism and services group in the world, employing 80,000 people in 500 companies around the world. The World of TUI is an innovative, customer-focused company which owns many of Europe's best-known holiday brands, including Thomson Holidays in the UK. The World of TUI has leadership positions in airline, inclusive tour operations and travel agency sectors. The group employs 17,500 people in the UK, Ireland, Sweden, Norway, Denmark and Finland. TUI UK employs around 9,000 people, 7,000 of whom work overseas in some 40 holiday destinations. TUI UK also includes the travel agents Thomson holiday shops, Callers Pegasus and Teletext agents Team Lincoln.

Thomson Holidays

Thomson Holidays sells more package holidays than any other UK-based tour operator, making it the market leader in the air-inclusive holiday sector, a position it has held since 1974. Its head office is in London, but the majority of its 3,000 employees work overseas. Its brands include Thomson Gold, Thomson Small and Friendly, Just and Thomson Young at Heart.

Retail distribution

The UK retail distribution businesses and channels within TUI UK include:

- Thomson travel shops – the UK's leading travel agency chain with 860 branches, including a flagship superstore in Leicester, Thomson Direct call centre, Thomson TV on Sky Digital and www.thomson.co.uk where bookings can be made online. Thomson retail shops sell around 2.7 million holidays and flights a year, accounting for approximately 20 per cent of the total market;

- Team Lincoln – is the UK's leading Teletext and Internet specialist selling in excess of 250,000 holidays a year from its base in the North-East of England from where it operates four call centres;
- Manchester Service Centre – specialises in selling flights via the Internet and Teletext, with a call centre operation based in Bury selling in excess of 300,000 flights per year;
- Travel House Group – a leading regional retailer and Teletext business with over 100 retail shops based in Scotland (Sibbald Travel), the North East (Callers Pegasus), and South Wales and the Midlands (Travel House). The Group sells around 300,000 holidays a year.

Airline operations

One of the fleet of Thomsonfly aircraft

For more than 40 years, Britannia Airways has been TUI UK/Thomson's charter airline and the world's leading holiday airline. This changed on May 1st 2005 when TUI UK's aircraft fleet was renamed and re-branded as Thomsonfly, to reflect the single Thomson name that now applies to all parts of the group's operations. This one brand now runs through the company's charter service and its growing low-fares airline Thomsonfly.com. Thomsonfly will continue with Britannia's fleet of 33 aircraft carrying in the region of 8 million passengers every year.

CASE STUDY QUESTIONS

1. What are the advantages to TUI UK of owning its own tour operations, travel agency and airline companies?

2. Log on to the TUI UK website (www.tui-uk.co.uk) and make a list of the different tour operating and retail travel agency brands that TUI UK offers. Why do you think it has so many brands available to customers?

3. How do you think TUI UK will need to develop its business in the next ten years to make sure that it retains its position as the UK's most popular holiday company?

4. Carry out some research to discover what work TUI UK and its parent company TUI AG are doing in the area of sustainable tourism (remember that TUI UK is also a member of the Federation of Tour Operators – look into what this body is doing in this area also).

Unit 11

Specialist tour operators

There is a growing demand for specialist tour operators from a travelling public that is looking for something more than the mass-market companies offer. There are literally hundreds of specialist tour operators in the UK travel and tourism industry, including:

Activity holidays are growing in popularity

- Companies offering holidays and other travel arrangements to a particular geographical region or destination, e.g. Magic of Spain and Magic of Italy;
- Those that cater for a particular segment of the market, e.g. PGL Adventure Holidays for young children and Saga Holidays who specialise in the 'senior' market;
- Operators that specialise in a particular type of activity, e.g. walking holidays offered by HF Holidays and Susi Madron's 'Cycling for Softies', which offers all-inclusive cycling packages to rural France;
- Tour operators that cater for the special interests of their clients, e.g. wine tasting holidays in the Loire and art history tours to Italy;
- Those that specialise in sporting holidays and breaks, e.g. Longshot Golfing Holidays and tours to see the Formula One Grand Prix around the world;
- Companies that use a specific type of accommodation or form of transport, e.g. Eurocamp, which organises self-drive camping holidays in the UK and on the Continent, and operators that offer tours on steam railways, e.g. Ffestiniog Travel.

Many specialist operators join the Association of Independent Tour Operators (AITO) to develop the interests of the sector (see case study in unit 1 on page 28).

(see case study in unit 1 on page 28)

ACTIVITY

Visit the AITO website (www.aito.co.uk) and carry out a holiday search for 'activity and sporting' holidays to Canada. Make a series of fact sheets on the companies featured.

Unit 11

Domestic tour operators

Domestic tour operators are companies that specialise in holidays in the UK for British people. They offer a very wide range of holiday products, from packages in holiday centres such as Center Parcs and Pontin's, to coach holidays in the Highlands of Scotland. Many domestic tour operators deal directly with their customers rather than selling through travel agents. This is partly to do with the fact that small, domestic operators are sometimes reluctant to pay commission to agents and also because many British people see travel agents as a place to go to book a holiday abroad. However, there are some domestic tour operators that sell packages through travel agents and pay commission, for example Butlin's, Superbreak, Hoseasons and Shearings.

WEBLINK

www.shearingsholidays.com

Check out this website for more information on Shearings Holidays.

FOCUS ON INDUSTRY – Shearings Holidays

Historically a coach-based company, Shearings has expanded its product range to include hotel breaks, plus air, cruise and rail travel. The company currently carries over 500,000 holidaymakers every year to a variety of destinations in the UK, Ireland, Continental Europe, Canada, the USA, Australia and New Zealand. The company's head office is in Wigan, Lancashire where it employs 250 people involved in creating, selling and managing its range of holiday programmes. In total, Shearings employs over 2,400 members of staff in 50 different locations.

Shearings is one of the UK's most popular tour operators

Special interest groups are well catered for by domestic operators. Activity holidays are growing in popularity and tour operators, large and small, are emerging to cater for the demand, for example YHA Holidays, Acorn Adventures, PGL, HF Holidays and Cycleactive. Companies offering specialist services and facilities, ranging from sketching holidays to ballooning breaks, are being increasingly sought by people looking for something unusual to do in their leisure time.

Unit 11

Inbound tour operators

Inbound, or incoming, UK tourism is concerned with meeting the needs of the increasing numbers of overseas visitors who choose to visit Britain; outbound tourism, on the other hand, deals with UK people taking holidays abroad. Just as we might visit a travel agency to book our annual overseas holiday or business trip abroad, so many overseas visitors do the same in their own country when they want to come to Britain. A travel agent in the USA, for example, who has a client wanting to spend a week in Scotland, has to contact a tour operator to make all the arrangements. This operator, who may be based in the USA or in Scotland, is known as an incoming tour operator, since it is providing a service for incoming visitors to Britain. Approximately 270 incoming tour operators in the UK are members of UKinbound (formerly BITOA – the British Incoming Tour Operators' Association).

Products and services

We have seen so far in this unit that the tour operations sector is extremely diverse with a wide range of products and services available to suit different types of customers. The following sections of this unit investigate package holidays, ancillary products and services, and tailor-made holiday products.

Package holidays

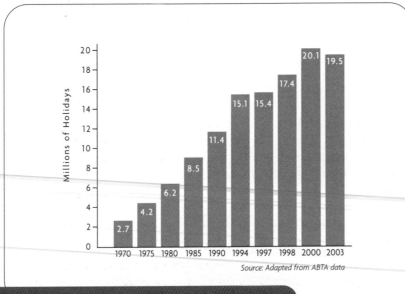

Fig. 11.4 Overseas package holidays taken by the British

Source: Adapted from ABTA data

The invention of the package holiday has been one of the great success stories of the travel and tourism industry in the last 50 years. Sales of package holidays really took off in the early 1970s and have continued to grow ever since (see Figure 11.4). Low prices gave millions of people the chance to travel abroad for the first time.

Today, however, package holidays are under threat from the growth of low-cost airlines and the Internet, which allow people to

Unit 11

assemble their own holidays, bypassing travel agents and tour operators altogether. Mintel's Travel Trends report showed that, for the first time in 2003, package holidays made up less than half of all overseas holidays sold to British people. Growing numbers of people are looking for the 'unpackaged holiday', individually tailored to their particular needs and desires.

Research carried out for ABTA found that the main reason Britons choose a package holiday is to relax in a sunny environment (71 per cent of the people surveyed had taken a summer sun holiday within the past 12 months). The next most popular type of package holiday was the winter sun holiday, but only 15 per cent of those surveyed had chosen this type of holiday. The research also highlighted the growth in popularity of activity packages and adventure holidays.

For the purposes of the Package Travel Regulations, a 'package' is defined as:

'....the pre-arranged combination of not fewer than two of the following when sold or offered for sale at an inclusive price and when the service covers a period of more than 24 hours or includes overnight accommodation – (1) transport, (2) accommodation and (3) other tourist services...'

Put simply, this means that a typical 10-day holiday that includes a flight, accommodation and the services of a representative in the resort qualifies as a 'package' under the Package Travel Regulations, entitling the holidaymakers to redress and compensation in the event of a problem. However, people who book individual parts of a holiday separately themselves, such as a flight and accommodation in a hotel, are not covered by any help available under the Package Travel Regulations if things go wrong. We look in more detail at the Package Travel Regulations later in this unit on page 360.

Ancillary products and services

The very competitive nature of the tour operations sector means that profit margins on holidays are often very low (sometimes non-existent!). This means that tour operators look for ways of supplementing their income through sales of ancillary products and services, either in-resort or before their clients travel. The income they make on the sale of add-ons can be greater than the profit margin on a holiday, so they are very important!

ACTIVITY

Look through a variety of tour operators' brochures (outbound and domestic) and draw up a list of the different types of ancillary products and services they offer. Make a note of the similarities and differences you find between operators.

This activity is designed to provide evidence for P1.

Tailor-made travel arrangements

Tailor-made travel arrangements involve designing all aspects of a customer's holiday on an individual basis rather than selling a ready-assembled package holiday. The customer benefits by getting a holiday that is individually tailored to their needs, but it does mean more work for the travel agent or tour operator. We saw in unit 7 that more travel agents are adopting this approach and some charge a fee for their service, which many customers are happy to pay since they come away with a tailor-made rather than 'off-the-shelf' product.

WEBLINK

www.national-holidays.co.uk

Check out this website for more information on National Holidays.

FOCUS ON INDUSTRY – Tailor-made arrangements at National Holidays

National Holidays specialises in coach-based holidays and short breaks in the UK and Continental Europe. For groups of 30 or more the company offers tailor-made travel and accommodation arrangements. Members of the group choose the resort, hotel, meal arrangements and excursions, and the company designs the holiday to meet the needs of the group. The group organiser can either discuss arrangements with a member of National Holidays' staff or complete an online form for a quotation.

More tour operators are using Internet-based systems to help them assemble tailor-made travel solutions for customers. This is known as 'dynamic packaging', since it is totally driven by the needs of the customer. This is a trend that will grow as travellers look for a more personal service from tour operators and the companies themselves react to developments in new technology.

Unit 11

SECTION 2: PLANNING, SELLING AND OPERATING PACKAGE HOLIDAY PROGRAMMES

All tour operators have to carry out certain functions in order to plan, sell and operate their package holiday programmes successfully. The same basic functions are carried out whether the company is a large, mass-market operator or a small, specialist firm employing just a few people.

Planning a package holiday programme

There are three key elements to planning a package holiday programme:

1. Research;
2. Contracting;
3. Pricing.

The next sections of this unit look at each in turn, based on how the functions are carried out in a typical mass-market tour operator.

Research

A great deal of background research is undertaken to make sure that tour operators' programmes have the best chance of meeting their sales potential. Sources of research data available to help with this process include:

- Internal sales data – gives a tour operator a clear idea of which products and destinations are in demand and which may need to be scrapped or revised;
- External sales data – available from commercial sources, this information gives a tour operator a 'benchmark' against which to measure its own performance;
- Analysis of competitors' programmes – can be very helpful in identifying new themes, destinations or product opportunities;
- Market research reports – from companies such as Deloitte & Touche, Mintel and Nielsen give useful information on future trends in the tour operating sector;
- Government data – is a useful tool for analysing past visitor numbers to particular destinations overseas, for example the International Passenger Survey (IPS);
- Analysis of customer satisfaction questionnaires – provides a tour operator with valuable feedback on a range of issues, such as quality of accommodation, customer service standards, etc.
- Financial analysis – essential for forecasting future revenue streams and profitability.

Unit 11

Staff with responsibility for market research work with marketing department personnel to identify potential new market opportunities, as well as assessing the changing needs and tastes of previous customers. This is achieved by studying sales statistics and market research surveys. They particularly look at the feedback collected from existing customers via CSQs (customer satisfaction questionnaires). Staff try to predict what holidaymakers will want, in terms of which resorts, what type and length of holiday, what standard of accommodation, which departure airports and what price they are prepared to pay.

Marketing department staff at TUI/Thomson

In large tour operating companies, it is staff employed in the marketing department who are responsible for researching, planning and developing the different holiday products, which are aimed at particular segments of the market. Product Managers focus on the selection of resorts, choice of accommodation and selection of regional UK departure airports. Typical segments of the market for which products are developed include:

- Singles;
- Families;
- Couples without children;
- Groups;
- Business travellers;
- Youth market;
- Senior market.

Planning and organising a holiday programme does not happen overnight. Staff in the marketing department start making plans for a season 12-18 months before the holidays go on sale. The first task is to assess the total number of holidays that will be taken during a season by all UK holidaymakers. Having calculated this total market figure, individual Brand Managers or Product Managers decide what share of the market it is realistic to sell (the programme capacity). Having decided on the capacity of the programme, detailed planning on how many holidays should be arranged in each resort and what accommodation and flights are needed can begin. Marketing staff are also responsible for the key activity of pricing the holidays, which can be very risky given the advance planning necessary before the launch of a programme and the potential for fluctuations in currency exchange rates.

Unit 11

ACTIVITY

Draw a flow chart of the main tasks involved in developing a package holiday programme to a new long-haul destination in South America. Include timescales and staff/departmental responsibilities in your chart.

This activity is designed to provide evidence for P2 and M2.

Contracting

Once the structure of a tour operator's programme is finalised, staff in the contracts department negotiate with accommodation providers over the number of beds and type of accommodation required. This function is often the responsibility of senior management, under the direction of the Overseas Regional Manager, who may be assisted by specific Product Managers. The staff involved in contracting the accommodation and related services have to negotiate on price, quantity and quality, within a very competitive environment. It is likely that other mass-market operators will be using the same hotels in their programmes. An operator may try to negotiate exclusive use of particular accommodation, but this will involve a financial commitment on behalf of the operator that it may not be willing to risk.

There are three main types of contracts used in tour operating:

- Commitment/guarantee – where the tour operator guarantees to pay for a certain number of bed spaces;
- Allocation and release back – where the tour operator agrees an allocation of a certain number of bed spaces with the hotel and agrees to give back any that it has not sold by a certain date;
- Ad hoc – this is a most flexible arrangement when a tour operator agrees a contract (discounted) rate with a hotelier and makes bookings as and when required.

Negotiations on contract terms usually start a year before the holidays are sold.

At the same time as accommodation contracting is under way, the flight programmes have to be negotiated, either with their own in-house airline in the case of the large operators, or with charter or scheduled airlines in the case of smaller operators. In large tour operating companies, teams working on different programmes and products liaise with the flight or aviation department over how many seats they will need, which regional airports are to be used and whether day or night flights are required. The flight department must make optimum use of its resources, which includes selling spare capacity in the flight-only market. Contracts are generally agreed more than 12 months in advance

Pricing

Pricing a package holiday programme is one of the most difficult and risky aspects of the business. Tour operators have to consider a number of important factors when determining the final selling price of a package holiday, including:

- The contracted rates that have been agreed with accommodation providers, car hire companies, transfer service providers, etc.
- Seasonal adjustments, e.g. low prices for the 'shoulder season' (either side of the peak) and higher prices for peak season demand;
- Load factor on the aircraft, i.e. the percentage of seats that need to be filled before the tour operator breaks even and begins to make a profit;
- Fixed costs, e.g. the cost of hiring a transfer coach is the same regardless of the number of passengers aboard;
- Variable costs, e.g. the cost per person for accommodation where the tour operator only pays for accommodation actually booked;
- Indirect costs, e.g. head office overheads;
- Direct operating costs, e.g. the cost of accommodation;
- Profit margins, i.e. the percentage added to the net selling price, covering all indirect costs and allowing for a profit.

Fixed Costs	Variable Costs
• Rates	• Postage
• Rent or mortgage	• Telephone, fax and Internet
• Interest on loans	• Computer and equipment hire
• Bonding monies	• Printing and stationery
• Maintenance	• Advertising and publicity
• Cleaning	• Part - time staff
• Insurance	• Professional fees and charges
• Staff salaries	• Bank charges
• Lighting and heating	• Lighting and heating
• Market research	• Transaction charges eg., credit cards

Fixed costs are costs that do not alter with changes in the level of activity, whereas variable costs alter in direct proportion to the volume of business generated by the tour operator. Examples of both types are given in Figure 11.5.

Fig. 11.5 Fixed and variable costs in tour operations

Pricing methods

Pricing has to be based on the best available knowledge and experience. A mass-market tour operator that sets the prices of its main summer programme holidays too high in relation to its competitors will not achieve optimum levels of sales. Too low, on the other hand, and it will find it difficult to produce an adequate profit.

There are two basic methods that can be adopted to arrive at the cost of a package holiday programme:

- Cost-based pricing;
- Market-based pricing.

Unit 11

Costing a package holiday to the Costa del Sol – 14 nights half-board

Flight costs	£
26 return flights during the season @ £18,000 per flight	468,000
Empty leg at beginning and end of season	18,000
Total flight costs	486,000
Cost per occupied flight (£486,000 divided by 26	18,692
Cost per seat based on 90% load factor on Boeing 737 with capacity of 168 passengers	123.62
Hotel costs per person for 14 nights	190.00
Transfers and handling fees per person	10.75
Total costs of package per person	**324.37**

The direct costs of the package holiday are £324.37. The tour operator uses this figure to determine a selling price that covers these costs plus an additional amount (mark up) to cover (1) a proportion of the fixed costs of the holiday; (2) the commission payment to travel agents and (3) a profit margin. The exact price charged will depend on a number of factors, including prices of similar holidays offered by competitors, the cost of the holiday last year and the season in which the holiday is taken.

If we assume a mark up of 20 per cent, the final brochure price of the above holiday would be £324.37 + £64.87 = £389.24.

This is the break-even point – the tour operator will sell the holiday above break-even when demand is high and below break-even when demand is low outside the peak season.

Fig. 11.6 Costing a package holiday to the Costa del Sol

Cost-based pricing involves calculating all the fixed and variable costs of a tour product, including any commission payments to agents, and setting the price at a level which covers all these costs and allows a profit margin. This is the method adopted by small, specialist operators who are unlikely to be operating in such a competitive environment as the mass-market holiday companies and whose products will have a degree of uniqueness. In large tour companies, it is not always easy to work out the exact proportion of fixed costs that should be levied on a tour programme.

Sometimes referred to as 'what the market will bear', market-based pricing sets pricing in a wider context by taking account of what competitors are charging when determining prices. Re-issuing brochures with revised prices is now commonplace among tour operators that are constantly checking competitor activity and making adjustments to maintain their market share. Following the market leader's pricing is a risky business, if a company has not fully taken into account its own costs of operation. The hope is that the economies of scale involved in tour operating will enable the larger operators to reduce their costs, but still allow a profit margin at the end of the day.

The example of a calculation for a typical package holiday programme shown in Figure 11.6 shows that pricing is often a combination of both market- and cost-based approaches.

Tour operators are becoming increasingly aware of the impacts (good and bad) that their activities have on the destinations they use in their tour programmes, in particular how tourism can have harmful effects in areas such as exploitation, poverty, corruption and unemployment. A number of initiatives have been established to try to make tourism in developing countries a force for good, by attempting to alleviate poverty and by promoting sustainable principles and practices. These include the work of the Travel Foundation, Tourism Concern and the Tearfund charity.

ACTIVITY

Log on to the Travel Foundation's website (www.thetravelfoundation.org.uk) and produce an information sheet on the Foundation's aims, work, structure, partners, etc.

This activity is designed to provide evidence for P4.

Legal factors

Tour operators must follow a variety of consumer protection and contract laws and regulations when carrying out their business activities, as the following sections of this unit explain.

Package Travel Regulations

The Package Travel, Package Holidays and Package Tours Directive was adopted in June 1990 and came into operation on 1 January 1993 in the then 12 Member States of the European Union as the Package Travel, Package Holidays and Package Tour Regulations. The main aim of the Regulations is to give people buying package holidays more protection and access to compensation when things go wrong, while at the same time harmonising the rules covering packages operated throughout European Union countries. The provisions of the Directive did not replace national laws and, in the case of the UK, simply consolidated existing legislation and industry codes of conduct. The Package Travel Directive has, nonetheless, caused something of a stir in the UK travel and tourism industry, given its wide-ranging powers and scope. Up to the introduction of the Regulations, tour operators had been able to disclaim responsibility when holiday arrangements went wrong, for example overbooking at a hotel or the failure of a coach transfer to arrive, on the grounds that they had no control over these unfortunate events. Under the terms of the Package Travel Regulations, tour organisers must accept legal responsibility for all the services they offer to travellers. Exceptions would be made in circumstances which could neither have been foreseen nor overcome, although in such circumstances, organisers must give all necessary assistance to consumers.

The Package Travel Regulations place a number of duties and responsibilities on the organisers of packages, namely:

- Providing information to customers on who is responsible for the package they have booked. That person or organisation is then liable in the event of failure to deliver any elements of the package;
- Providing clear contract terms;
- Giving emergency telephone numbers;
- Providing proof of the organiser's security against insolvency and information on any available insurance policies;
- Giving immediate notification with explanation of any increase in prices permitted within the terms of the contract;
- Providing a variety of compensation options if agreed services are not supplied;
- Producing accurate promotional material including brochures.

The Regulations apply to packages sold or offered for sale in the UK, regardless of the operator's place of establishment. They do not apply to packages sold in other countries by operators established in the UK, although similar provisions apply in other member states of the European Union and in those countries that are part of the European Economic Area (EEA). The Regulations do not apply to packages sold in the Channel Islands or the Isle of Man, although the regulations do apply to organisers based in these areas, or anywhere else in the world, who sell their packages within the UK.

Trade Descriptions Act 1968

This Act protects consumers against false descriptions made knowingly or recklessly by anybody selling products and services, including holidays and other travel products. Any description of, for example, a hotel or resort must be truthful at the time it was written (if circumstances change, then the company must inform the customer of the nature of the changes). The Act places a duty on owners and operators of travel and tourism facilities to produce brochures, websites and other promotional materials that are not intended to deceive customers.

Supply of Goods and Services Act 1982 (as amended by the Sale and Supply of Goods Act 1994)

This legislation states that any contract for a holiday should be carried out using 'reasonable care and skill'. The tour operator and travel agent should ensure that the booking is carried out correctly and that the holiday itself should be of a generally satisfactory standard, complying with any descriptions made. Tour operators must take great care when selecting accommodation, transport and any services they provide as part of their package holidays.

Unit 11

Consumer Protection Act 1987

The Consumer Protection Act makes it a criminal offence for an organisation or individual to give misleading price information about goods, services, accommodation or facilities they are offering for sale. The Act defines a 'misleading' price as one which:

- Is greater than the price given in any promotional material;
- Is described as being generally available, but in reality is only available in certain circumstances;
- Does not fully state what facilities are included in the price and the fact than surcharges will be payable after booking.

The Act has special significance for tour operators, which must ensure the accuracy of any price information in their brochures and other publicity material. This is because it is an offence to include incorrect price information even if the inclusion was innocently undertaken, but is later shown to be misleading.

Unfair Contract Terms Act 1977 and Unfair Contract Terms in Consumer Contracts Regulations 1999

These laws allow customers to challenge any terms in a contract that they consider to be unfair or unreasonable, unfairly weighted against them, or that are ambiguous. Standard contract terms should be written in clear, understandable language. It is illegal to have a contract term that attempts to restrict the customers' statutory rights or avoids responsibility for death or personal injury. In certain cases, the Office of Fair Trading (OFT) may be able to prevent a company from using an unfair contract term in the future.

Fair Trading Act 1973

The Fair Trading Act forbids any unfair or unreasonable conditions or terms being imposed on customers, e.g. tour operators cannot say in their booking conditions that all complaints must be reported within 24 hours of returning from holiday. This is clearly unreasonable since holidaymakers may have suffered injury or distress, thereby making it difficult for them to complain within such a short time period.

Licensing and bonding

All tour operator members of ABTA must provide a bond securing their liability in respect of all forms of transportation, accommodation, travel and holiday arrangements, whether

outside or within the UK. The bond is a formal undertaking from an approved bank or insurance company to pay a sum of money to ABTA or the Civil Aviation Authority (CAA) in the event of the company's financial failure. The bond monies are used primarily for the purpose of reimbursing customers who would otherwise lose money that they had already paid, so that:

- Clients whose holidays are actually taking place when a tour operator ceases trading can continue with their holiday as planned or be brought back to the UK;
- Clients who have yet to travel on holidays already paid for can get their money back when an operator fails;
- Alternative holiday arrangements can be made for clients, who have paid for trips that have yet to take place, when a tour operator ceases trading.

For bonding purposes, tour operators are classed as either 'licensable' or 'non-licensable'. Licensable activities are those that require the operator to hold an Air Travel Organisers' Licence (ATOL); all other tour operations are classed as non-licensable. The CAA bonds provided by ATOL holders provide the first line of defence for licensable activities when things go wrong, whereas ABTA bonds provided by members fulfil the same function in respect of non-licensable activities.

WEBLINK

www.caa.co.uk

Check out this website for more information on ATOLs.

FOCUS ON INDUSTRY – ATOL

An ATOL is a licence issued by the Civil Aviation Authority (CAA) and is required by all individuals and companies selling holidays and seats on charter flights. Applicants must show that they are fit to hold an ATOL, have adequate financial arrangements and must lodge a bond with the CAA. In the event of company failure, the bond money is used to repatriate clients who might otherwise be stranded overseas and to refund, as far as possible, passengers who have paid in advance but have yet to travel. Where the bond is insufficient to meet all claims, the Air Travel Reserve Fund, managed by the CAA, meets the shortfall.

SECTION 4: DESIGNING, PLANNING AND COSTING A PACKAGE

This final section of the unit will give you practice in designing, planning and costing a package holiday.

Scenario

Your uncle has always wanted to set up a business offering walking holidays in the Pyrenees, after many years of enjoying similar holidays with HF Holidays, Headwater and Ramblers' Holidays. He has asked you to help him research the idea and put together a programme for six week-long tours in May and September. If these go well, he hopes to expand the number of weeks in future years. He will lead the tours himself and take no more than 12 walkers on each tour.

Design and plan

You will need to carry out some in-depth research to address the following points:

1. Which destination(s) to use in the Pyrenees;
2. What transport arrangements to get to the Pyrenees would suit best;
3. What type of accommodation is needed and on what accommodation basis;
4. What excursions and activities should be included in the package;
5. What precise dates and timescales should be agreed.

You can assume that all suppliers will give you discounted, inclusive tour (IT) rates for accommodation, travel, excursions, etc., but as this is a new venture you are only likely to be offered a discount of 25 per cent off their brochure rates, e.g. you will be charged £37.50 for a room that would appear in a hotel's tariff as £50.

Cost

Having designed and planned your package, you are now in a position to cost it. As with the example of the package holiday to the Costa del Sol on page 353, you will need to calculate all the direct costs of the holiday and add a mark-up of 20 per cent to cover fixed costs and a margin for profit. If you choose to fly your holidaymakers to the destination, you need not worry about load factors as you will be using a scheduled carrier (which could be one of the low-cost airlines).

Points to be bear in mind when costing include:

1. Variations in accommodation and travel prices depending on the season;
2. How your final prices compare with similar packages offered by other operators.

Present your designing, planning and costing of the package as a short feasibility study, including all the information you have collected.

Unit 11

UNIT SUMMARY

This unit has examined the important role that tour operators play in the travel and tourism industry. You have examined the structure of the sector and considered the work of trade associations and regulatory bodies. The package holiday was considered in detail, along with the many types of tour operators that service both UK and overseas tourists. You have seen that planning, selling and operating a package holiday programme is a complex business, often giving only small profit margins. The impact of environmental, political and legal factors was discussed in details, showing how tour operators can have positive and negative impacts on destination areas. Finally, you were given the chance to design, plan and cost a package of your own. Throughout the unit you have been shown examples of good practice in UK tour operations. The case studies on the FTO and TUI UK gave an insight into the activities of a trade association and a mass-market tour operator.

If you have worked methodically, by the end of this unit you should have:

- Examined the UK tour operations environment;
- Investigated how tour operators plan, sell and operate a package holiday programme;
- Examined the external factors that affect the planning, selling and operation of a package holiday programme;
- Designed, planned and costed a package for inclusion in a tour operator's programme.

You are now in a position to complete the assignment for the unit, under the direction of your tutor. Before you tackle the assignment you may like to have a go at the following questions to help build your knowledge on tour operations in travel and tourism.

Test your knowledge

1. Why are tour operators sometimes thought of as 'wholesalers'?
2. What is the difference between horizontal and vertical integration?
3. What is UKinbound and what activities does it undertake?
4. Name six members of the Federation of Tour Operators.
5. What is 'consolidation'?
6. What is an outbound tour operator?
7. Why are ancillary sales important to tour operators?
8. What is a 'package' as defined by the Package Travel Regulations?
9. What is an ATOL?
10. What sources of research are available to tour operators to help them plan their programmes?
11. What is the difference between a tour operator's fixed and variable costs?
12. List the main stages in the production of a tour operator's brochure.
13. What environmental and political events have affected tour operators in the last 5 years?
14. What is a 'bond'?
15. How do you think the tour operations sector will change in the next 10 years?

Unit 21

Work-based Experience within the Travel and Tourism Industry

INTRODUCTION TO THE UNIT

This unit has a very practical outcome – a chance for you to gain some experience of working in the travel and tourism industry. It gives you the opportunity of putting some of the 'theory' that you have been studying on your course into practice in the workplace. You will be expected to spend a minimum of 10 days on work experience; this could be in a block, at weekends, on day-release from college, in evenings or during a vacation.

In this unit you will investigate the many opportunities that exist for work-based experience, using a range of information sources. You will consider the opportunities for skills and career development, plus the constraints surrounding your placement. You will reflect on the objectives of your work-based experience and appropriate codes of behaviour in the workplace. As part of the placement, you are expected to plan, carry out and present an agreed project of mutual benefit to you and the placement provider. Finally, the unit explains how to carry out a personal review of your work-based experience and your own performance while on placement.

WHAT YOU WILL STUDY

During the course of this unit you will:

1. Investigate opportunities for a **work-based experience** in the travel and tourism industry;
2. **Prepare** to obtain a work-based experience;
3. Plan, complete and present an approved **project;**
4. Undertake a **personal review** of the work-based experience and your own performance.

You will be guided through the main topics in this unit with the help of the latest industry examples. You should also check out the weblinks throughout the unit for extra information on particular organisations or topic areas and use the activities to help you learn more.

ASSESSMENT FOR THIS UNIT

This unit is internally assessed, meaning that you will be given an assignment (or series of assignments) to complete by your tutor(s) to show that you have fully understood the content of the unit. A grading scale of pass, merit or distinction is used for all internally assessed units, with higher grades awarded to students who show greater depth in analysis and evaluation in their assignments. An assignment for this unit, which covers all the grading criteria, can be found on page 383. Don't forget to visit www.tandtONLine.co.uk for all the latest industry news, developments, statistics and tips to help you with your assignments.

Unit 21

ACTIVITY

Log on to these websites and make notes on key tips for getting a placement and search for particular placements that interest you.
www.connexions-direct.com; www.work-experience.org; www.support4learning.org.uk

This activity is designed to provide evidence for P1.

You may be lucky enough to work at an airport on your placement

Constraints

Most students on short periods of work-based experience tend not to travel outside their immediate area. Your location will have a bearing on the number and type of placement opportunities open to you. If you live in a town or city, you are likely to have a good choice of placement types, for example transport providers, hotels, travel agencies, airports, etc. In a country area there may not be the same number of placements on offer, so you may have to travel further to secure one that suits you. Countryside placements include National Parks, stately homes, outdoor activity centres, farm accommodation and tourist information centres.

Other constraints that may affect your choice of placement may include:

- Personal issues – perhaps concerning mobility or health-related matters that may affect where you can go for your placement;
- Transport – having access to public transport or other means of getting to the placement will need to be taken into account. This could be a particular problem in a rural area;
- Travelling time – this should be kept to a minimum unless you have chosen to travel further afield to work with a particular company;
- Hours of work – these need to agreed before the start of your placement, in line with the custom and practice at the workplace and subject to legal requirements. To make the work-based experience as realistic as possible it is normal for students on placement to work the same hours as permanent staff;
- Shifts – you may be asked to work shifts in certain placements, for example hotels, airports, large attractions, etc;

Unit 21

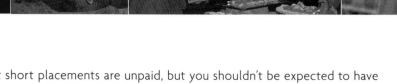

> • Finance – most short placements are unpaid, but you shouldn't be expected to have to pay for equipment or special clothing – this should be provided by the employer as necessary. Placement employers sometimes offer to cover students' travel costs or your college/school may have a system to help with this expenditure.

ACTIVITY

Working with another member of your group, make a list of the constraints that each of you will need to take into account when deciding on your work-based experience.

This activity is designed to provide evidence for P1.

Opportunities for skills development

Work-based experience gives you the opportunity of developing new workplace skills or brushing up existing skills. In the 'preparation for employment' section of Unit 6 Working in the Travel and Tourism Industry, you were shown how to carry out a self-evaluation of your current skills levels in areas such as communication, IT, numeracy and working with others. You were also asked to assess yourself in a variety of personal qualities and attributes, including:

- Attitude to work;
- Personal presentation;
- Assertiveness;
- Personality type;
- Body language;
- Time management.

It is worth going back to see how you assessed yourself in these skills, qualities and attributes, and use the information to help you select a placement that is likely to help you improve in areas of weakness.

Depending on the type of work-based experience that you choose, you will have the chance to develop a full range of workplace and personal skills, such as:

- Technical and practical – computer skills, putting up displays, etc;
- Social and personal – communicating professionally with work colleagues, etc;
- Analytical and critical – you may be asked to comment on data, new products, etc;
- Problem-solving – this could be anything from finding information for a customer to working out an itinerary for a business trip;
- Self-motivation – your placement will let you see if you can be motivated in the workplace;

Unit 21

WEBLINK

www.springboarduk.org.uk;
www.itt.co.uk

*Check out these websites
for more information on
careers in the travel and
tourism industry.*

- Prioritising and action-planning – these are important work and life skills that you can develop on your work-based experience;
- Customer care and relating to people – these skills are important and transferable to most sectors of the travel and tourism industry;
- Time-keeping and presentation – although you are not a full-time employee you must act in a professional manner at all times, including being punctual and wearing appropriate dress while on placement;
- Research skills – this could be finding out the prices charged by a competitor company, interviewing visitors, etc.

Opportunities for career development

Your work-based experience is a good opportunity to gain more information about a particular sector of the travel and tourism industry and to consider if a career in the sector would interest you. Don't be too downhearted if the placement doesn't live up to your expectations and you decide that it's not the type of organisation you want to work for in the future. At least you will have gained experience of the workplace and can concentrate on other sectors for future placements and jobs. If you do well on the placement, despite the fact that it may not be your first choice of career, the employer is likely to offer to provide a reference for you in the future; this is very valuable when moving on to other employment, training or education opportunities.

Health, safety and security requirements

Encouraging good health and safety practices in the workplace is important for employers and employees. By law, organisations are obliged to:

You could get a placement at a tourist information centre

1. Assess health and safety risks at work, e.g. by nominating a health and safety officer;
2. Have control measures in place to monitor health and safety issues;
3. Maintain minimum levels of hygiene and comfort by making sure that the workplace is clean, well-ventilated, complies with minimum temperature requirements and has mains drinking water;

Unit 21

4. Record and report certain health and safety incidents in the workplace, for example a serious accident involving staff and/or customers. This can be done by a nominated first-aider or fire safety officer;

5. Comply with regulations to protect the environment, for example the rules on waste storage and trade effluent.

The induction to the organisation when you first start should include details of the organisation's policies and procedures on health, safety and security. Make sure you listen carefully and ask questions if there is anything that you don't understand. If you are asked to wear a security badge or tag, make sure you wear it at all times for security reasons and to save your embarrassment if you accidentally trigger an alarm!

Securing your placement

Having used a variety of resources, discussed any constraints, considered opportunities for skills and career development, and examined health, safety and security requirements, you are now in a position to make contact with a potential placement organisation and convince them that you are the person for the job! Depending on the organisation, you may have to consider doing one or more of the following:

1. Sending a CV;
2. Attending an interview;
3. Sending a letter or email confirming acceptance of the placement.

ACTIVITY

Working in small groups, role play a series of placement interviews for the following scenarios:

1. A student hoping to secure a placement at a tourist information centre;
2. A student wanting a period of work-based experience in the marketing department of a major mass-market tour operator;
3. A student being interviewed by the owner of a travel agency for a two-week placement.

You should take it in turns to play the role of the interviewer and interviewee. Tips on interview skills for both the interviewer and interviewee can be found in the 'preparation for employment' section of Unit 6 Working in the Travel and Tourism Industry

Unit 21

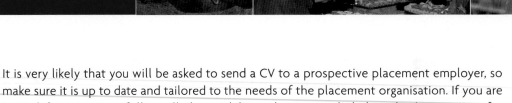

It is very likely that you will be asked to send a CV to a prospective placement employer, so make sure it is up to date and tailored to the needs of the placement organisation. If you are invited for interview, follow all the guidelines that are included in the 'preparation for employment' section of Unit 6 Working in the Travel and Tourism Industry, which also has tips on writing a CV and an example of a business letter that you could use as a template when writing a letter of acceptance to the placement employer.

ACTIVITY

Use the sources described earlier in this unit to investigate three different work-based experience opportunities that appeal to you, giving details of job roles, location, opportunities for projects, skills development opportunities, etc. Explain how each of the possible placements has the potential to help you achieve your personal, career and curriculum objectives.

This activity is designed to provide evidence for M1.

Unit 21

SECTION 2: PREPARING FOR A WORK-BASED EXPERIENCE

Having secured a placement, you can now turn your attention to some of the practicalities of the arrangement. It may sound obvious, but make sure you can find the placement easily and you know how long it takes to get there! If it's some way from where you live, you might like to visit the area a few days before the placement starts to familiarise yourself with the route. Don't leave it until the last minute if you need to ask somebody else for a lift or buy a ticket for travel. The same goes for any accommodation you may need to arrange with friends or relatives close to the placement. Finally, make sure you know what time you are expected at the placement on the first day and create a good first impression by not being late!

Code of behaviour

All travel and tourism organisations have codes of behaviour that they expect all staff to follow, covering such matters as

- Timekeeping and attendance;
- Appropriate dress;
- Honesty and reliability;
- Accepting authority and responsibility;
- Responding to instructions and carrying out tasks;
- Following health, safety and security guidelines;
- Appropriate language in the workplace;
- Courteous and non-discriminatory behaviour;
- Use of company facilities (particularly telephone, email and the Internet);
- Dealing with customers and suppliers.

Most of these points will be covered in your induction to the organisation when you first arrive or may be discussed as appropriate so as not to overload you with information at the start of your work-based experience.

Setting objectives

To get the best out of a period of work-based experience it's important to have clear idea of what you want to achieve. You do this by setting objectives for the placement. These could be related to you as an individual (personal objectives), where you would like to work in the future (career objectives) or related to the BTEC course you are following (curriculum objectives). Figure 21.2 gives some examples of these objectives.

Unit 21

Personal	Career	Curriculum
• Learn more about yourself as a person at work • Gain extra confidence in dealing with people • Develop telephone technique • Learn customer service skills	• Make contacts for the future • Learn more about the organisation • Learn more about the travel and tourism industry • Find out about qualifications and training from work colleagues at the placement	• Gather information to complete the assignment for the work-based experience unit • Collect information that could be useful for other unit assignments • Use information from any special projects that you complete to help with your studies back at college/school

Fig. 21.2 Objectives for work-based experience

Objectives should always be SMART, i.e.

- Specific;
- Measurable;
- Achievable;
- Realistic;
- Time-limited.

You might like to talk with friends, relatives and staff at your college or school before completing the next activity.

ACTIVITY

Using the information in Figure 21.2 as a guide, draw up your own chart of the personal, career and curriculum objectives you hope to achieve on your period of work-based experience. Remember, they must be SMART!

This activity is designed to provide evidence for P2.

Unit 21

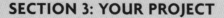

SECTION 3: YOUR PROJECT

The placement that you complete for this unit includes a project that should be agreed in advance with your placement provider. The assessment for the unit requires you to plan, carry out and make a presentation on the agreed project.

Planning a project

The topic of the project that you undertake should be agreed between you, your tutor and your placement employer. It may be that the placement provider has already chosen a topic and agreed it with your tutor. If this is the case, make sure you are happy with it, since you are the one who will be doing the work!

Topics that you could consider for the project include:

- Examining customer care provision in the placement organisation;
- Carrying out a review of their website and suggesting improvements;
- Developing a marketing plan for the organisation;
- Drawing up a training scheme for new members of staff;
- Producing a staff guide to teamwork, leadership and motivation in the workplace;
- Developing some new menu options;
- Carrying out a review of current products and services, with suggestions for improvements.

Your project might investigate developing business tourism

Your project should have clear objectives and outcomes that can be achieved while on placement. You need to be realistic about what can be achieved with the time you have available, bearing in mind that the placement provider will want you to be working most of the time.

Undertaking the project

You should treat your project in just the same way that you complete assignments at college or school. Plan your time well, prioritise tasks and keep to any deadlines you, your placement employer or tutor sets. It's likely that you will be given periods of time to work on the project while on placement, but when things get busy there may not be much time available. Try to involve as many staff as possible at your placement so that you can benefit from their experience and helpful advice. They will happily answer your questions if you ask them at a time when they are not too busy. Review the progress on your project from time to time with the placement provider, agreeing any actions that need completing. Keep a full record of all your investigations to do with the project.

Depending on the type of project you decide to complete, you should make full use of the resources available at the placement. This could be members of staff, Internet access, books and manuals, computer and telephone systems, etc. Always get permission from a member of staff before you use any equipment.

ACTIVITY

Draw up a proposal for a project that you would be interested in completing while on your period of work-based experience. This should be agreed with your tutor and/or placement provider and should include key objectives, proposed outcomes, timescales and resources needed.

This activity is designed to provide evidence for P3.

Presentation

Having completed your project you must make a presentation that covers:

1. The objectives of the project;
2. The methods you used to achieve the objectives;
3. Timescales involved;
4. Resources consulted;
5. Outcomes of the project.

The presentation could be to your placement employer and staff, your tutor or your college/school group, or any combination of the three. The format of the presentation will depend on the type of project you carried out, but could be a written report, an individual or group presentation (with or without PowerPoint), a display, a leaflet, a video/DVD or any other method that suits your project. Where appropriate, make recommendations for future actions and include relevant graphics and data.

Unit 21

SECTION 4: PERSONAL REVIEW

It's fair to say that we all learn from our experiences in life and it's likely that you will have learned a lot from your period of work-based experience (although it may not be obvious to you just now!). This section of the unit gives you guidance on carrying out a personal review of your placement once it has finished. The review should take the form of a written account of all aspects of the placement.

Your own performance on placement

If you spent time completing the chart discussed earlier in this unit, with the expected personal, career and curriculum objectives for the placement, reviewing your performance won't take too long. Take each of the objectives in turn and state whether or not it was achieved. If you were successful give some details of how the objective was achieved. If unsuccessful, explain why. You should also go beyond these objectives when reflecting back on your placement performance. There may be examples of activities that you were unaware of before you started the placement, but which were of interest to you in terms of your personal or career development. Also, more subjective aspects of the placement, for example how you felt about being in a work setting or your feelings about working inside/outside for 7 or 8 hours a day, should be built into your review.

ACTIVITY

Make a list of your strengths and weaknesses while on placement. How could you build on your strengths even further and address the weaknesses you have identified?

This activity is designed to provide evidence for P5.

Monitoring progress on placement

To be able to complete your placement review, you will need to look back on any documents or evidence that you gathered while on placement. One of the most useful of these is a log book, completed on a daily basis to record the activities you undertook and skills practised, plus any action points for future reference. Other reference materials could include transcripts of interviews carried out while on placement, witness testimonies, project reviews, video and audio recordings. Your college/school may have a purpose-designed logbook that is used by all placement students.

2. The project you must complete as part of your work-based experience;

3. Reviewing and evaluating your period of work-based experience.

Task 1

(a) Research and deliver an illustrated presentation describing the range of opportunities for work-based experience in the travel and tourism industry.

This task is designed to provide evidence for P1.

(b) As part of your presentation, explain how three work-based experience opportunities can help meet personal, career and curriculum (course-related) objectives.

This task is designed to provide evidence for M1.

(c) Prepare for work-based experience by producing a written document that includes the objectives that you have set for your placement and a personal code of behaviour.

This task is designed to provide evidence for P2.

Task 2

(a) Negotiate a work-based project and produce a written plan for its completion, listing key objectives, proposed outcomes, timescales and resources.

This task is designed to provide evidence for P3.

(b) Present the project in an agreed format.

This task is designed to provide evidence for P4.

If your presentation shows how the project met its objectives and you demonstrate a range of research techniques and you present in-depth findings coherently and accurately, this will provide evidence for M2. If you present the project showing analysis of key issues and make justified recommendations for future action, this will provide evidence for D1.

Task 3

(a) Complete a written personal review of your work-based experience and your own performance while on placement.

This task is designed to provide evidence for P5.

(b) As part of your review, evaluate how the work-based experience met its objectives and evaluate the effectiveness of your own performance.

This task is designed to provide evidence for M3.

Critically evaluate your own performance while completing your work-based experience and your project, making recommendations for future personal development that are justified.

This task is designed to provide evidence for D2

Unit 22

First and foremost, the visit is part of your BTEC course of study, meaning that is a learning experience just like on all the other units you are studying. It's obviously different to your other units in that it includes a period of time away from your college or school as a member of a group. As well as learning more about the travel and tourism industry first hand, the visit is a great way to forge new friendships and take part in new experiences. You may be visiting a new part of the UK or going abroad for the first time, so it's an exciting time as well!

This is likely to be one of the most challenging units on your course. Equally, it should be one of the most rewarding, enjoyable and memorable, as long as you plan well ahead and work as part of a team. In completing this unit you will be developing and applying many of the skills that employers in travel and tourism say they are looking for in new recruits, such as communication skills, problem solving, team working and project management.

Agreeing aims and objectives

The residential study visit is very much a team effort, so members of your group must get used to working together from the outset. You must all be clear about what the study visit is trying to achieve. In other words, you must have a clear aim and objectives.

An aim is a general statement about the overall target of a project. For example, the aim of your study visit could be *'to organise and take part in a successful study visit that is both educational and enjoyable'*. Anybody reading this aim will be clear as to what you are trying to achieve.

Objectives are more specific and give greater detail about the study visit. Taking the example of a visit to Manchester, the objectives could be to:

1. Learn about the different types of tourists that visit Manchester;
2. Find out about the range and quality of accommodation on offer in the city;
3. Discover how Manchester is marketed to tourists;
4. Learn about the structure of public sector tourism in the city;
5. Find out what plans Manchester has for developing tourism in the next ten years.

You may also have objectives that relate to your course or future career development, for example to gather information to complete assignments or to interview people working in the travel and tourism industry in the destination you are visiting, to find out more about their jobs.

You will need to work with the other members of your group and your tutor to agree the objectives of your particular study visit. Whatever objectives you decide upon, remember that they must be SMART, in other words:

Unit 22

- Specific – it's no use having 'woolly' ideas that are not well thought through or clearly defined;
- Measurable – objectives must be capable of being measured so that you know if you have achieved your target;
- Achievable – setting objectives that are wildly optimistic wastes everybody's time;
- Realistic – objectives must fit in with your aims for the visit;
- Timed – it is important to set time deadlines within which your objectives must be achieved, either during the visit or to be completed when you return to base.

ACTIVITY

Working with the rest of your group, hold a meeting to discuss the overall aim and specific objectives of your residential study visit. Remember that at this stage you haven't agreed a destination, so make sure your aim and objectives can apply to any area you visit. Agree a set of objectives and, after the meeting, add any personal or career-related objectives of your own to the group list to develop a list of objectives that are specific to you.

This activity is designed to provide evidence for P1.

Holding meetings

You should hold regular meetings as a group to discuss the planning of the study visit, although you are responsible for completing the unit assignment on an individual basis. So as not to waste anybody's time, the meetings should be run in a business-like manner, with:

- A written notice of each meeting – this is sent out in advance, giving the date, time and venue;
- An agenda – this is the list of items to be discussed at the meeting. It is helpful if it is distributed before the meeting, but may be given out on the day;
- Minutes – these are a written record of what was discussed and agreed at the meeting. At the next meeting, the minutes of the previous meeting are discussed and agreed as a true record of events.

You should elect somebody to chair the meetings and a person to take the minutes. To share the workload, it would be a good idea if different people could take on these roles at each meeting.

Unit 22

SECTION 2: PROPOSAL FOR AN EFFECTIVE STUDY VISIT

Having agreed the objectives for the study visit you can now turn to thinking about where to go. Many factors will need to be considered and any constraints taken into account, as the next section of this unit explains.

Deciding on a suitable study visit destination

Your tutor is likely to have already decided if the study visit will be in the UK or abroad, so that's one less thing for you to think about! It's worth spending some time as a group deciding on the type of destination you would like to visit, before thinking about an actual location. There are many different types of destinations you could choose from, including:

- Towns and cities – these destinations have a wide variety of facilities for tourists, including accommodation of all types, attractions, entertainment and tourist information services. They are generally well-served by public transport, such as rail, bus, air, coach and tram services;

- Coastal/seaside areas – have been popular with tourists since Victorian times and continue to be so today. The growth of package holidays from the 1960s onwards gave coastal resorts in the Mediterranean a major boost for tourism. In the UK, seaside resorts continue to be popular with the family market;

- Purpose-built resorts – companies such as Disney, Center Parcs and Butlins offer purpose-built facilities for their visitors, where accommodation, entertainment, activities, catering and information are all provided on site;

- Natural and rural areas – have long been a magnet for visitors of all types who want to get away from the stresses and strains of everyday life. National Parks and other protected areas are found in many countries, offering visitors the opportunity of experiencing fresh air and exercise in natural surroundings;

- Historical and cultural areas – 'heritage' is one of the main reasons why overseas visitors come to Britain and visit many other destinations around the world. As many people look beyond the 'sun, sea and sand' destinations for a more enriching experience, historical and cultural destinations are increasing in popularity.

Any one of these destination types would be suitable for a residential study visit.

> ### WEBLINK
>
> www.wtgonline.com;
> www.antor.com;
> www.travelocity.com;
> www.abtanet.com;
> www.aito.co.uk;
> www.lonelyplanet.com;
> www.oag.com;
> www.roughguides.com
>
> *Check out any of these websites for information on destinations around the world.*

Considerations and constraints

As choosing the destination for the study visit is a group task, you need to consider everybody's feelings, ideas and circumstances. There could, for example, be medical or personal reasons why some members of the group are not able to travel to a particular area or use a certain type of transport. Other considerations to bear in mind when deciding on a destination include:

Unit 22

Spain's Costa Blanca is a popular study visit destination abroad

• Budget – it is likely that you will have to pay the whole of the cost of the trip yourself, plus spending money on top. The amount you have available (your budget) will have a bearing on the type of accommodation you choose, the length of the trip, mode of travel and what activities you can take part in when in the destination;

• Legal – you may need to investigate visa, passport and health requirements for certain destinations, as well as issues such as drinking, driving and religious codes;

• Distance – be realistic in how far you can travel in the time that you have available. Remember that you will be working hard while at the destination, so don't be too ambitious in selecting an area;

• Tourist board help and support – some tourist boards encourage group trips by students and can help to arrange visits to hotels, attractions, etc. and suggest guest speakers for talks in the destination;

• Season – travel and accommodation will be cheaper out of peak season, but you must weigh this up against the fact that a resort will not be as busy and some facilities may not be open. This could restrict the number of travel and tourism facilities you can visit as part of the study visit. Choosing a time either side of the peak season is likely to be best, but don't pick a time when you will have lots of college/school work to finish!

• Cultural issues – you need to be sensitive to cultural issues in many destinations, e.g. drinking, improper language and dress code;

• Climate and weather – it's best to avoid extremes of weather, so don't pick a time of year that is likely to be very hot, very humid, very cold or very wet in the destinations you are considering;

• Health, safety and security – these are of the utmost importance on any study visit, whether in the UK or abroad. Your tutors will brief you fully on health, safety and security before you go on the trip, but at this stage you need to consider issues such as personal safety, natural disasters and political instability when deciding where to choose for your study visit;

• Availability of staff – your tutors will have work commitments and constraints that will affect when they can be away, so make sure you consult them at an early stage in the planning of your trip.

WEBLINK

www.fco.gov.uk

Check out this Foreign and Commonwealth Office website for the latest information on areas in the world where tourists are considered at risk.

Unit 22

ACTIVITY

To help you narrow down the search for a suitable destination, have a brainstorming session with the other members of your group, listing as many destinations as possible that could provide opportunities to meet the objectives you agreed earlier. When you have finished your list, take each destination in turn and ask each group member to give it a rating of between 1-10 (where 10 is the best and 1 the worst) against each objective. If all goes according to plan, you should be able to draw up a league table of the most suitable destinations for your trip. If you run into problems, ask your tutor to advise on the best course of action.

Making your final choice

Now that you have considered the aim and objectives of your study visit, the type of destination that you would like to visit and discussed other considerations/constraints affecting your choice of area, you need to think about the features and benefits of different destinations before making your final choice. Features are facts about the destination and benefits are what this means for visitors (see Figure 22.1).

Feature	Benefit
Good transport links	Fast journey times
Close to the mountains	Excellent scenery and opportunities for activities
Long stretches of sandy beaches	Opportunities for watersports
Many different accommodation types	Suitable for a wide variety of visitors

Fig. 22.1 Examples of features and benefits of destinations

ACTIVITY

Still working as a group, carry out a features and benefits analysis of the top three destinations from your league table. Present the information in the form of a chart similar to that shown in Figure 22.1. Use this information to agree finally on the destination for your study visit.

This activity is designed to provide evidence for P2.

Unit 22

Formulating your proposal

Having agreed the destination as a group activity you must now draw up you own proposal for the study visit individually. This should be a detailed document that includes information on the following:

1. A full itinerary for the visit, giving details of arrival and departure points;
2. The features and benefits of your chosen destination;
3. The transport you will use to travel to and from the destination, including any transfers;
4. Details of the accommodation to be used on the visit;
5. What activities are to be undertaken while at the destination;
6. Full costings of the various parts of the trip;
7. How the objectives you developed for the trip are going to be met;
8. What course-related opportunities are offered by your study visit;
9. How considerations and constraints have been addressed.

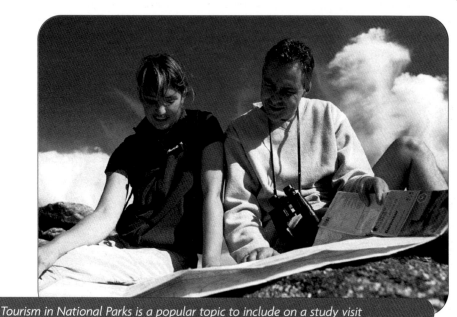

Tourism in National Parks is a popular topic to include on a study visit

You should consult a wide range of relevant information sources when compiling your proposal, e.g. transport operators, accommodation providers, the Internet, travel gazetteers, guide books, atlases, etc.

Essential information and documentation

Your proposal should include details of essential information and documents that you and other group members must consider before and while taking part in the study visit, including:

- Emergency numbers;
- Medical details;
- Permission forms (from college/school, parents/guardians);
- Money (in an appropriate foreign currency if travelling abroad);
- General information (suitable clothing, insurance and E111 form, passport, etc.);
- Code of conduct while on the study visit.

Unit 22

Travel checklist

- Check the FCO website or call the FCO travel helpline for advice before you travel.

- Get travel insurance and check that the cover is appropriate.

- Check what vaccinations you need at least 6 weeks before you go and consider whether you need to take extra health precautions.

- Get a good guidebook and get to know your destination. Find out about local laws and customs.

- Ensure you have a valid passport that is in good condition and has the necessary visas.

- Make copies of your passport, insurance policy (plus 24-hour emergency number) and ticket details. Leave these copies, your itinerary and contact details with family and friends.

- Take enough money for your trip and some back-up funds, e.g. travellers' cheques, Sterling or US Dollars.

- Make sure your travel organiser can provide sufficient evidence of security for the refunding and repatriation of consumers in the event of insolvency.

- If your travel involves passage on airlines with which you are unfamiliar, you may wish to check their safety and reliability with a reputable travel agent.

Source: FCO website

Fig. 22.2 Travel checklist from the Foreign and Commonwealth Office

The Foreign and Commonwealth Office's website (www.fco.gov.uk) has excellent information on a range of travel-related issues, such as insurance, drugs, travel health, terrorism and travel money. The FCO also produces a useful travel checklist (see Figure 22.2).

ACTIVITY

Working as a group, produce a code of conduct for your study visit. Consult your tutors to get their views on what you have devised.

Risk assessments

A risk assessment is a systematic investigation of the potential risks of any activity, to:

1. Identify hazards and potential risks;
2. Put measures in place to reduce potential risks;
3. Have contingency plans in case of incidents.

In your case, the activity is participating in a residential study visit, which as any member of staff will tell you can be a risky business at the best of times! Your college/school will have a policy on completing risk assessment forms for supervised trips, so discuss this with your tutor.

SECTION 3: PARTICIPATION IN THE STUDY VISIT

Having spent a long time planning the visit, the time has finally arrived to set off on your journey. Let's hope that you have played a full and active part in helping plan the study visit and will carry your enthusiasm with you while actually at the destination. It's very important to remember that, while on the visit, you are representing your institution and course, as well as yourself. Having a positive approach to the visit will ensure that you gain the most from the experience and your group are seen as ambassadors for your college/school.

Making an impression

Figure 22.3 highlights some of the main areas that you as an individual can make an impression, in a positive or negative way, while on your study visit.

Personal presentation

Meeting and greeting

Making an Impression

Attitude and responsibilities

Working environment

Fig. 22.3 Making an impression on your study visit

- Personal presentation – throughout the visit you should take care with such matters as personal hygiene, grooming, appropriate clothing, etc;
- Meeting and greeting – be polite at all times and make a point of meeting people in a positive manner, using a little of the local language if abroad;
- Attitude and responsibilities – make sure your time management is good and that you take on any responsibilities given by your tutors in a good spirit;
- Working environment – while carrying out project work in the destination, always respect the local traditions and cultures, and reflect on the impact you are making on the people living in the destination.

Communications skills with customers and colleagues

The study visit is an ideal way of developing your communication skills, as you will be meeting lots of new people and taking part in a range of activities. Be positive when dealing with people on your trip and always ask questions when visiting facilities or listening to guest speakers.

Unit 22

Gathering evidence

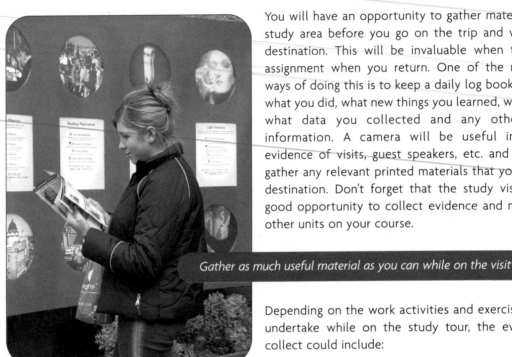

You will have an opportunity to gather material on your study area before you go on the trip and while in the destination. This will be invaluable when tackling the assignment when you return. One of the most useful ways of doing this is to keep a daily log book, which lists what you did, what new things you learned, who you met, what data you collected and any other relevant information. A camera will be useful in capturing evidence of visits, guest speakers, etc. and you should gather any relevant printed materials that you see in the destination. Don't forget that the study visit is also a good opportunity to collect evidence and materials for other units on your course.

Gather as much useful material as you can while on the visit

Depending on the work activities and exercises that you undertake while on the study tour, the evidence you collect could include:

- Trends in visitor numbers to the destination;
- Profiles of visitors to the destination
- Information on visitor motivations;
- Descriptions of the range and quality of tourist facilities;
- Roles of key organisations within the travel and tourism industry;
- Information on funding sources for tourism, including constraints;
- Details of geographical and cultural features in the destination;
- Plans for future tourism development;
- A PEST analysis (political, economic, social, technological factors affecting tourism);
- Information on environmental issues in relation to tourism.

This evidence will come from a range of secondary sources, e.g. data held by the local tourism organisation or economic development agency, and your own primary data collection, e.g. visitor and business surveys, and audits of tourism facilities.

Unit 22

SECTION 4: EVALUATION OF THE STUDY VISIT

You should start your evaluation by looking back at the aims and objectives you devised for the study visit (remember that you used the agreed set of objectives developed by your group and added your own personal or career-related objectives, to come up with a list of objectives that were specific to you). You should review each objective and decide whether or not the objective had been fully met, giving reasons for your comments.

In addition to your own personal evaluation you may be asked to take part in a group evaluation of the success of the planning and operation of the study visit. This will focus on:

- The suitability of the destination;
- Travel arrangements;
- Suitability of accommodation used;
- Value for money of the whole visit;
- Comments on quality and quantity of research opportunities;
- Access to tourist facilities and guest speakers in the destination.

Your tutor may also wish to hold one-to-one interviews with members of the group, giving feedback on individual performance.

UNIT SUMMARY

This unit has given you the opportunity of planning, taking part in and evaluating a travel and tourism residential study visit in the UK or abroad. You have considered the aims and objectives of the study visit, which can be personal, career-related or specific to your course of study. You have worked as a member of a group to decide which destination to choose for your study visit, having consulted a number of reference sources. Due attention has been paid to the various considerations and constraints that can affect your choice of destination, including your budget, time of year to travel, climate and availability of staff. You have participated in the study visit after guidance on the best ways to make a positive impression on the hosts in the destination area. You have been alerted to the different types of research evidence that can be collected in the destination, including primary and secondary data. Finally, you have reflected on the whole experience by carrying out an evaluation of the study visit.

If you have worked methodically, by the end of this unit you should have:

- Established the aims and objectives for a study visit;
- Developed a proposal for an effective study visit;
- Participated positively in a study visit;
- Evaluated the study visit.